From Hinton
to *Hamlet*

From Hinton to *Hamlet*

BUILDING BRIDGES BETWEEN YOUNG ADULT LITERATURE AND THE CLASSICS

Second Edition, Revised and Expanded

Sarah K. Herz
and Donald R. Gallo

GREENWOOD PRESS
Westport, Connecticut • London

Library of Congress Cataloging-in-Publication Data

Herz, Sarah K.
      From Hinton to Hamlet : building bridges between young adult
   literature and the classics / Sarah K. Herz and Donald R. Gallo.— 2nd ed.,
   rev. and expanded.
            p.   cm.
      Includes bibliographical references and index.
      ISBN 0-313-32452-2 (alk. paper)
      1. Young adult literature—Study and teaching (Secondary)
   2. Literature—Study and teaching (Secondary)   3. Youth—Books and
   reading.   I. Gallo, Donald R.   II. Title.
   PN1009.A1H47 2005
   809'.89283'0712—dc22   2005012728

British Library Cataloguing in Publication Data is available.

Library of Congress Catalog Card Number: 2005012728
ISBN: 0-313-32452-2

First published in 2005

Greenwood Press, 88 Post Road West, Westport, CT 06881
An imprint of Greenwood Publishing Group, Inc.
www.greenwood.com

Printed in the United States of America

The paper used in this book complies with the
Permanent Paper Standard issued by the National
Information Standards Organization (Z39.48–1984).

10   9   8   7   6   5

For all the students who have shared their reading lives with us...
thank you for your inspiration, your enthusiasm, and your trust.

CONTENTS

PREFACE

Perhaps you are asking why a second edition?

So much top-quality young adult literature (YAL) has been published since we wrote *From Hinton to* Hamlet in 1996 that we felt compelled to share this bounty with you. YAL is better than ever. In the past few years there has been an explosion of well-crafted literature for secondary students, especially at the high school level, with stories that focus on the precarious journey from adolescence to adulthood. Although the theme connectors and other recommended readings in the first edition are still valid, we are now suggesting new titles that offer you stronger choices to bridge the classics. We believe your students want to read literature that focuses on concerns they have about themselves and contemporary society. With a wider selection of titles, the interests of every type of reader in your classroom can be met with ease.

Besides including many new YAL titles that bridge the classics, the Thematic Extensions section in chapter 5 is much more extensive, along with annotated YAL titles that connect to archetypes, and an Author Paper model using YAL. Chapter 7, "Other Backyards," provides lengthy lists of fiction and nonfiction titles for interdisciplinary approaches with literally hundreds of annotated titles. In chapter 6 we have profiled five school and public libraries whose exciting programs exemplify the possibilities of middle and high school student involvement. We've also included Web sites of professional organizations, journals, review sources, and individual authors, which did not exist when we wrote the first edition. This second edition is thereby filled with lots of new material that reinforces YAL as a tool that provides your students an opportunity to reflect where and how this literature bridges the literary canon.

So here are new titles, pre- and post-millennium, that we think are provocative, exciting, heartbreaking, thoughtful, mind-blowing—they are almost guaranteed to grab the attention of you and your students; they will test the limits of the reader's interpretation; they will delve into the depths of the reader's imagination. And many of these stories will haunt the reader's memory.

You may also be wondering how we shared the workload—who wrote which chapters, who contributed what insights.

First, we share common perspectives about YAL as well as teaching methodology, so we never had to argue about whose point of view would dominate any section of this book. Second, as we did with the first edition, we divided the work assignments, with Sarah revising the first three chapters as well as chapter 6. Don expanded and revised chapter 8 and most of chapter 5 and constructed the Works Cited section. We both revised and wrote several new Theme Connectors for chapter 4, with Sarah writing about three times as many as Don, and we both contributed new titles and annotations for chapter 7. We also critiqued and edited each other's work, and so you will see us using "we" throughout most of this text, since this has been a cooperative effort. Where you occasionally see "I," especially in the introduction and chapter 1, it will be Sarah speaking about her personal experiences as a teacher. We both contributed to this preface.

Finally, writing about YAL and convincing teachers that it can be a pathway to lifetime reading for teens is really our goal. We hope that you become readers of YAL along with your students and realize how these powerful stories touch their lives.

Donald R. Gallo and Sarah K. Herz

Acknowledgments

Thanks to the publishers who sent us advance galleys as well as copies of YAL titles so that we could keep up to date on the newest novels, short stories, poetry, and informational books, especially the late Bill Morris (HarperCollins), John Mason (Scholastic), Liz Rhynerson (Random House), Andrea Cruise (Penguin Putnam), Jeanne T. McDermott (Farrar, Straus & Giroux), Anne Irza-Leggat and Sharon Hancock (Candlewick), Angus Killick (Hyperion), Ellen Greene (Harcourt), Kathleen Doherty (Tor), Lauren Wohl (Roaring Brook), Lisa DiSarro (Houghton Mifflin), Barbara Witke (Peachtree), Michelle Fadlalla (Simon & Schuster), Lisa Nadel (Henry Holt), Stephen Roxburgh (Front Street), Kate Kubert (Bloomsbury), and Andrew Woodridge (Orca). Your generosity is much appreciated.

Special thanks to the extraordinary librarians—Michelle Hasenfratz, Kay Hones, Mary Long, and Connie Mitchell—who took time from their busy end-of-the-year schedules to answer all of Sarah's persistent questions. A special thank-you to Diane Tuccillo, who shared her knowledge about these outstanding school programs.

And we want to thank all the authors whose imaginations fuel teenagers with amazing stories that convince them that reading is a crucial part of their lives.

Sarah Herz and Don Gallo

INTRODUCTION

What kinds of readers are in your classroom? Excited avid readers who devour all kinds of books, magazines, newspapers? Students who tune out classroom chatter because they are so focused on their reading? These readers interpret and discuss literature with confidence and authority; most of us dote on them and count on them to rev up the discussion in our classroom.

But what about the nonreaders? They hate to read; reading is academic torture for them. In the early stages of reading, they could not find the "magic" to unlock the mystery of reading, and they probably sensed that their teacher was disappointed in their weak performance. Their struggles during their elementary school years reinforced their negative feelings about finding any pleasure in reading. The opportunity to enjoy a good story, to wonder, "And then what happened?" eluded them. By middle school and high school these nonreaders are unable to connect to the required literature curriculum; they slither through literature class, probably using *Cliffs Notes* and *Masterplots,* videos and DVDs, anything that circumvents reading.

And what about aliterate readers—capable readers who read to complete the coursework, but who rarely read for pleasure? They resent control—the required number of pages for homework, the daily quizzes to check up on their reading, the required titles, the interpretation dictated by the teacher, the lack of student-shared discussion or response during class—but manage to pass the course. They are the invisible readers in the classroom, capable and perceptive, cranking out tests and essays, but rejecting the notion that literature serves any useful purpose in their lives.

I met up with these readers during the 24 years I taught English, and I confess that I never considered my students' attitudes about reading until I observed their response to YAL. When I accepted and understood the possibilities of YAL, I found a powerful tool to help students take pride in their reading and to help them develop into confident, critical readers.

YAL's value lies in its ability to connect students to the story immediately, because it deals with real problems and issues that are central to their lives. It helps teenagers in their search for understanding the complex world of today. The questions *Who am I?* and *Where do I fit in?* plague most adolescents during most of their formative years. As developing readers, many students cannot find answers to these questions in such challenging classics as *Jane Eyre, Pride and Prejudice, Tom Jones, Green Dolphin Street, Moby Dick, Babbitt,* or *Hamlet*...yet.

In addition to the usual literary elements of adult literature—plot, setting, point of view, characterization, dialogue, style, and theme—YAL offers teen readers a comfortable reading experience that provides them an opportunity to begin to perceive the complex nature of human relationships. By using a teenage narrator, most YAL creates an immediate and intimate contact between reader and author because the story is about a teenager's problem or relationship, and the reader is hooked. Readers also feel confident in sharing their interpretation with friends and in engaging in literary discussions in and out of the classroom.

YAL has gone through a transformation; what used to be used only as supportive reading for less able and less motivated students has become a rich literary source that meets the abilities of all types of readers. But before you begin to investigate the possibilities of YAL in your classes, if you are not already familiar with a variety of books, it is important that you confer with a school or town librarian and read several award-winning titles. Better yet, ask your students for some titles of the best books they've read in the past two years. In many instances, you will find that their favorite titles are *not* what a teacher taught to the whole class, but rather are particular titles recommended by classmates. In checking many of my students' favorite titles with school librarians, I found that most students' choices were YAL.

Sixteen years ago I started reading YAL, and I haven't stopped. Through the years I have learned more about the world of adolescents through these stories, poems, and novels than I learned in psychology courses. And when I listened to my students discussing books, I heard the meaning they made from reading YAL. YAL liberated my classroom and me—I was no longer the authority figure dominating their reading life. But the most satisfying bonus of all was my acceptance into their discussions, seeing their willingness to risk and to trust writing and speaking their opinions in our classroom. I learned to bridge my own reading, switching back and forth between YAL and adult books, and I too took pride in sharing my reading life with my students. Now that I am retired, I reflect on the shared talks about books with my excited students and believe more than ever that YAL is the key to unlocking the magic of reading for our students. At conferences and staff development workshops I booktalk the most exciting, poignant, mesmerizing YAL for teachers and librarians, so they can experience the joy of helping teenagers become lifetime readers.

Sarah K. Herz

Chapter 1

HOW I FOUND A TREASURE TROVE OF READERS WITH YOUNG ADULT LITERATURE

Young adult literature (YAL) bullied its way into my teaching life in 1987 when a group of 7th graders staged a rebellion during the assigned reading of *Lilies of the Field*. They questioned their reading rights—*What right did I have to force this lousy book down their throats? What about their rights?* We made a deal, and they instituted free reading choices; they could pick the books they wanted to read. And they agreed to my two requirements: they had to discuss the book with the class, and they had to answer some response questions in their reading journal. The result was a remarkable change in our class: cooperation, respect, independence, motivation, and excitement about reading and sharing.

Most of the students read YAL; we had the advantage of an outstanding librarian who knew YAL, and she booktalked stacks of books to my class—every genre was covered. She also included appropriate adult books. As I began to read more and more YAL, I too became a devoted fan. With the freedom to choose their own titles, my students became readers, begging for time to read in class. And with confidence and poise, they shared their responses, recommendations, and critiques during Book Forums. As I observed students of various reading abilities talking about literature with critical authority, using such literary terms as *setting, conflict, character development,* and *foreshadowing,* I realized the effect of YAL on their joy of reading. Looking around the classroom, I kept thinking to myself that I was really dense—why had it taken me 15 years to let go? What was happening in my classroom at that moment was the best I could hope to achieve in any class!

This experience caused me to reverse my attitude about YAL. Previously I thought of these books as sentimental exaggerated stories about gangs, friendships, relationships, drugs, and divorce. Why would my students be interested in this pap—wasn't it the same as reading comic books? (An ironic statement from me, incidentally; I loved comic books when I was a kid, and probably even read them through 8th grade.) And the covers were ridiculous (but my students read them because the covers enticed them)! So how could my students learn or read quality literature with this stuff? I was so wrong! Through YAL I finally began to understand the pleasure they could find in reading. And once they became empowered readers, the required curriculum was not so daunting; they whipped through *A Midsummer Night's Dream,* listening to one another's explanations and acting out parts without feeling self-conscious. Wow—what a shift in studying Shakespeare with 7th graders!

I also observed that students chose to read a wide variety of literature—fiction, nonfiction, adult fiction, poetry, and plays, sort of like circling a salad bar at a restaurant. By validating their reading choices, I became a reading peer of sorts—listening, sharing, commenting, agreeing and disagreeing, recommending titles to others. Sometimes the kids' comments were more astute and enthusiastic than the discussions in my adult reading group. As I reflect on the exciting and stimulating atmosphere in those classrooms, I am certain that the catalyst was the quality of YAL my students eagerly read and wrote about with ease and confidence.

Next I turned my attention to my two high school classes, where reading classics, such as *The Scarlet Letter, Ethan Frome,* and *Death of a Salesman,* was a daily grind. Unlike my 7th and 8th graders, who were evolving into enthusiastic and independent readers, many of my high school students were what I would call "lost readers." I doubted that many of them would ever read any kind of book as adults. They found no pleasure in reading. How could I help them become "found readers"?

Two *English Journal* articles crystallized my thinking about my high school nonreaders. The first article, "The Natural Reading Life: A High School Anomaly" by Anne McCrary Sullivan, jolted my consciousness about students' reading experiences in and out of school. Sullivan describes the results of an assignment that asked her high school students to write their reading histories. When she eagerly sat down to read them after school, she states, "The longer I read, the greater my distress grew. Finally, I cried. The details varied, but in one account after another I found this recurring thread: I loved reading when I was young; school made me hate it" (40). What an indictment!

Sullivan's students described their reading experiences in elementary school as positive—their teachers had read to them, they chose books from the library to read alone—and then, *crash!* From 6th grade through high school, students agreed with Louis, who wrote, "I was told what, when, and how to read" (41). Some of these students continued to read outside of school, but many did not find the time to continue to read for pleasure.

One student confessed that he used Mr. Cliff (*Cliffs Notes*) for assigned reading in order to find time for his own reading. When I finished reading the reading histories of those 15 students, I was distressed too. Distressed because I wondered if my students' reading histories would echo these same bleak comments.

I began to think about the readers in my literature classes during my years as a teacher. I realized that I had neglected to ask my students to share their opinions and experiences about reading. Each year I had plunged into the curriculum without considering their past reading experiences. Why hadn't I ever considered the building blocks of their reading history?

The other article, "The Story World of Adolescents in *and* out of the Classroom" by Mark Vogel and Don Zancanella, provides interesting data from the literary lives of four adolescents. Each interview reflects the students' other experiences, such as films, television programs, comic books, and personal family histories, experiences that are not usually part of classroom writing and discussion. The four students reveal distinct personal reading preferences; however, their reading interests were not fulfilled in class assignments. And their classroom work did not begin to reflect their enthusiasm for a wide range of reading and viewing interests, nor their opinions about literature and understanding of those experiences.

From these in-depth interviews, the researchers conclude that unless teachers try to integrate students' outside literary experiences with classroom readings so that students begin to find connections in themes or subjects or genres, many students will not find much meaning in the prescribed literature curriculum. This article emphasizes that teachers need to investigate a wide range of reading and viewing (film and television) activities students engage in, and insure that the literature classroom honors their perceptions and choices about all kinds of reading experiences. Not an easy task for any literature teacher.

After reading these articles, I wanted to explore my own students' reading histories. It was important for me to find out what they did and did not like about reading and discussing literature. What kinds of reading activities did they enjoy? I gathered my courage and asked them to share their reading lives from earliest memories to the present. I was shocked and elated by their candor. Shocked because they related similar experiences to Sullivan's students, and elated because they trusted me enough to be honest. Here is an excerpt from one of their histories:

"Chris, you're ... a little slow."

"What do you mean Mrs. R.?"

"Well you aren't as good as the rest of the class and you're falling behind in your work."

"What should I do?"

"Well, I think I am going to have to put you in the low class. They don't read as much there and you'll be able to keep up with them. I'm sorry. You're just not the reading type. So here is your new book. Now get over there and I want you to be caught up by Wednesday."

"But, but...Mrs. R.?"

She was gone and so was my interest in reading. First grade was the worst year of my life. Mrs. R. put me in the low reading class. None of my friends were in it...I never liked that reading group, mostly because it made me feel stupid. To this day, I don't like to read.

Here's an excerpt from a 7th grader's reading life kept for three years:

The level of reading we had to do compared to last year skyrocketed! Not to mention, my teacher made me absolutely despise reading! I felt like reading was a huge responsibility and burden. Since I didn't practice my reading the last three years, I was a slow reader and couldn't comprehend either. I read through books and worked hard to understand them. That was the turning point in my reading life. From that year on, I read through every book completely and comprehended it superbly. My speed wasn't too fast, although it set me back. Sixth grade was the best year reading. I enjoyed the books more because I was faster...we had reading journals writing about the summary and character development during the chapter. I actually liked doing these. I liked doing the journals because I had a lot of opinions about the book that I wanted to express. The next year was very different. The books, the journals, and the reader response questions were very new to me. The books were the biggest change. Books like *The Pigman, The Giver,* and *The Miracle Worker.* They have all been unique in their themes; the main point these books are trying to tell you are much different than the books I read in earlier years...

Overall, I would say, yes, I like to read. As long as the book is interesting and as long as I am not forced to read something that I despise...reading puts me into a whole New World.

An avid reader writes:

Before fifth grade, no teacher had really motivated me to read. But in fifth grade, Mrs. K. was always excited about books. As I discovered the wonder of books, I began to really enjoy reading. If I read a book which I liked, I would keep on reading books by that author. This would continue, like a domino effect, until I had almost read all the books.

I also became a member of the Westport Library, with a library card as proof. I joined the Young Critics group at the library. In this group, everyone discusses a good book which they read. Of, if they consider the book bad, they have the responsibility of warning the rest of us. By the end of the year, the leader organizes the list of good books that we shared, and we vote on them. These votes are used in formulating a list which is printed onto a bookmark. After a while, I noticed that if I didn't go to these meetings, my interest in reading began to wear off.

My favorite books in eighth grade were *Cold Sassy Tree, A Tree Grows in Brooklyn, Briar Rose.* I wonder if I will ever read all the books which I want to read.

A possibly aliterate student comments:

In eighth grade I was introduced to the horrible world of quizzes practically every time we read a chapter. I hated quizzes...I like when we had a hands-on experience at the end of certain books. I like making a game board for *To Kill a Mockingbird* or acting out scenes from *Monster.* We were also introduced to the horrible world of book reports (ick!).

In seventh grade I pretty much got into mysteries and adventures. But I think what encouraged me to read was that no one forced me to read what I didn't want; I was free to discover all of the adventures and wonders of a good book by myself.

Another aliterate reader recognizes his frustration:

My parents used to read books to me almost every night before they tucked me in. It used to be my favorite part of the day. When I got a bit older my parents not only read to me, but I read to them...it gave me a feeling of pride knowing I could read.

After a couple of grades, the teachers made me, forced me to read a certain amount in a time period. I usually found this frustrating and gave up on reading completely because their demands made me so angry. This experience developed a prejudice about reading, so I did not read in my free time, only when teachers made assignments. I tried to stay away from books and to exclude them from my life, but this did not work since reading is part of every subject. I reintroduced myself to books and learned not to relate them to any form of homework.

As the reading lives assignment continued through the years, I collected enough recurring comments to reach the following conclusions:

- Reading groups based on skills can destroy students' confidence about reading.
- Choice and self-selection are an important component of reading development. Students want to choose all kinds of books, from YAL to classic or contemporary literature.
- Students like to pace their reading; they are passionate and literate in expressing their likes and dislikes.
- Students like to write about their reading in journals, they like to reflect on what they have read, and if they are in the middle of a good book, they don't want to stop to take tests and quizzes.
- As they begin to analyze stories, students have the ability to distinguish between easy and demanding books.

- A teacher's enthusiasm about reading counts; a teacher who is excited about reading transmits the importance of stories.
- Book discussion with peers is crucial to teen readers; it makes reading a part of the socialization process. It also focuses on the importance of listening to varied opinions.
- Many required titles in high school are a real turn-off for struggling readers; they need a bridge to required classics.

I found the inventory of my students' reading lives insightful and disturbing. I cringed when I read about the effects of harmful groupings and testing for comprehension on their reading lives. Yes, some of these histories are skewed—a teacher's comment taken out of context, for instance—but these classroom events remain with them. And only a positive reading experience can erase all the negative memories. By reading their histories and engaging them to reflect on their reading histories, I was gathering valuable information to empower us to work together so they could find pleasure in reading. I had to retool my teaching style in order to change the negative attitudes.

As I gathered my students' reading histories each year and learned to change my teaching strategies, I noticed subtle changes in their reading. There were two avenues of reading in our class—the freedom to choose any title (though I booktalked various genres of YAL that I thought would appeal to them) and the required curriculum, which we read and discussed together. Tests and quizzes were verboten; they developed their written responses into well-organized essays, and our classroom became a community of independent readers who took charge of their discussion and writing about literature. There were few inhibitions about sharing their writing and opinions about literature. All types of readers could participate with ease because no one's opinion or ability level was threatened; there was such respect, honesty, and trust that questioning each other's ideas about interpretation was a shared learning experience. The classroom atmosphere was relaxed, yet students were engaged in making meaning. These classes were the most satisfying in my teaching career. But it was YAL—all those well-crafted novels by authors such as Chris Crutcher, Karen Hesse, Robert Cormier, Will Hobbs, Alden R. Carter, Harry Mazer, Han Nolan, Sue Ellen Bridgers, Ron Koertge, Sarah Dessen, Will Weaver, Walter Dean Myers, Norma Fox Mazer, M. E. Kerr, Randy Powell, Kathryn Lasky, and Jacqueline Woodson, to name a few—that helped me recapture those "lost readers." My students discovered books that connected to their lives, but now they could discuss these teenage concerns and issues in meaningful ways with peers. They wrote their responses to YAL with fervor, rereading the texts and rediscovering the importance of stories, whether fantasy, mystery, adventure, history, or reality, stories that could transport their imaginations into new realms.

My treasure trove of readers recharged our English classroom; they validated my belief that reading and discussing literature helps us to discover what it means to be human.

Chapter 2

WHAT IS YOUNG ADULT LITERATURE, ANYWAY?

WHAT YOUNG ADULT LITERATURE IS

Trying to explain or define Young Adult Literature to teachers who have not read it or who have a negative attitude about it (like I did initially) is very difficult. It's even more difficult because many teachers perceive YA books as a supermarket shelf stocked with romances, mysteries, or horror series with garish covers. Please don't rely on supermarkets or drug stores for the best selection of teen books. In the past few years, many bookstores have set aside a separate teen section featuring well-written YAL for middle and high school readers. YAL used to be shelved with children's books, but many bookstores realized that teen readers would not browse among younger children's books. Now the teen section at bookstores is packed with every genre of YA book imaginable, and teen readers head right for this section to select books.

Years ago, before the advent of YAL in the late 1960s, Nancy Drew, the Hardy Boys, Tom Swift, and the adventures of Frank Merriwell were considered teen literature. These novels avoided controversial topics such as sexuality, substance abuse, divorce, and death. They focused on one socio-economic class, for the most part—white middle-class teenagers engaged in white middle-class activities. They were considered superficial by many literary critics because they lacked credibility in portraying the true nature of adolescents' lives. And they were never part of the school curriculum. For years, English classes in most high schools taught Charles Dickens, William Shakespeare, Nathaniel Hawthorne, and other adult novelists whose writing perplexed struggling readers. Before YAL appeared on the scene, there were a few titles slanted for teenage readers, such as *Seventeenth Summer* by Maureen Daly, *Johnny Tremain* by Esther Forbes, sports novels by John Tunis, and hot-rod books by Henry Gregor Felsen. However, few if any of those were included in school curricula.

The turning point for YAL came in 1967 with the publication of *The Outsiders* by S. E. Hinton, which describes the problems of alienated youth; *The Contender* by Robert Lipsyte, which reflects the hope and the despair of African American urban youths; *The Chosen* by Chaim Potok, which describes the inner conflicts of two Jewish adolescents; and *Mr and Mrs Bo Jo Jones* by Ann Head, dealing with teen pregnancy. Other authors began to change the focus of YAL as more novels addressed the realities of teenage life and offered readers an honest view of the main characters' hopes, fears, and dilemmas.

It is important to note that as YAL gained popularity among teenage readers, the literary talents of the authors also became more evident. YAL authors incorporated into their books the same elements as those in adult novels: a consistent point of view, a significant setting, a well-delineated but not complicated plot, vivid characterization, realistic and lively dialogue, and an attractive style.

Here are Don Gallo's characteristics of good fiction for young adults:

- The main characters are teenagers.
- The length of the average book is around 200 pages, though it may be as brief as 100 pages or (as in the case of the Harry Potter novels) as long as 900 pages.
- The point of view is most often first person, and it is usually that of a teenager.
- The narrator is most often the main character.
- The story is usually told in the voice of a teenager, not the voice of an adult looking back as a young person (as it is in *To Kill a Mockingbird* or *A Separate Peace*).
- The language is typical of contemporary teenagers, and the vocabulary, unlike that of adult classics, is manageable by readers of average ability.
- The setting is most often contemporary, but also can be historical, futuristic (as in science fiction), or imaginative (as in fantasy); it takes place most often in the United States but is occasionally set in foreign countries.
- The books contain characters and issues to which teenagers can relate.
- In a majority of the books, parents play a minor role or are "the enemy."
- The plot and literary style are uncomplicated but never simplistic, though the plots of a few books are quite complex (for example, those of Robert Cormier, M. E. Kerr, Chris Lynch, and E. R. Frank).
- The outcome of the story is usually dependent upon the decisions and actions of the main character.
- The tone and outcome of the novels are usually upbeat, but not in all instances. (Since 2000, there has been an increase in the number of darker, grittier novels for and about teens.)

- With the exception of complicated plotting, all the traditional literary elements typical of classical literature are present in most contemporary novels for young adults—well-rounded characters, flashbacks, foreshadowing, allusions, irony, metaphorical language—though they are used less frequently and at less sophisticated levels to match the experiential levels of readers.
- The very best YA books can be as appealing to adult readers as they are to teens.

Using these characteristics and comparing them with the elements of adult fiction, we begin to realize that many YAL authors—such as Walter Dean Myers, Chris Crutcher, Karen Hesse, David Klass, Laurie Halse Anderson, Jerry Spinelli, Joan Bauer, Tamora Pierce, Ron Koertge, Han Nolan, and Jeanette Ingold—reflect mastery of the novel form combined with well-crafted writing.

There is no agreed-upon literal definition of YAL. Some have defined it as any kind of literature read voluntarily by teenagers; others delineate it as books with teenage protagonists, or books written for a teenage audience. Suffice it to say that YAL covers a broad spectrum of books, including books written for adults that are read by both adults and teenagers. An example of this type of crossover is J. D. Salinger's *The Catcher in the Rye,* published in 1951. Did Salinger write this book primarily for young adults? Which age group mostly reads this book? Another example is Bobbie Ann Mason's *In Country,* which was nominated for the National Book Award in 1988. Esmeralda Santiago's *When I Was Puerto Rican,* Orson Scott Card's *Ender's Game,* and Alice Sebold's *The Lovely Bones* are more recent examples of crossover novels. Salinger and Mason do not write for young adult readers per se. Publishers categorize these novels as adult novels, but they appeal to young adult readers because they include some of the YA novel characteristics mentioned previously.

Regardless of the conflicting points of view among teachers, librarians, critics, and publishers, there is clearly a distinct body of literature written specifically for young adults and being read by them. And the contents of the books in the YA genre has grown better with each decade, with more high-quality, hard-hitting books being published in the past five years than ever before.

SOME TEACHER PERCEPTIONS

Too many teachers in middle and high schools still perceive YAL as supportive reading or as an alternative literature curriculum for lower-level English classes. Not all YAL is for the remedial reader or the unmotivated reader who cannot handle the prescribed readings in the traditional English curriculum. Nor is it an expurgated version of a required classic. It is true that some of these novels are ideal for low-ability readers and students with short attention spans who cannot engage in traditional class-room literature. But that attitude leads to the belief that these titles are not comparable to the "normal" class texts. Thus YAL, like some stock charac-ter actor, is typecast by many teachers as being inferior reading and lack-ing the necessary qualities of great works of literature. Many teachers equate YAL with boxed sets of controlled vocabulary reading books, some-times referred to as "hi-lo" books, with no literary qualities.

This attitude about YAL is further reinforced because the traditional secondary school English curriculum in most schools has not included many—if any—YAL titles. In his 1989 study of the top 10 titles taught in public, private, and parochial schools in grades 9–12, Arthur N. Apple-bee, codirector of the Center for the Learning and Teaching of Literature at the State University of New York–Albany, confirmed that traditional classics dominate the English curriculum. Comparing his 1989 survey with a 1963 survey, Applebee concluded that "Shakespeare dominated the list in 1963 and continued to do so" (*Study of Book-Length Works,* 9). The only title to have dropped in popularity is *Silas Marner!* The top 10 titles in the 1989 survey were Shakespeare's *Macbeth, Julius Caesar, Hamlet,* and *Romeo and Juliet; The Adventures of Huckleberry Finn* by Mark Twain; *The Scarlet Letter* by Nathaniel Hawthorne; *Of Mice and Men* by John Steinbeck; *The Great Gatsby* by F. Scott Fitzgerald; *Lord of the Flies* by William Golding; and *To Kill a Mockingbird* by Harper Lee.

These findings corroborate the case in many senior high schools. While I frequently heard teachers state a need for more appropriate literature for average 9th and 10th grade classes, the traditional classics remained in place. Although I heard a distraught colleague swear she would never again teach Dickens's *Great Expectations* to an average-level 10th grade class, I found that most of us ignored YAL, didn't even attempt to con-sider it viable in the English curriculum, and, if it was mentioned, assumed it was appropriate for 7th and 8th graders—*not* for high school, and definitely *not* for the college-bound. This attitude still exists today among too many secondary teachers. I have heard and observed English teachers speak of YAL with disdain, emphasizing that the classics are important and necessary. It is important to question whose needs are being met in the literature classroom—students' or teachers'?

Applebee has not surveyed schools concerning the top 10 titles since 1989; however, based on curriculum lists and our conversations with high school teachers, the classics and a few contemporary adult novels still dominate the curriculum. YAL is likely to be more prevalent in mid-dle school literature courses, along with such classics as *The Pearl, Inherit the Wind,* and *To Kill a Mockingbird.*

Over the past 30 years, many authors of YAL have proven their liter-ary mettle by telling their stories from an adolescent's point of view and drawing readers immediately into the book, whether the story is fantasy, mystery, science fiction, historical fiction, or adventure/survival. An example of this kind of writing that grabs adolescents follows, from Chris Crutcher's *Chinese Handcuffs*:

Dear Preston:
    Gotta tell you this feels weird. I got the idea from a book called *The Color Purple*, by a lady named Alice Walker. It's a good book—a really good book—but that's not the point. The main character didn't have anyone in the world to talk to, no one she could trust, so she started writing letters to God, because It (that's the pronoun she used for God because she wasn't all sure of His or Her gender) was about the only thing left she believed in. Since you've been gone, I've been running around so full of that day and everything that probably led up to it that if I don't tell somebody about it, I might explode. Only there's no one to tell. I can't burden Dad with it; he certainly has enough other things to worry about, what with Mom and Christy having left.

Crutcher's use of an adolescent first-person narrator writing a letter to his dead brother about his life, their father, their mother and sister, mentioning he's ready to explode, is powerful. The narrator, Dillon, draws the reader in by sharing his most intimate feelings about death, love, fear, and insecurities. Crutcher sustains this intimate style with his readers, reassuring them that their rollercoaster feelings are not unique among their age group. The novel is well written, the characters are well developed, and through Dillon's struggle, Crutcher succeeds in proving that adolescents can survive if they learn to compromise with amoral situations.

As a way to familiarize educators with YAL in the teen section, a colleague of ours, who teaches a Young Adult Literature course at a state university, started a teacher reading group that reads a YA title and meets every month for discussion in the café of their local Borders bookstore. Many of them discuss these newest titles with their students and encourage them to browse in the YAL section at libraries as well as bookstores. It's a neat idea to get kids into the habit of going to bookstores to browse and read books, especially since there's a place to sit and read (and eat!). And it's not a bad place to hang out with a group of friends.

Other colleagues have a YA reading group of middle school, high school, and college teachers and librarians that meets in their home every month to read and discuss new YA titles. Reading group discussions help us to gain a perspective on our responses versus student responses to YAL books. And it's a good way to keep up-to-date on newly published titles and authors.

The more educators read and discuss current YAL, the more they begin to realize the amazing changes in YAL in the past 10 years. At staff development workshops, I've often recommended teacher reading groups as a method of learning about new titles and new authors. The more teachers read and discuss titles, the easier it is for them to decide which books are suitable for the appropriate grade levels. I suggest they buy five copies each of various titles and rotate them among themselves to determine which title is a bridge to the curriculum and for which grade level. Then they can order class sets of two or more titles that meet the ability level of their students. Or they can group several titles around a theme. There are lots of ways for teachers to find YAL titles to bridge the required curriculum.

THEMES AND ARCHETYPES IN YOUNG ADULT LITERATURE

Like well-written adult literature, YAL contains many universal themes, including the eternal questions *Who am I?* and *Where do I fit in?* Other themes include alienation from one's society or group; survival or meeting a challenge; social and/or political concerns about sexual, racial, or ethnic discrimination; and social concerns about AIDS, teenage pregnancy, divorce, substance abuse, terrorism, family conflicts, dealing with death, and political injustice. These are issues and topics that *all* students can benefit from reading and discussing, not just students at lower academic levels.

And like adult best sellers, some of the literature is intended for pure escape or entertainment, while other stories are grounded in more universal themes. According to recent research, as the next chapter will show, YAL has proven to be an effective means to motivate adolescents to read all kinds of literature, including the classics. YAL is not a stepchild of the classics or of contemporary literature. Furthermore, if our students want to read, discuss, and write about YAL, don't their opinions warrant consideration? If we hope to help students become lifetime readers and to help them realize the importance of literature in understanding themselves in relation to the complexities of their world, don't we need to use all the resources available to us? To engage today's students in reading, we need to consider quality adolescent literature as a means to meet the needs of those individuals in our English classes who are not reading—especially students of average or high ability who choose not to read and students who have not developed any interest in reading literature since they were in middle school. We are not advocating that YAL replace the classics entirely; rather, we are asking you to consider the possibility of using some YAL, at least as an entry or bridge to the prescribed plays, novels, short stories, and nonfiction in your curriculum.

Chapter 3

DIRECTING VERSUS EXPLORING:
HOW TO GET TO WHERE YOU'RE
GOING WITHOUT A LITERARY MAP

TEACHING WHAT A BOOK "MEANS"

In the traditional English class, most teachers want students to acquire knowledge about literary genres, such as novels, short stories, drama, essays, and poetry. We want students to be able to identify the elements of literature: setting, character, plot, style, and theme. We want them to become familiar with literary terms such as *crisis, climax, foreshadowing, flashback, figurative language,* and *denouement.* When the whole class reads a title from the traditional curriculum, we pointedly ask questions related to this literary knowledge, often in preparation for a test. Some teachers produce chapter-by-chapter study questions that students must answer on a daily basis. In a sense, these questions are telling students what is important, how they should comprehend the novel, and what the book "means."

Although the teacher believes he or she is being helpful in giving students these materials, in fact, by discussing the answers to these questions on a daily basis, the teacher has stolen the students' freedom to express their personal reactions to the novel. Students have not revealed their own discoveries about the novel through their private reading, nor have they been allowed to share their ideas or personal reactions with other students. In this type of English class, the teacher has transmitted what he or she (or the accompanying curriculum guide) considers the "correct interpretation" of the novel; the teacher's interpretation might be based on literary criticism, college coursework, or publishers' teaching guides. If the students do well on the teacher's test, then the teacher concludes that those students have acquired literary knowledge. The teacher probably feels good about this type of teaching experience, thinking he or she has fulfilled the goal of teaching students to understand and appreciate a work of literature.

Granted, this example might sound extreme, but teaching guides and teacher-led interpretations of prescribed curriculum titles are more the rule than the exception in our profession. The template of "teach and test" exists in too many English classes. Some teachers know what they want students to learn from a work of literature before the first paragraph, stanza, or act has been read. There are expected answers to teacher-generated questions. Yet the goal most of us have in mind is to assist, help, force, and convince our students to appreciate good literature, whatever good means.

Early on our students get a clear message from us: if they want to be considered literate and educated adults, they must learn to appreciate good literature. Enjoyment of reading is not a consideration, discovery and exploration by students are immaterial, and allowing them to select what they want to read or are interested in is ignored by many of us. Our own love of reading and literature presupposes that what *we* select and what *we* interpret is best for our students. Too often reading for pleasure is not a goal, and students' opinions are irrelevant.

Many of us are convinced that we are leading our students into an appreciation of traditional literature, but there is qualitative and quantitative research to prove us wrong. Two reader surveys reflect the effects of traditional literature on students' reading attitudes as well as their reactions to prescribed traditional assignments.

WHAT STUDENTS SAY ABOUT REQUIRED BOOKS

G. Robert Carlsen and Anne Sherrill's book *Voices of Readers: How We Come to Love Books* (1988) reveals a wide array of responses from individuals about their reading experiences in junior and senior high school. One adult reports,

During my high school days, I read most of the classroom assignments, but was bored by the masterpieces, or perhaps I failed to understand them. They seemed to be written in another language and seemed not to entertain, but confuse. (132)

Another individual recalls,

I hated almost all of the books we studied in English classes... I hated Charlotte Bronte the most. I was to read *Jane Eyre* for a seventh grade book report, but I couldn't finish it and have never been able to force myself to try it again. (131)

Carlsen and Sherrill's respondents cited numerous reasons for not enjoying assigned literature, including the difficulty of understanding the reading in the first place, then having to dissect the texts, "rehashing the same material for days," and having to search for the "meaning" the teacher expected, without acknowledging their own feelings, and being forced to read sophisticated texts when the students lacked the experience and maturity to fully understand them (129–36).

Don Gallo, then a professor of English at Central Connecticut State University, studied the reading interests of nearly 3,400 students in grades 4–12 in over 50 schools in 37 towns throughout Connecticut in 1982. In his study, students were asked if they liked the novels and other books they were assigned to read. Gallo reports,

In junior high schools, 40 percent of the boys and 35 percent of the girls indicated that they *seldom* or *never* liked required selections. In senior high schools, 41 percent of the boys and 23 percent of the girls said *seldom* or *never*. In comparison, only one student in every five *usually* or *always* liked the assigned books. ("Listening to Readers" 20)

Many of the students surveyed by Gallo noted the same reaction to the classics as did the respondents in the Carlsen and Sherrill study. The Connecticut students complained that the traditional classics were "antiquated," contained unfamiliar words, and were too historical, old-fashioned, and dull. One 10th grade boy exclaimed, "These books have nothing to do with me," and a 10th grade girl commented, "Reading literature is keeping in touch with the dead." Many students agreed with another 10th grader, who stated, "Our teacher doesn't *want* you to enjoy literature; she wants you to read it for the details and themes" (20). As a teacher who loves literature, I cringe at these comments and wonder how many of my students felt the same way.

Even though these surveys are more than 20 years old, and readers' interests have changed somewhat, the essence of these findings and the patterns they reveal are not unlike the results of recent reading surveys.

Shouldn't a major purpose in teaching literature be to help students find pleasure in reading and to become lifetime readers? Certainly the above comments are convincing reasons to modify the traditional literature curriculum in order to meet the needs of students who are not yet ready for the classics.

We can best help nonreading, turned-off, bored students by first trying to understand where they are developmentally. To do so, it will help to review G. Robert Carlsen's research about the stages of developing readers, Louise Rosenblatt's transactional theory about the reader and the literary text, and Robert Probst's observations about the student's personal response to literature as a first step in understanding students' ability to make meaning or take meaning from literature.

STAGES OF GROWTH IN LITERARY APPRECIATION

G. Robert Carlsen's *Books and the Teenage Reader* (1980) explains the idiosyncratic reading patterns of adolescent readers based on their emotional and intellectual development. Carlsen, a former professor of English at the University of Iowa, based his conclusions on his own experiences with students in Iowa public schools. His theories are significant because they consider the psychological and/or social development of adolescents and their impact on students' reading choices. Carlsen matched story choices with particular age groups in order to begin to make sense of adolescents' preferences. For example, in early adolescence, between the ages of 11 and 14 years, Carlsen found the most favored types of stories were about animals, adventure, mystery, the supernatural, sports, home and family life, broad slapstick, fantasy, and historical settings. At age 15 or 16 the reading interests among Carlsen's students included nonfiction accounts of adventure, historical novels, romances, and stories of adolescent life. By late adolescence, during the last two years of high school, students chose books read by adults as well as books written for teenagers. Some of the subject matter at that time included the search for personal values, topics of social significance, strange human experiences, and the transition to adult life (36–42).

Carlsen's description of stages of reading development makes sense to us based on our own classroom experiences with student readers. In a 1974 *English Journal* article titled "Literature Is," Carlsen cited reading patterns that have been mapped through observations of thousands of adolescent subjects. He proposed five stages of developing readers (23–27):

1. *Unconscious delight:* The typical response of elementary to middle school readers. They read for enjoyment without analyzing why; they have not yet developed a vocabulary for discussing emotional responses.
2. *Living vicariously:* Action and escape seem to dominate for middle school and junior high readers—horror, mystery, romance, fantasy, and true adventures.
3. *Seeing oneself:* The typical response of readers in junior high school into high school is more egocentric. Now readers are concerned with what's happening in their personal and social lives. YAL has a strong appeal at this stage.
4. *Philosophical speculations:* Upper-level high school students shift from focusing on self to an interest in others, looking for relationships, examining why. Some are still reading stories of adolescent life.
5. *Aesthetic delight:* In late high school to adulthood, readers have acquired critical awareness and begin to recognize universal themes. By this stage readers have developed the vocabulary to describe literary elements. They can delight in, recognize, and appreciate the qualities of writing.

These stages describe the norm. Students with reading problems and lower social and intellectual abilities may reach these levels at a later age. Conversely, students with stronger reading and social abilities may attain higher levels sooner.

In one way, these stages build on one another; in another way, all five levels of response can operate at the same time in varying degrees. As adult readers, we float among the various stages of development, depending on the subject matter. It is doubtful that as educated adults we respond on an aesthetic level consistently; after all, we all like to relax with a good escapist story. We often lose ourselves in best sellers by such well-known authors as John Grisham, Stephen King, Robert Ludlum, John LeCarre, Dan Brown, or Nora Roberts. Yet many of us expect our students to respond continually at an aesthetic level to adult-oriented literature even though some of them have not matured beyond the "personal problem" stage, or lack the advanced reading skills necessary to handle many of the classics included in the traditional curriculum (for example, *The Scarlet Letter, Hamlet, Great Expectations, Ethan Frome, The Great Gatsby,* or *The Grapes of Wrath*). Thus, when we select literature for our classes, we need to consider our students' stages of reading development. And we need to remember that students move among these various reading stages, depending on the subject matter, the genre, and their interest level, as well as their individual reading ability and habits.

Accepting Carlsen's stages of literary development does not mean we have to provide an entire curriculum suited to students' tastes (that could mean reading six consecutive Lemony Snicket or Stephen King novels!), but it does mean that we ought to provide a *comfort* level in students' reading choices by providing *quality* literature that is *accessible* to them regardless of whether it fulfills *our* notion of what great literature is.

Whether we feel more comfortable teaching the classics is not a prime consideration if we truly want our students to enjoy reading and become habitual readers. Too often in the past, we have graduated students from our high schools who have read the required classics and passed the obligatory quizzes and tests but who never read a significant literary work—or even a contemporary best seller—during the remainder of their lives. We have taught them the best literature of the past, but we have failed to help them become lovers of literature. By what we require them to read and how we teach it, we have failed to convince them of the power of literature to help them learn about themselves or to help them survive in a complex world.

But how will they learn to interpret and appreciate literature if they don't study the best that literature has to offer? The first step involves helping them to become readers, to enjoy the act of reading, and to realize that reading is experiential. Through their reading experiences they can begin to understand the nature of human relationships; they can begin to conjecture and explore some answers about their primary question—*Who am I?*

YAL provides teenagers an opportunity to read books that speak to them; these books allow the reader to compare himself or herself to the struggles of the main character. Sometimes the story exemplifies the very problem that the reader has been wrestling with and is unable to see objectively. By allowing students to read a wide variety of YAL as well as adult contemporary and classic literature, we are saying, "Pick what you like to read, what you are comfortable with, and enjoy a good read." And by supporting their choices, we are helping them move through their own personal maturation as serious, committed readers. This process encourages independence and respect for the individual reader and helps them to understand how literature might be useful in their struggle to comprehend the complexities in human relationships and contemporary society.

TRANSACTIONAL THEORY

It will further our understanding of students' engagement in the reading of literature if we consider two seminal works by Louise Rosenblatt, professor emeritus of English Education at New York University. *Literature as Exploration*, first published in 1938, emphasizes the importance of the literary experience in the education of the student. Among the important theories she advances is the notion that literature teaches the student about his or her culture, that stories of America and its people offer the student a variety of opportunities to learn about America and its diverse population. The literary experience also helps the student to develop sensitivity and understanding about the human condition; it relates experiences that aid the emotional maturation of the developing reader and allows him or her to listen to and exchange ideas with other students. However, Rosenblatt adds, "Like the beginning reader, the adolescent needs to encounter literature for which he possesses the intellectual, emotional, and experiential equipment" (26). When the students use past experiences to respond to literature, they are in the process of building new experiences as a guide to understanding society. Rosenblatt emphasizes the need to encourage students to feel free to respond on an emotional as well as a judgmental level. As the students exchange responses with other students, they begin to clarify, reconsider, or reaffirm their personal responses. In this atmosphere, students are making personal meaning from reading literature and are beginning to participate in the exploration of the powerful ideas transmitted by literature. But Rosenblatt warns, "Books must be provided that hold out some link with the young reader's past and present occupations, anxieties, ambitions" (72). And it is in this context that we must consider accommodating the needs of developing adolescent readers.

In *The Reader, the Text, the Poem*, Rosenblatt explains the process of reading as a transaction between the reader and the text. She believes that a work of literature has no meaning to a reader until he or she has experienced a personal response. It is important to consider this explanation carefully, because many students in traditional classrooms are not offered the opportunity to have a personal response. Instead, they are lectured to or they study and accept selected literary criticism; in many cases they become passive receptors of teachers' lectures. If we consider Rosenblatt's thought-provoking explanation about the act of reading, it becomes clear to us that we must allow our students to become active readers.

Using "poem" to refer to the "whole category of aesthetic transactions between readers and text," Rosenblatt describes the poem "as an event in time...during a coming-together, a compenetration, of a reader and a text" (12). The words of the literature enter a student's consciousness and tap into his or her personal experience. The words and the reader's experiences begin a process of meaning that evokes a personal response in the reader. This meaning is highly personal, asserts Rosenblatt; until it is shared, it remains a private meaning. It is not likely to coincide with teacher meaning or critic meaning or any other imposed meaning. But its importance is the first step in the reader's "reading life"; it must be accepted and respected as a beginning step in the reader's response to the text.

In this transaction between reader and text, the reader is actively engaged in thinking about the words on the page; the reader is making meaning from reading literature, meaning that should have an opportunity to be shared and discussed in the classroom. As teachers of literature, we must accept the wide range of responses to a text based on the wide range of students' experiences. It is this exchange of responses to literature that often motivates students to become readers.

As teachers, we need to remember that the act of reading is first a private experience; each reader uses his or her own personal experience as a bridge or connection to begin to make meaning from a work of literature. If we acknowledge Rosenblatt's transactional theory of reading and agree that reading offers the adolescent an opportunity to test his or her life experiences against the experiences offered in the text, then we must consider seriously Rosenblatt's comment in *Literature as Exploration* that "choices must reflect a sense of the possible links between these materials and the students' past experience and present level of emotional maturity" (42).

Simply put, we cannot determine what students ought to read without considering their ability to respond to a work of literature on the basis of their personal experiences. What can they relate to in the book? How many teenagers can relate to Arthur Dimmesdale's particular brand of guilt and sin? How many 10th graders can relate to Ethan Frome's acceptance of his stark life caring for Maddie and Zenobia? In what way can a contemporary urban teenager, possibly raised in a welfare family, relate to Lear's losses? But sometimes a high school student can empathize with Nick's need to leave the East and get away from the Buchanans after Gatsby's death. Or a son who has a difficult parental relationship can understand Biff's shame and disrespect for his father, Willie Loman.

For students who are not ready or who cannot yet respond to Shakespeare, Hemingway, Fitzgerald, James, Wharton, Miller, and other authors of demanding literature, there is a body of quality YAL that invites them to become confident readers, responding readers, and makers of meaning. For example, most 7th or 8th graders from any socioeconomic group can relate to Ponyboy and Sodapop in S. E. Hinton's *The Outsiders*—to their struggle to fit in and their feelings of alienation, seeing perhaps a parallel to Steinbeck's characters George and Lennie in *Of Mice and Men*. Richard Peck's *Remembering the Good Times* describes in compassionate detail the effect of a boy's suicide on his two best friends, something many of today's students can relate to. Many teenage readers can identify with Zoe in Annette Curtis Klause's *The Silver Kiss* as she faces her mother's death from cancer. And other powerful writers—such as Jerry Spinelli, Will Hobbs, Walter Dean Myers, Alex Flinn, Joan Bauer, Gail Giles, Jacqueline Woodson, Sonya Sones, Chris Crutcher, and Carol Plum-Ucci—provide a compassionate view of teenagers struggling to make sense of a world that tests their perception of morality. As students become makers of meaning in the literature they read, they gain the knowledge to discover and measure their own feelings and beliefs against those of their classmates and to reconsider those opinions and beliefs.

Imagine the act of reading as a series of moments, of words flashing through these moments, stacking up in our memory bank—flashing ideas and images that connect to some event in our past experience, perhaps an event in childhood; we read on and on, weaving a vast mural of these events, and the mural becomes our picture...with language it becomes our story. Our students should be weaving their own stories when they respond to a text.

Rosenblatt's theory is important because she validates the reader's personal response as a genuine and authentic beginning in making meaning. The world of the reader is an important component in understanding, enjoying, and respecting literature as a source of knowledge. Rosenblatt reminds us of the possibilities of a literary experience as a social force in the life of the developing reader. She reminds us that the reader's response to the text is not static; as readers mature and wrestle with new ideas and challenges, they are preparing themselves for more insightful transactions with more demanding literature. Rosenblatt uses the phrase "developing social sensitivity"; we might also call it developing a social conscience, a feeling of compassion for the human condition.

Rosenblatt comments, "When the young reader considers why he has responded in a certain way, he is learning both to read more adequately and to seek personal meaning in literature" (*Literature as Exploration* 70). Perhaps the reader then is moving into what Carlsen calls the philosophical stage; perhaps the reader is moving from an emotional to a cognitive response, independently considering the structure of literature. The more that maturing readers read, the more they begin to recognize patterns in the literature. They begin to connect settings, characters, and plots from other readings. The process continues through personal response as well as through classroom discussion, which can inspire meaningful interaction among readers.

It is during this discussion stage—and it truly must be a discussion, not a question-answer session—that students *share* their individual, personal responses. For example, if several students have read *Ironman* by Chris Crutcher, they might argue about the father-son relationship, comparing it to their relationship with their own parents. They may question, argue, agree with, or defend their personal feelings about the behavior of particular characters in the novel. They might support or refute a father's right to give orders to a son. They may agree or disagree with each other's responses, going back into the text, reading passages out loud to one another, and at the same time begin to sift out particular details through dialogue and description while reconsidering their responses and interpretations. At this point, students are sharing personal responses as well as discussing literary techniques such as dialogue, character relationships, point of view, and setting. They argue and discuss with conviction, going back into the text to validate opinions. There is no doubt that this kind of student-led discussion provides the most exciting moments in a classroom—it is the essence of why we teach literature.

RESPONSE-BASED TEACHING

Most of us have led our students to the so-called correct meaning of the prescribed literature. And many of us have used published teacher guides, reading aids, packaged quizzes, and tests that encourage a kind of dead-end approach to reading. How do we move away from this comfortable stance and, instead, risk changing to a response-based classroom? It isn't easy.

We need to find a starting point, a comfort zone for our students as well as for ourselves. So how do we begin to rethink our time-tested (but time-worn) habits and attitudes about teaching literature? First, you might want to read Carlsen and Rosenblatt to make your own sense of their theories, observations, and conclusions; as readers, we should have a personal response to their texts and speculate for ourselves what kinds of changes we need to consider if we want to meet the needs of our students.

Although our students are in a constant state of change, we teachers are suspicious of change. But changing our whole approach to teaching literature can unhinge the most seasoned veteran. And changing from a teacher-centered classroom to a student-centered, response-based classroom is scary. Our students will probably be more open to change than we will.

Fortunately, Robert E. Probst, research fellow at the Center for Urban Education and Innovation, Florida International University, has written a comprehensive book that encompasses research and application about response-based teaching. In *Response and Analysis: Teaching Literature in Secondary School*, he explains clearly the nature and structure of response-based teaching as a means of engaging students in their reading of literature. Using Rosenblatt's theory of the transaction between reader and text, Probst describes the reader's response in isolation, the reader's response with other readers, and the reader's relationship with texts. He provides model lessons using reader response, demonstrating how it encourages honest responses from students, invites speculation, and develops discussion skills among students as they begin to formulate their own interpretations of a text. He emphasizes that

the teaching of literature must be grounded in the students' responses to the text, so they need the opportunity to articulate those responses. The ideas and concepts in the literature classroom do not have identity and substance independent of the students; rather, they are produced by the students as they interact with the text. Unless students read and respond, there is no literature to teach—only text and information about texts. (73)

Thus students must engage with the text, they must articulate some response, and their responses must be accepted and discussed with serious intent so they begin to trust their judgment and are willing to have a dialogue with peers.

After pinpointing techniques for encouraging students to respond and work with their responses, Probst explains several categories of responses: Personal, Interpretive, Topical, Formal, and Broader Literary Concerns. These varied responses will lead to insights, perspectives, and analytical ideas that students can consider and discuss among themselves. Thus, a dialogue about the text has begun, and students are engaged in "making the poem."

In his chapter "Literature for Young Adults" (YAL in this text), Probst explains why YAL is important in the teaching of literature. With sexuality and violence as topics, Probst uses several YAL titles within each category to illustrate how provocative they can be in eliciting responses and interest in discussion and writing.

Because YAL focuses on controversial and contemporary issues that are meaningful to adolescent readers, it constructs a bridge to the traditional English curriculum. Using Arthur N. Applebee's report, *A Study of Book-Length Works Taught in High School English Courses*, we can begin to pair or group some titles from YAL with several of the most widely taught traditional titles. Some YAL titles that could be used to tie into *To Kill a Mockingbird*, for example, might include *Betsey Brown* by Ntozake Shange, *Many Stones* by Carolyn Coman, *Spite Fences* by Trudy Krisher, or *Who Will Tell My Brother?* by Marlene Carvell. All deal with family relationships, loneliness, and personal identity.

For *Lord of the Flies,* some novels with common ideas could include *The Chocolate War* by Robert Cormier, *Out of Control* by Norma Fox Mazer, *Give a Boy a Gun* by Todd Strasser, or *Whale Talk* by Chris Crutcher. All focus on the conflict between going along with the crowd or being an individual.

Hamlet could be preceded by reading *Simon Says* by Elaine Marie Alphin, *The Crazy Horse Electric Game* by Chris Crutcher, *Freewill* by Chris Lynch, *America* by E. R. Frank, or *Forgotten Fire* by Adam Bagdasarian. All deal with young people surviving alone, without parental or adult support, searching for their place in an indifferent society.

Shattering Glass by Gail Giles, *The Rag and Bone Shop* by Robert Cormier, *Slot Machine* by Chris Lynch, *Lord of the Deep* by Graham Salisbury, and *Breaking Point* by Alex Flinn provide the reader with a view of characters struggling to understand a society interested in self-gratification, a society that exploits its less powerful members, just as Nick, the narrator, tries to understand his milieu in *The Great Gatsby*. Nick describes Gatsby's need to impress his golden girl, Daisy Buchanan, at any cost. Yet Nick is overwhelmed by Tom Buchanan's treatment of Mabel and Daisy's indifference to Gatsby's death. These YAL novels are good starting points before reading *Gatsby* because they, too, present main characters in situations that reflect the cruelty and selfish behaviors of dispassionate people.

Many of these novels can be bridged by theme, setting, character predicaments, and other common threads. Our next chapter will include many more examples of grouping YAL with traditional titles from the literary canon. As Probst states:

The suggestion that adolescent literature be granted a place in the literature curriculum is not a compromise. It doesn't weaken the curriculum by displacing the great works. Rather, it strengthens it by offering students the emotional and intellectual experiences of significant reading—the same sorts of experiences that skilled adults may have with the established great books of the culture. It invites them to participate at their own level in the ongoing dialog abut the major issues of human life. (224)

Chapter 4

Building Bridges: Getting Students from Wherever They Are to Where the Curriculum Says They Should Be

RESTRUCTURING THE CLASSROOM

As former students, most of us who teach English and reading experienced only one way of teaching literature: one book at a time, studied usually for a three-week period. We call that a *unit*. Some of us, usually on our own, have learned the value of a thematic approach where the *ideas* are viewed as more important than the individual literary work. Instead of reading and discussing one book in excruciating detail, we examine more broadly two or more works that deal with the same theme or themes.

Teaching in this way, as you no doubt realize, requires not only a change in attitude but also modifications in class structure. You probably have been asking yourself, *If I can't get my students to read* Great Expectations *(or* Hamlet *or whatever) all the way through on their own to begin with, how am I supposed to get them to read* two *books for the same assignment? And where does the extra time come from to do that anyway?* Important questions. Here are some comments that will help you answer them.

Nobody ever has to force teenagers to go to a movie. They go because they know from experience that movies are interesting. They are attracted by the ads they see on television or by recommendations from their friends. In contrast, the word around your school—if your school is like most other schools in this country—is that many, if not most, of the required books are not very interesting, and so students need to be prodded, cajoled, and threatened (with quizzes) before they'll start reading. We need to prove to students that books can be exciting, understandable, and worth their time.

When we teachers select required books that most students can handle and do enjoy, then students are more likely to want to read other similar books. And if we constantly recommend all kinds of books to our students, and if we provide time for the students in our classes to talk with others in class about good books they have read or are reading, we create a positive atmosphere that will carry over to the required reading.

In other words, if we prove to our students that we understand the kinds of books they are interested in reading, they will begin to trust our judgment about other books. Similarly, if the students in our classes have heard good things from older students about the books those students read in our previous classes, the students in our current classrooms will be more willing to read the books we require and recommend. And carefully chosen Young Adult novels and stories are those kinds of literary works.

So, by introducing our students to exciting, readable, rewarding novels (and other types of literary works) from the start, they will more likely be interested and more willing to read those literary works. After all, when we do something willingly and with a certain amount of personal interest in the activity, we are likely to do it more quickly and more competently than if we are not enthusiastic about the task. In addition, because YA novels are almost always shorter and easier to read than the complex, adult-oriented classics, our students will be able to finish the books in a much shorter amount of time than we normally set aside for the reading of a book that they may view as little more than drudgery. A week or so is sufficient time for most students to read and discuss the main issues in most YA books. (You can decide to spend more time—or less—on a book according to its length and complexity as well as the ability of the students in that class and their level of interest and involvement.)

Print isn't the only useful "literature" we can recommend. Videos, CDs, audiotapes, and CD-ROM programs on the same themes should also be considered.

Within the traditional three-week unit, if we've spent about a week on the YA materials, we will still have approximately two weeks to examine the classic that will follow. How can we manage the former three weeks of reading and assignments in only two weeks?

First, because our students (we expect) have been so successful in reading and discussing the YA novel, theoretically they should be somewhat more interested in reading the classic—with the same themes and issues—than they otherwise might have been, and they therefore will read the book with greater commitment and, possibly, with greater speed.

Second, because the class already will have examined the major themes and issues of the unit during discussion of the YA novel and other shorter selections, the students will have a focus when they read the more complex classic.

Third, because the specific themes and issues in the classic have already been identified, class activities and discussions should concentrate on those instead of on more picky elements. For example, the class can discuss the personalities and motivations of characters instead of recalling what they wore in chapter 1. The class can examine the manner in which the protagonist deals with the moral dilemma in the classic and compare that with the manner in which the protagonist in the YA novel dealt with her or his dilemma. Big issues. Major themes. Not picky details, line by line, scene by scene, chapter by chapter.

Moreover, if you accept the value of helping students to become more responsible for their own learning—through self-selected goals, small-group assignments, cooperative learning activities, and the like—and your students have demonstrated their ability to do those things at least adequately during the reading of the YA novel, then those same students should be able to use the same skills to examine the classic in the same manner. Thus, *they* will decide which are the most important issues to discuss and explore, with you recommending others if the students have missed any you deem important. Daily quizzes on minor details designed to punish (or embarrass) unprepared students and "motivate" recalcitrant readers will not be necessary. (In fact, if you have discovered the value of response journals—in which students write their personal reactions to the literature as they read—you will already have eliminated pop quizzes.)

Remember, our goal is to help students find pleasure in reading and to make them lifelong readers. Using YA novels and other shorter works as bridges to the classics or to other required literature will help us to achieve that goal. Once you get over the insecurity of doing something so different, you'll see how much more involved your students are in their work, how much more they enjoy it, and how much more they are learning. And you are likely to discover an excitement about teaching that you haven't felt in years.

MAKING CONNECTIONS

Let's consider some Young Adult Literature that connects with the traditional titles required in the majority of English programs in the United States.

—————————————— / / / ——————————————

The Adventures of Huckleberry Finn by Mark Twain

Themes

1. Innocent's initiation into the evil world
2. Journey to find self
3. Finding harmony and peace in nature as opposed to "civilized society"
4. Surviving in an intolerant and prejudiced society

5. Coming of age among charlatans, liars, cheaters
6. Surviving without adult role models

Suggested YAL titles that share some of these key themes:

STEVERMER, CAROLINE. *River Rats.*

The Mississippi River is a toxic brown river and the City is a desolate wasteland as a result of the Flash, which occurred 15 years ago. Traveling up and down the river on a paddle wheeler, the *River Rat,* a band of young orphans who survived the nuclear holocaust call themselves River Rats. Esteban (the male pilot) and Toby (the female captain) run the boat, while Tomcat (the narrator), Lindy, Spike, and Jake make up the crew. They barter their services by carrying mail and playing their dissonant rock-and-roll music for food, fresh water, and firewood at various ports, such as Fountains, Dresbach, and Thebes; they avoid the City and other ports occupied by savage gangs. The River Rats' most challenging journey begins on the day they save a disheveled old man from the river, who is running away from hunting hounds and men with clubs. While docked at Fountains to replenish their water supply, the old man, King, tries to escape with Lindy's guitar. Tomcat follows him and finds out he is being pursued by the Lesters, who want the old man to lead them to guns stored in the Pharaoh's Tomb. Eventually the Lesters capture the River Rats and their boat and force the crew and the old man to lead them to the Tomb. Their journey through the City combating Wild Boys is a harrowing and suspenseful adventure. Eventually they reach the Tombs, outwit the Lesters, and get back the *River Rat.*

Theme Connector

Like Huck, the River Rats travel the Mississippi River, selecting ports where they can find food and water and where the inhabitants are civilized. And like Huck, the River Rats learn to cope with charlatans who try to deceive them. When challenged to survive, they use all of their inner resources to outwit evil adults—in Huck's case the Duke and the Dauphin, while the River Rats outwit the Lesters after a horrendous journey through the desolate city. Both Huck and the River Rats face challenging circumstances that test their survival skills.

CRUTCHER, CHRIS. *The Crazy Horse Electric Game.*

When Willie, a top athlete in Coho, Montana, has a water-skiing accident that at first paralyzes him and later impairs his coordination and gait, his friends tolerate him, but he has to live life from a very different perspective. And his father, a former athletic hero, is ashamed of him.

When the situation becomes unbearable, Willie gets on a bus and runs away to Oakland, California. He lives in the ghetto and attends a "last chance" high school where a gym teacher helps him to exercise and rebuild his body. Although Willie does not regain his former athletic ability, he does gain knowledge about his inner strengths. He learns to appreciate his mind and his ability to concentrate, and most of all, to appreciate the kindness and acceptance of the people in this very different community. He returns to Montana a whole person, but his parents are no longer together. He considers the people in the ghetto fighting for a better life his family because they helped him realize the meaning of his own life.

Theme Connector

Willie and Huck are adolescents who witness the inhumane behavior of individuals against the uneducated, the disabled, and the poor, and begin to understand intolerance. When Willie feels he is no longer accepted by his father or friends and leaves home, he is alone. Huck's father is not supportive and exploits Huck at every opportunity. Ironically, both meet up with black men who help them: Willie meets a pimp, Lacey, who gives him shelter and food; Huck travels with Jim, a runaway slave. Lacey and Jim offer Willie and Huck protection and emotional support, which help them gain knowledge and wisdom through these experiences.

NIX, GARTH. *Shade's Children.*

The Change has destroyed civilization. The Overlords rule, using non-human forms to control society: Trackers (robots) police the children in the Dorm (orphanage), Wingers (who roam the skies at night), and Myrmidons (combat soldiers). Fourteen-year-old Gold-Eye has escaped from the Dorm with the aid of a spike and is crawling under a train track; he knows that he will be sent to the Meat Factory if he is caught. He escapes capture by climbing an embankment and is pulled up by three young people—Ella, Drum, and Ninde. They take him to their leader, Shade, where they live in a submarine wedged between two rotting piers. Shade's children are the children who have escaped the Overlords' plan to remove their brains and vital reproductive parts on their 14th birthdays for making Trackers or Myrmidons to control society. Shade is no longer human—he's a hologram—but he has devised weapons to combat the Overlords. Using his human intelligence, he has organized and trained his children to fight the Overlords; he sends them on missions to find the source of the Overlords' power.

Gold-Eye joins Ella, Drum, and Ninde, and together they go on dangerous missions, using their cunning and skill to discover the source of the Overlords' power. However, by the time they achieve their goal, they have to make a moral decision regarding their allegiance to Shade, who becomes more ruthless and demanding with each mission. Gold-Eye and Ninde use all of their abilities to reject the use of power; instead, they retrieve their humanity and help to restore peace to the city.

Theme Connector

Both Gold-Eye and Huck face what seem to be insurmountable circumstances, but they persevere and learn to use their inner resources to combat evil adults. Gold-Eye has three friends who aid and protect him; Huck has Jim, who provides him with emotional and physical support. Both Gold-Eye and Huck learn the importance of human relationships based on trust and honesty. Though Huck travels the river to find his sense of morality, Gold-Eye's journey in a desolate wasteland tests his concept of right and wrong. Both Huck and Gold-Eye find trusted friends to help them realize their inner strengths.

HOBBS, WILL. *Jason's Gold.*

The Klondike Gold Rush of 1897 starts 15-year-old Jason Hawthorn on his journey to catch up to his brothers, who left two days earlier for Dawson City. As a stowaway on a ship leaving Seattle for Skagway, Jason is discovered by a group of charlatans, who threaten to expose him as a stowaway unless he helps them cheat and steal. He refuses and is thrown off the ship in Juneau, where he continues heading north, hitching rides and working along the way. During the trip up Chilkoot Pass, the avalanche of people with their packs, horses, and dogs becomes a trial for Jason, and he saves a dog whose owner is ready to shoot it. With King as his companion, Jason manages to pick up work, grub, and a canoe. After packing food and equipment in the canoe, he and King follow the many lakes to the Yukon River. But winter is closing in, and when a moose gores Jason, his injuries prevent him from further travel. He and King retreat to a cabin to spend the winter until the spring thaw. A group of men burst into the cabin and leave Charlie, a young boy whose leg is amputated, and he and Jason manage to survive the winter. Jason helps Charlie regain his independence; Jason knows that he has to hunt for food, and when he confronts a hibernating bear, he loses his closest companion, King. Eventually Charlie and Jason arrive in Dawson City, where Jason is reunited with his brothers and the friends who helped him in Skagway. Although Jason and Charlie have forged a close bond, Charlie chooses to return to his family. Both boys have learned to respect nature and to make important decisions without adult interference, using their combined abilities to survive threatening circumstances.

Theme Connector

Jason and Huck share similar character traits: they are perceptive about deceitful adults trying to take advantage of them, willing to work, and willing to share food and shelter with those in need. They have a sense of morality that is obvious when they reveal their innermost thoughts. They are adolescents who are exposed to liars, cheaters, and destructive adults; however, they have a sense of compassion and fulfill their commitments. Their journey on the river tests their survival skills and their perseverance—their achievements are commendable, and as they come of age they prove they are responsible and humane.

Other YAL titles that mesh with themes in *Huckleberry Finn* include the following:

Ayres, Katherine. *Stealing South: A Story of the Underground Railroad.* When 16-year-old Will seeks his fortune as a peddler in Ohio, he is asked by a runaway slave to help two other slaves in Kentucky reach safety in Canada.

Brooks, Kevin. *Kissing the Rain.* The bullying that Moo experiences in school every day suddenly stops after he is the only witness to a road-rage incident where a man is killed, but then adults for both sides begin to put undue pressure on him to support their side in court, and Moo is in a losing position no matter what he does.

Carbone, Elisa. *Stealing Freedom.* The daughter of a slave mother and a freeman father in Maryland, 13-year-old Anna Maria Weems undertakes a long journey to freedom on the Underground Railroad in 1853.

Curtis, Christopher Paul. *Bucking the Sarge.* Fifteen-year-old Luther is determined to win the science fair and find a way out of Flint, Michigan, where his domineering and not very ethical mother, Sarge, runs an empire of slum houses and group homes.

Farmer, Nancy. *The House of the Scorpion.* Matt, the young clone of sinister drug lord El Patron, must first fight for his identity and then struggle to avoid being murdered in a country called Opium.

Frank, E. R. *America.* Abandoned by his mother and separated from his foster mother, a severely disturbed boy named America spends most of his youth in mental institutions, slowly making sense of his life with the help of a caring psychiatrist.

Goobie, Beth. *Flux.* Twelve-year-old Nellie is able to shape-shift and travel to parallel worlds in this frightening novel about a society where young children are abducted for science experiments.

Hobbs, Will. *Down the Yukon.* In this sequel to *Jason's Gold,* Jason and his girlfriend Jamie leave Dawson for the new gold fields in Nome by paddling down the Yukon River.

Lasky, Kathryn. *True North: A Novel of the Underground Railroad.* A young slave girl named Afrika runs away to Canada with the aid of a 14-year-old girl in

Boston who discovers that members of her family are helping runaway slaves.

Lowry, Lois. *Gathering Blue.* In a futuristic society, lame and orphaned Kira is brought to special living quarters where she is expected to carry on the tradition of sewing the special robe of the Singer, but then she discovers what lies behind other doors.

Pearsall, Shelley. *Trouble Don't Last.* A young boy and an old man, both slaves in Kentucky, escape and make their way to Canada via the Underground Railroad.

Philbrick, Rodman. *The Last Book in the Universe.* In a future time without hope, Spaz tries to rescue his little sister with the help of Ryter and a proov (genetically perfected) girl who lives in Eden.

Spinelli, Jerry. *Milkweed.* A young, naive, orphaned gypsy boy in Poland steals to survive in the Warsaw Ghetto during the Nazi occupation.

Spooner, Michael. *Daniel's Walk.* In hope of locating his long-missing father, young Daniel joins a wagon train on the Oregon Trail in 1846, facing all sorts of dangers and adventures along the way.

Note: Huckleberry Finn appears frequently on censored lists in various school districts. An interesting novel to introduce the *Huckleberry Finn* censorship dilemma is Nat Hentoff's *The Day They Came to Arrest the Book.* In this story, the new librarian, Ms. Fitzgerald, and a history teacher, Ms. Baines, confront the school principal when he listens to parental requests to ban *The Adventures of Huckleberry Finn* from the school library. The principal ignores the policy of the review committee because he is willing to bow to political pressure. The novel presents the points of view of students, parents, and faculty members regarding the censorship of books in school classrooms and the library.

———————————————— / / / ————————————————

The Grapes of Wrath by John Steinbeck

Themes

1. Denial of the American dream
2. Exclusion from the American mainstream
3. Importance of family and home
4. Displaced people
5. Exploitation of poor people

Suggested YAL titles that share some of these key themes:

PAULSEN, GARY. *The Beet Fields: Memories of a Sixteenth Summer.*

The boy is 16 years old when he runs away, no longer able to tolerate his drunken mother and his absent father. He finds himself on a North Dakota beet farm, hoeing and thinning beets with Mexican migrant workers. He cannot keep up with them; his hands bleed and he is physically exhausted. When the farmer tells him he will earn $11 an acre, he thinks he can make a lot of money, but the farmer charges him for stale food, gloves, a hoe, and lodging—sleeping on some gunny sacks in a shed. And he owes the farmer money. He is alone. Eventually the Mexicans invite him to eat with them; he kills pigeons from the barn rafters to contribute to the evening stew. He won't give up; he hoes and thins, despite his bloody hands. He travels with the Mexicans to the next farm, where the farmer hires him to drive a tractor in his wheat fields. He saves his money, but a deputy jails him as a runaway and steals his money. After escaping from jail, the boy is given food and shelter by an old woman, Hazel. When she takes him to the county fair, he sees the deputy and is on the run again. At the fair, a carnival man, Taylor, hires him. The boy experiences the underbelly of carnival life—he is a shill to get people into the sideshows for Taylor and runs the Tilt-a-Whirl. The boy thinks he is learning about life from Taylor; Taylor's brother, Bobby; and Ruby, the exotic dancer. He realizes that working the beet fields with the Mexicans, driving the tractor from sunup to sundown, and working and traveling with the carnies has hardened him. But he is completely ignorant. He doesn't understand people at all; he is disconnected from society. He tumbles along like the weeds in the fields, a displaced person who has no roots. Because he is tired of being chased and he wants to avoid prison, he enlists in the army the following year. He wants to find a place for himself.

Theme Connector

The boy's experiences and the Joads' experiences illustrate harsh living conditions and overt exploitation by farmers. They are displaced people, moving around, trying to find a sense of place. They are barely tolerated by their employers, who are inhumane; neither the boy nor the Joads receive any respect. Both are vulnerable in a society that revolves around economics, a society that lacks social justice. While the Joads manage to maintain a sense of family, the boy is utterly isolated, overwhelmed, and confused by the farmers and the carnival people.

Both novels convey strong images to illustrate the injustices that are part of the characters' lives. The boy finally seeks refuge in the army; he feels like a fugitive on the run. Yet he is an honest, hardworking boy in an ironic circumstance who has committed no crime. The Joads want an honest day's work but are denied their right to participate in a society that lacks a social conscience; they are honest people who maintain their dignity despite their rejection by mainstream society.

RYAN, PAM MUÑOZ. *Esperanza Rising.*

On her 13th birthday, Esperanza Ortega's life changes abruptly. Her father, owner of El Rancho de las Rosas in a small village in Mexico, is murdered; the ranch burns down; and Esperanza and her mother are forced to leave their luxurious life and flee to California with trusted servants. They settle in a company farm labor camp during the Great Depression, working night and day, living in squalor, trying to adjust to the grind of their daily life. The camp is segregated—Mexicans, Japanese, Filipinos, Chinese, and other groups live separately. But when the Okies come, a school, electricity, and running water are installed, because they are Caucasian. Despite her education, Esperanza is a member of the "brown group, Mexicans who are good for only manual labor," says her friend Miguel. Esperanza's mother, Ramona, understands their circumstances; her spoiled and indulged daughter has to learn how to adapt to this community: the migrant workers live in decrepit cabins, cooking their peasant food and sharing their chores. Esperanza learns from the community and becomes a hardworking young woman who appreciates their support. When her mother becomes very ill and is hospitalized, Esperanza rises to the challenge and becomes a compassionate and responsible human being.

Theme Connector

The Mexican migrant workers and the Okies share a desire to work hard for a day's wages. They are families who seek to participate in the American dream—working hard to achieve success. But they are denied access to the American dream, the Mexicans because of their skin color and the Okies because of their socioeconomic status. The Joads and Esperanza's community consistently display honest and compassionate behavior; the families maintain their pride and dignity under the most difficult conditions. Despite their meager existence, they unconditionally share with those in need. Parallel situations occur in the novels that illustrate the families' strength to survive challenging situations. They are people who live with honor and respect; their strength and tenacity are admirable.

HESSE, KAREN. *Out of the Dust.*

In a series of narrative poems, 14-year-old, freckle-faced Billie Jo Kelby relates the tragedy that nearly destroys her family during the Great Depression. Trying to survive the horrendous dust storms in the

Oklahoma panhandle, Billie Jo's mother and father struggle to fight the 70 days of wind and sun that destroy the wheat crop; the dust pervades every facet of their lives. When Billie Jo's mother dies in a horrible accident, she and her father withdraw from each other and barely communicate. In order to heal and to escape the tyranny of the Dust Bowl, Billie Jo hops a freight train and heads west with other migrants. But when she reaches Arizona, she realizes that "getting away, it wasn't any better." She is lonely for her father. When she returns home, they show their love and become a family again.

Theme Connector

The Joads are forced to leave their permanent home to become migrant workers because of the dust storms and the bank foreclosures. Despite the brutal dust storms, Billie Jo and her family continue their daily lives on their farm, hoping for rain. There is a strong sense of humanity about both families that is revealed in their respect for one another and the strangers with whom they share their food and shelter. While the Joads are excluded from the mainstream, Billie Jo's family and their ravaged community refuse to give in to the dust storms, showing a will to survive. Their crops are ruined, they receive very little rain, and the continuous dust storms challenge their very existence, but they remain on their land. Billie Jo says, "Hard times are about losing spirit, and hope, and what happens when dreams dry up." The Joads exemplify a strong spirit; though they are denied jobs, they carry on, searching for a place to put down new roots. Both families display a spirit of hope and a belief in a better future. Their tenacity under these circumstances is extraordinary; they refuse to give up.

Other YAL titles that mesh with themes from *The Grapes of Wrath* include the following:

DeFelice, Cynthia. *Nowhere to Call Home.* After her father commits suicide following the bankruptcy of his factory business, 12-year-old Frances Barrows disguises herself as a boy and becomes a hobo, riding freight trains during the Great Depression.

DuPrau, Jeanne. *The People of Sparks.* After Lina and Doon find a way out of the City of Ember, they are joined by 400 other former residents who find temporary shelter in a nearby town of Sparks, until the local residents feel their existence is threatened by the presence of the newcomers.

Durbin, William. *The Journal of C.J. Jackson, a Dust Bowl Migrant, Oklahoma to California, 1935.* Leaving their family farm in Oklahoma, the Jackson family endures the life of migrant workers in filthy camps as they seek a better life in California.

Haseley, Dennis. *The Amazing Thinking Machine.* While their father is away looking for work and hobos are passing through their neighborhood almost daily during the Depression, young Patrick and Roy build a machine that promises to answer whatever questions it is asked.

Janke, Katelan. *Survival in the Storm: The Dust Bowl Diary of Grace Edwards, Dalhart, Texas, 1935.* Based on first-person interviews with people who lived during the era, 15-year-old author Katelan Janke uses the perspective of a 12-year-old girl to describe the hardships of a Texas family during the Dust Bowl era.

Meltzer, Milton. *Driven from the Land: The Story of the Dust Bowl.* Meltzer describes the journeys of various families during the Dust Bowl era, including first-person accounts and black-and-white photographs.

Paterson, Katherine. *Jip: His Story.* In 1855–56 Vermont, young Jip, an abandoned orphan, befriends the town lunatic, who lives in a cage, and later learns that he himself is half black and is about to be sold as a slave.

_____. *Lyddie.* In a society that constantly tries to exploit her, Lyddie, a former Vermont farm girl, survives the horribly difficult work of the textile mills in Lowell, Massachusetts, in the 1840s and reunites with her family.

Peck, Richard. *A Long Way from Chicago.* Two city kids from Chicago, Mary Alice and her younger brother Joey, spend summers with their Grandma Dowdel in a small Illinois farm community during the Great Depression.

Porter, Tracey. *Treasures in the Dust.* In alternating chapters, two 11-year-old best friends—Annie and Violet—describe their experiences in rural Oklahoma during the Dust Bowl era.

Soto, Gary. *Jesse.* Wanting to escape the prospects of working as migrant laborers, two Mexican American brothers try to support themselves while attending a community college as the Vietnam War threatens.

------------------------------ / / / ------------------------------

Great Expectations by Charles Dickens

Themes

1. The value of loyal and trustworthy friends
2. The illusion that money brings happiness
3. The influence of wealth on class structure
4. The search for one's place in society

Suggested YAL titles that share some of these key themes:

PULLMAN, PHILIP. *Ruby in the Smoke.*

In 1872 Victorian London, 16-year-old Sally Lockhart investigates her father's death. She visits the shipping firm he owned with a partner, Mr. Selby, where she is referred to a Mr. Higgs. When she questions him about the phrase "the Seven Blessings," he gasps and dies. So starts Sally's intense investigation of her father's past. Without any parents, Sally is placed in the care of a distant cousin, Miss Rees, who is indifferent and cruel to her. In the course of trying to unravel the mystery of her father's death on a ship out of Singapore, Sally comes into contact with seedy and life-threatening characters—such as the evil Mrs. Holland, who is out to kill Sally for the Ruby of Agrapur, and Hendrik van Eden, alias Ah Ling. With the help of her new friends— the photographer Frederick Garland, his sister Rosa, and a young clerk named Jim—she uncovers more and more details about the ruby and her father's accidental death. Sally is a well-developed character who consistently demonstrates tenacity, intelligence, and independence. By the end of the novel she solves her father's murder, finds her inheritance, and establishes a family relationship with Frederick, Rosa, and Jim. (Pullman's *Shadow in the North* and *Tiger in the Well* complete this exciting trilogy).

Theme Connector

The settings of both *Ruby in the Smoke* and *Great Expectations* offer striking images of Victorian London. Although *Ruby in the Smoke* uses more mystery and suspense, Pullman's images of London, with coaches clattering on foggy, cobblestone streets, along with dark alleys and isolated wharves on the river, are reminiscent of Dickens's London. Both authors place the orphaned main characters in challenging situations with sinister, deceitful people. Adelaide, an orphan who is terrified of the unmerciful Mrs. Holland, conjures up images of Dickensian mudlarks along the waterfronts of London.

Both Sally and Pip share common experiences as they seek their true identity; during the course of their journeys their systems of honesty, trust, and fairness are tested again and again. As they grow and develop from these experiences, they learn the truth about themselves and their families. Sally learns that Mr. Marchbanks, her real father, was an opium addict who in a blind moment gave her to Lockhart in exchange for the ruby. Pip learns that his benefactor was a convict, not the class-conscious Miss Havisham. His infatuation with Estella is manipulated cruelly by Miss Havisham, but when he returns from his experiences trying to be a London gentleman, Pip begins to appreciate the value of love, friendship, and loyalty offered by his country friends, Biddy and Joe. Sally becomes wary of most people after her experiences with her guardian, Miss Rees; the opium dealer, Ah Ling; and her father's partner, Mr. Selby. But by the end of the novel she realizes that Frederick, Rosa, and Jim are her loyal friends. Both Pip and Sally share similar traits such as loyalty, honesty, and commitment.

WHELAN, GLORIA. *Homeless Bird.*

When she learns of her arranged marriage, 13-year-old Koly has no choice but to obey Hindu tradition. She loves her family, but after her marriage celebration, she feels empty as she watches her parents leave. After a few days she learns that her husband, Hari, is very ill, and his parents deceived Koly's parents because they wanted Koly's dowry to try to save his life. After Hari dies, his mother treats Koly with resentment and disdain; she steals Koly's widow's pension and uses it as a dowry for her own daughter. Finally, on a train trip she deliberately abandons Koly in the "city of the widows." When she learns that she is abandoned, Koly is frantic after sleeping on the street for two nights. Raji, a young rickshaw driver, befriends her and takes her to a home for widows, where she makes friends and finds a job in the bazaar. Eventually her talent in embroidery enables her to get a better job in an elegant sari shop.

The novel reveals a tradition of Indian family life: a daughter may never return after she is widowed. Because Raji befriends Koly, along with Maa Kamala, "the housemother" who operates the house for widows; Mrs. Devi, the patron who supports the house; and Mr. Das, who owns the exclusive sari shop, Koly forges a new life. She learns to use her intelligence and artistry to appreciate friends and to gain confidence in herself. She is no longer a homeless bird; she has matured into a young woman with a future.

Theme Connector

Despite their difference in age, Pip and Koly exhibit similar character traits. They are honest, loyal, hardworking, and trustworthy people. Pip leaves the country to become a London gentleman, thanks to a nameless benefactor. Koly endures the taunts of a cruel mother-in-law who finally abandons her in the city of the widows. She is alone, sleeping on the street, until a young man, Raji, takes her to a home for widows where she finds friends and a job. Pip is impressed with his London friends and tries to emulate them. However, when he senses their taunts and cruelty, he realizes their insincerity; he realizes his money cannot make him into a sophisticated gentleman. He learns that true friends are hard to come by, and so he returns to his old friends, Joe and Biddy. Koly finds friendship and loyalty among her friends in the widows' house, and with Raji, a young man who comforts her and respects her intelligence. She teaches him to read and write, and when she gets a better job, she remains close to him. She realizes that she has found a place in society—she is an artisan working with saris, and she has close friends in Raji and Tanu, as well as a kind patron in Mrs. Devi. When she was widowed and living with her in-laws, she saw her life slipping away...there was no hope. Pip is treated cruelly, too: Miss Havisham teases and taunts him through his infatuation with her ward, Estella. Both Koly and Pip are tossed about in cities; they experience situations that test their endurance and spirit. Because they are compassionate, caring, genuine people, they survive with grace and honor, and both appreciate their devoted friends.

AVI. *The True Confessions of Charlotte Doyle.*
    In 1832, a 13-year-old proper young lady, Miss Charlotte Doyle, is traveling from Liverpool, England, to Providence, Rhode Island, to rejoin her family. Her father has booked passage for her on one of his company's ships, the *Seahawk.* Although Charlotte is alarmed that she is the only passenger, she starts out on the journey. When one of the crew members, Zachariah, tries to befriend her, she rebuffs him because he is a Negro and is beneath her social station. With her white gloves and her desire to associate only with Captain Jaggery, Charlotte reveals her snobbery to the crew. Although Zachariah helps her when she falls ill and warns her about Jaggery's evil disposition, she refuses to believe him. Finally, however, she witnesses Jaggery's cruel behavior. When she confronts Jaggery, he ignores her. The crew refuses to accept her because she has betrayed them. But after proving herself, she becomes a crew member and moves to their quarters, where she learns about trust, loyalty, and friendship. Jaggery tries her for murder, but when he attempts to kill her, Zachariah saves her life. After the voyage, she returns home to her family but finds their upper-class snobbery intolerable; she returns to the *Seahawk* to be with her loving friends, especially Zachariah.

Theme Connector

    Through a painful journey, both Charlotte and Pip discover the truth about upper-class society. Pip is mercilessly ridiculed by so-called gentlemen and the beautiful ward of Miss Havisham, Estella, until he realizes that Biddy and Joe are true friends who love him as he is. Charlotte has attended private school and presumes that her family's position in society makes her superior to the crew members. However, when she witnesses the cruelty and violence of Jaggery against the crew, she begins to realize his evil nature. When she returns to her family and tries to share what she has learned from her journey on the *Seahawk,* they reject her explanations and accuse her of an overly active imagination. Because she cannot tolerate their attitude and snobbishness, she leaves home and returns to her new family—Zachariah and the crew. Both Charlotte and Pip reject a society that values wealth and position more than honest and meaningful human relationships.

Other YAL titles that mesh with themes from *Great Expectations* include the following:

Brugman, Alyssa. *Finding Grace.* After high school graduation, Rachel takes a job as live-in caretaker for Grace, a brain-damaged woman who cannot communicate, where she attempts to reconstruct the woman's past while she develops her own identity.

Buss, Fran Leeper. *Journey of the Sparrows.* Fourteen-year-old Maria and her family, refugees from El Salvador, journey through Mexico and try to survive in Chicago without a green card.

Curtis, Christopher Paul. *Bucking the Sarge.* Fifteen-year-old Luther is determined to win the science fair and find a way out of Flint, Michigan, where his domineering and not very ethical mother, Sarge, runs an empire of slum houses and group homes.

Flinn, Alex. *Breaking Point.* As a new student in an exclusive private school, Paul is subjected to all sorts of harassment until the charismatic Charlie steps in—but Charlie's friendship comes at a very high cost.

Gavin, Jamila. *Coram Boy.* In eighteenth-century England, Otis Gardiner makes a living by disposing of unwanted and illegitimate children until his simple-minded son, Meshak, takes a liking to the son of a young aristocrat who's been disinherited by his family.

Haddix, Margaret Peterson. *Just Ella.* After Prince Charming discovers the identity of the owner of the glass slipper, Ella moves into the castle, discovers how confining and depressing life is there, and plots her escape.

Hartinger, Brent. *The Last Chance Texaco.* Feisty Lucy Pitt faces new challenges—and finds acceptance—at a last-chance group home for orphans and troubled teens.

Holt, Kimberly Willis. *My Louisiana Sky.* Tiger Ann is embarrassed by her mentally slow parents and dominated by her strong grandmother, but when Granny dies, Aunt Dorie Kay takes over, and things begin to change for Tiger Ann.

Levine, Gail Carson. *Dave at Night.* An orphan at the restrictive Hebrew Home for Boys sneaks out at night and experiences the music and culture of the Harlem Renaissance.

Nolan, Han. *Born Blue.* Raised by drug dealers and addicts, Leshaya is determined to overcome her horrible life by singing—the only thing that makes her feel whole.

Pullman, Philip. *Shadow in the North.* In this sequel to *Ruby in the Smoke*, Sally Lockhart, now 22 and an established financial consultant in London, falls in love with her photographer friend, Frederick, and begins an investigation into the destructive dealings of financier Axel Bellman.

_____. *Tiger in the Well.* After losing her home, business, and bank accounts, Sally Lockhart, living in a women's shelter, exposes the sinister business run by Arthur Parrish's boss, who exploits poor young women from Eastern Europe and forces them into prostitution.

Strasser, Todd. *Can't Get There from Here.* The painful stories of several homeless teenagers living (and dying) on the streets of New York City reveal their place in society and their search for someplace to belong.

Weaver, Beth Nixon. *Rooster.* Tired of the unpleasant surroundings of her family's struggling citrus farm and dealing with Rooster, a 13-year-old brain-damaged Cuban neighbor, 15-year-old Cady is easily attracted to Jon, the rich boy from across the lake, even if she can't fit comfortably into his snobby crowd.

Wolff, Virginia Euwer. *Make Lemonade.* When 14-year-old LaVaughn babysits the two young children of a 17-year-old unmarried girl, all their lives are changed.

———————————————— / / / ————————————————

The Great Gatsby by F. Scott Fitzgerald

Themes

1. Initiation into an amoral society
2. The need to compromise in order to survive
3. The excesses of winning at all costs
4. The acceptance of amoral behavior as the norm
5. Testing one's sense of morality; making a moral choice
6. Denial of the American dream

Suggested YAL titles that share some of these key themes:

CRUTCHER, CHRIS. *Running Loose.*

Louie Banks, a senior in high school, is the narrator of this coming-of-age story. Like most adolescents, Louie is involved in sports, with a peer group and a special girlfriend, Becky. As narrator, Louie tells his story about the unraveling of his world and how he manages to survive. Louie plays by the rules—he has a strong sense of morality—but he learns that some adults in society are corrupt and self-serving. In order to win an important football game, the coach tells the team to deliberately injure the star of the opponent's team. When the star player is carried off on a stretcher, Louie decides to take a moral stand and report the coach to the referee. Louie's moral choice alienates him from his peers as well as from the coach and the school principal. Because he chooses not to compromise his values, Louie cannot find acceptance within his community. When Becky, his only confidante and friend, dies, he is shattered. The last pages of the novel are riveting—Louie shares "what I have learned," the knowledge he has gained about surviving in a corrupt world.

Theme Connector

Although Louie is a teenager and Nick, the narrator of *The Great Gatsby,* is an Ivy League graduate working on Wall Street, they share naive views of adult behaviors and relationships. When they encounter amoral people—in Nick's case, Daisy, Tom Buchanan, and Jordan Baker; in Louie's case, the football coach, school principal, and members of the football team—the reader can almost feel Nick and Louie reeling in shock. Both Nick and Louie share some solid values (honesty, fair play, loyalty, trust), and when these values are tested as they interact with other characters, Nick and Louie are confused and repelled by the indifference of these characters. They go through a transformation: Nick must leave the East and "cleanse" himself in the Midwest; Louie will continue to stand up for what he believes in at all costs, because ultimately he has to live with himself.

The novels share some common techniques: a strong first-person narrator, flashbacks, secondary characters who demonstrate guile and deceit without remorse, and lots of dialogue between the protagonists and antagonists as well as introspective comments. Nick and Louie's voices are vibrant and realistic as they draw the reader into their shock and disgust with the behavior of other characters.

SALISBURY, GRAHAM. *Lord of the Deep.*

At 13 years of age, Mikey works on his stepfather's charter fishing boat in Hawaii. Even though Mikey is the youngest deckhand in the harbor, his stepfather, Bill, believes in Mikey's ability and good judgment. In turn, Mikey looks up to Bill, and from him learns not only about fishing but also about taking risks and making sacrifices. But Mikey is disillusioned when two wealthy, offensive men charter Bill's boat for three days, expecting to catch a prizewinning marlin. Their actions test Bill's values when he allows them to lie about catching a record-setting mahimahi. Bill's silence stuns Mikey. Mikey remains silent about the lie too, so Bill will not get into trouble. But his respect for Bill has changed dramatically, and Mikey is not willing to compromise his sense of morality to accommodate commercial gain. The experience has damaged their relationship.

Theme Connector

Though Nick, the narrator in *The Great Gatsby,* and Mikey, in *Lord of the Deep,* represent different age groups and social classes, they share the same dilemma as they witness dishonest behavior. They both value honest and fair play, expecting the same in others. But Mikey's encounter with the two callous charter fisherman, Cal and Ernie, forces him to realize that the end does not justify the means. Nick's experiences with Tom, Daisy, and Jordan help him to realize that they lack any kind of human compassion and step over or ignore unpleasant situations without any remorse. Both Mikey and Nick are disappointed by the actions of people they admire—Mikey admires Bill, while Nick admires Jay Gatsby; both Bill and Gatsby compromise their sense of decency without hesitation. Nick escapes the amoral actions of the Buchanans by returning to the Midwest, and Mikey rejects the deceitful situation on the boat by jumping overboard and swimming to shore. Both characters are unwilling to sacrifice their sense of right and wrong; they choose to sever their relationship before they will compromise their sense of morality.

GALLO, DONALD R., ed. *No Easy Answers: Short Stories about Teenagers Making Tough Choices.*

The 16 short stories in this collection show teenagers in a variety of situations that require them to make a moral choice. Some, like Cory in Virginia Euwer Wolff's "The Un-Numbing of Cory Wilhouse" and Smythe in Graham Salisbury's "The Doi Store Monkey," face the consequences of their actions honestly, while others, like Belinda in Rita Williams-Garcia's "Wishing It Away," are too emotionally troubled to face reality and make a rational decision. The topics of these challenging stories range from peer pressure, gang violence, unwanted pregnancy, and drug abuse to cheating on a test, betraying a trust, and computer blackmail. The stories give readers an opportunity to discuss the morality of each situation and to debate the character's choice: Was it a wise choice? How did it affect others? What has the character learned from his or her experience? What other choices might the character have considered?

Theme Connector

By discussing the merits of each character's choices in *No Easy Answers*—characters their age facing contemporary problems they can identify with—teenage students are better prepared to examine the morality of the adult characters' actions in *The Great Gatsby*. Readers can begin to group characters that exemplify a sense of morality and characters that are irresponsible and insensitive. For example, which characters in *Gatsby* are similar to the narrator in Jack Gantos's "The X-15s"? Which stories have characters who connect to Daisy Buchanan? What similarities are evident between Will Weaver's "The Photograph" and Fitzgerald's *The Great Gatsby*? How are adults in *The Great Gatsby* affected by peer pressure compared to teenagers in several of the stories? Nick, in *Gatsby,* has to decide how he will act in his amoral world; how are characters such as Bliss, Michael, Eva, Martha, and Duke able to deal with their moral choices? Which characters in these short stories are likely to grow up to be like Tom Buchanan, Daisy Buchanan, Jordan Baker, or other characters in *The Great Gatsby*? Why? This short-story collection is a rich source of character analysis for bridging the sophisticated characters in *The Great Gatsby*. By comparing characters in the short stories and the novel, students can grasp the universality of human behavior and can begin to draw parallels between the two texts.

KORMAN, GORDON. *Jake, Reinvented.*

High school junior Rick Paradis is the kicker and backup quarterback on the football team at Fitzgerald High. He admits that he is a follower, allowing Todd Buckley, the quarterback and leader of the "in group," to order him around. And as he tells the story of Jake Garrett and his experience with Todd Buckley and Didi Ray, it's evident that Rick is the ultimate "insider/outsider." He goes along with the group, but doesn't always approve of their actions or attitudes. Jake Garrett, a new student who has joined the football team, is very sophisticated in his J. Crew and Banana Republic wardrobe, and best of all, he throws wild keg parties every Friday while his father is away. No holds are barred—there is plenty of beer, liquor, and pizza—and the whole house is used by party-goers, from basement to bedrooms. He is the perfect host, smiling and welcoming all. Rick is alarmed at the destructive behavior of the crowd, but Jake assures him everything is fine.

During one of the parties, Nelson, a huge football player, accuses Jake of being a phony and blows his cover. Jake, alias Jacob, transferred from another high school, where he was an academic nerd, wore glasses, and previously tutored Didi Ray, Todd Buckley's steady girlfriend. Jake is infatuated with Didi and throws Friday parties, hoping Didi will attend. When she does and they meet again, Jake hopes she will be impressed with his new persona—a preppy, popular football player, accepted by the group. She vacillates between Jake and Todd, and when an ugly confrontation occurs and Jake is being strangled, she hits Nelson over the head with a champagne bottle. When the police come, Jake takes the blame for the assault; Didi never volunteers to testify on his behalf. Rick is furious at all the partygoers who witnessed the situation but remain silent. He is particularly angry at Todd Buckley and Didi Ray, who ignore the whole affair. On the date of Jake's court hearing, Rick and one other student show up; none of the partygoers take the time to give Jake moral support. Jake receives a suspended sentence and is sent to live with his mother in Texas. When they say goodbye on the courthouse steps, Jake hands Rick his phone number and address in Texas and reminds him to give it to Didi. Rick is stunned, but realizes that Jake has not learned from his experience with Todd and Didi.

Theme Connector

Nick's keen observations about the Buchanans and their friends parallel Rick's observations of his high school peers. The Buchanans' treatment of Gatsby is callous, particularly Daisy, who allows Jay Gatsby to use all of his resources to impress her. She leads him on, and when she kills Mabel, her husband's mistress, while driving Gatsby's car, she allows him to take responsibility for the accident. Jake takes the blame for severely injuring a football player, because he believes his "golden girl" Didi is saving his life. Both Daisy and Didi are self-centered and use their feminine wiles to toy with men. And both lack a moral conscience, ignoring the consequences of their destructive behavior. Jay Gatsby and Jake Garrett try to reinvent themselves for the women they love, but to no avail. They are left alone, rejected by the very people who pretended to be their friends. Ironically, both characters are not bothered by this treatment; they only focus on their fantasy of the women they adore. Rick and Nick, the narrators of both novels, have similar personalities. They see through the pretense and deceit, but they are powerless. Nick returns to the Midwest to distance himself from the amoral Buchanans, while Rick manages to face his peers with more confidence because he is aware of the need to respect all human beings. He has transcended adolescent intolerance and the need for group approval.

LOWRY, LOIS. *The Giver.*

Twelve-year-old Jonas lives in a futuristic community where all of society's ills, such as lies, deceit, disrespect, and disease, are under control. Also controlled are sexual awakening, memory, and emotion. No one in this controlled society can experience the feeling of love; no one has experienced snow, colors, or flowers; and only black and white exist, literally and figuratively. By the time children reach the age of 12 they are assigned their lifetime jobs in the community by the Committee of Elders, based on their performance from birth to 12 years of age. As Jonas sits in the auditorium waiting with his classmates, he is the last student assigned. To his surprise, he is assigned Receiver of Memory, the most prestigious job in the community! His life changes dramatically as he attends daily meetings with the aged Receiver of Memory, who now calls himself The Giver. Slowly, The Giver introduces Jonas to colors, flowers, snow, and other beautiful wonders of the world; however, he also has to give horrible memories to Jonas, such as death, disease, suffering, intolerance, and cruelty. As Jonas absorbs the intense evil and ugliness, he becomes sensitized to the horrors in his community. For example, he learns that "to be released" means to be killed.

Jonas's father, who works at the Nurturing Center, brings home a young baby, Gabriel, who is not sleeping well, cries a lot, and is developing too slowly. Even though Jonas's family has the permissible number of family members—mother, father, sister, brother—his father has permission to try to assist Gabriel. Jonas helps Gabriel sleep through the night by transmitting some pleasant, beautiful memories that The Giver has shared with him. Because The Giver has access to all procedures, decisions, and actions in the community, Jonas sees his own father kill a young baby by injection. Because Jonas's training allows him to experience pain, sorrow, and compassion, and because he is developing a sense of morality outside of the community's rules and values, he is tortured by what he begins to realize about his community. When his father decides that the baby Gabriel must be returned to the Nurturing Center, Jonas shares his concern with The Giver, who supports Jonas's decision to leave the community in order to save Gabriel.

Theme Connector

Although *The Giver* has a futuristic setting, the community is as callous and indifferent as Daisy, Tom Buchanan, and Jordan Baker are in *The Great Gatsby*. Nick and Jonas share similar character traits: compassion, honesty, caring, loyalty, and trust. The plots of the novels peel away an amoral world; Nick and Jonas have to interact with characters who refuse to acknowledge their amoral acts. Of course, in Jonas's community, the adults and young people take drugs to suppress their emotions so that they do not confront any sense of morality. But in a sense, the characters in *The Great Gatsby* also use a drug—bootleg alcohol—to suppress their sense of right and wrong. Both protagonists leave the community when their consciences will not allow them to tolerate the moral corruption. Jonas plots his escape in order to force his community to change, while Nick leaves the east to "cleanse" himself after Gatsby's death. Jonas and Nick realize the pain and pleasure of the truth and make a moral choice to remove themselves from intolerable circumstances.

The denial of the American dream could also be included in studying *The Giver*, because Jonas's training sessions as the Receiver of Memory have made him realize the value of each individual's life. Nick cannot tolerate the Buchanans' indifference to the death of Gatsby and Mabel. Although he realizes that Gatsby's fantasy and obsession with Daisy are distorted, he feels compassion for Gatsby as a human being.

Other YAL titles that mesh with themes in *The Great Gatsby* include the following:

Cormier, Robert. *The Rag and Bone Shop.* Cormier's last work places an innocent 12-year-old boy in a small room with a ruthless investigator who is determined to get a murder confession out of his subject.

Crowe, Chris. *Getting Away with Murder: The True Story of the Emmett Till Case.* The perfect companion piece for Crowe's *Mississippi Trial, 1955,* this carefully detailed book recounts the true events behind his historical novel and includes photographs.

_____. *Mississippi Trial, 1955.* While visiting his beloved grandfather in Mississippi, a white teenaged boy meets Emmett Till, a feisty black teen from Chicago, who is soon murdered for whistling at a white woman.

Crutcher, Chris. *Whale Talk.* Behind the triumphs of a high school swim team composed of misfits lurk painful lives and present dangers that culminate in a shocking and surprising ending.

Donnelly, Jennifer. *A Northern Light.* Sixteen-year-old Mattie faces a number of moral dilemmas, both on her family farm in upstate New York in 1906 and at the resort hotel where she works for the summer, when a young unmarried woman drowns under suspicious conditions.

Flinn, Alex. *Breaking Point.* As a new student in an exclusive private school, Paul is subjected to all sorts of harassment until the charismatic Charlie steps in— but Charlie's friendship comes at a very high cost.

Giles, Gail. *Shattering Glass.* A tension-filled story about conformity and popularity, this novel recounts the events of a school year that resulted in the murder of a classmate, told mainly from the point of view of one of the participants, with comments from other students.

Klass, David. *Wrestling with Honor.* When the captain of the wrestling team, Ron Woods, fails a mandatory drug test but knows he will pass it on a retest, he decides not to do it because it is a violation of his civil rights.

Koja, Kathe. *The Blue Mirror.* Tired of dealing with her alcoholic mother, a talented 16-year-old artist seeks solace in a downtown café, where she encounters a charismatic homeless boy named Cole, who draws her into his warped world.

Lynch, Chris. *Slot Machine.* Although Elvin tries to find his niche in the Christian Brothers Academy camp for incoming freshman, he fails miserably at every sport he tries.

Randle, Kristen D. *Breaking Rank.* This is a modern Romeo and Juliet story about a poor working-class kid named Baby and honors student Casey, whose relationship causes their different worlds to clash.

Tashjian, Janet. *The Gospel According to Larry.* After creating a hugely popular Web site that attacks commercialism in contemporary society, 17-year-old Josh Swensen becomes consumed by the greed and superficiality he has opposed and must find a way to normalcy.

_____. *Vote for Larry.* In this sequel to *The Gospel According to Larry,* "Larry" returns from his self-imposed exile to run for president of the United States in an attempt to overhaul the American political system.

Werlin, Nancy. *Double Helix.* Following high school graduation, Eli lands a summer job at Wyatt Transgenics to work under a legendary but amoral molecular biologist who knows secrets about Eli's birth.

——————————————————————————— / / / ———————————————————————————

Hamlet by William Shakespeare

Themes

1. Initiation of the innocent into an evil world
2. Dealing with loss of a parent
3. Abandoning one's sense of morality to seek revenge
4. Risking one's place in the community to take a stand
5. Surviving without parental support

Suggested YAL titles that share some of these key themes:

FIEDLER, LISA. *Dating Hamlet: Ophelia's Story.*
   Ophelia, Lady of the Court, and Hamlet, Prince of Denmark, are very much in love. Since his return to Elsinore to mourn his father's recent death, he confides to Ophelia his shock at his mother's marriage to his Uncle Claudius. Ophelia tells Hamlet that she and her servant, Ann, observed the ghost of his father on the ramparts the previous night. When his father's ghost appears to Hamlet on the ramparts that night, he tells his son he was poisoned by Claudius. Now Hamlet plots revenge— he and Ophelia feign madness in order to trick Claudius and Hamlet's mother, Gertrude. Ophelia's father, Polonius, forbids her to see Hamlet, but she ignores him. When a group of players come to Elsinore, Hamlet rewrites their play so that it is a reenactment of his father's murder. Ophelia, who knows about herbal potions, gives Hamlet a poisonous potion to kill Claudius. In the meantime, she feigns drowning in the river, while Laertes, her brother, and Hamlet duel before the court. Both are wounded and presumed to be dead. While watching the duel, Claudius and Gertrude drink the poisoned wine and die. Laertes, Hamlet, and Ophelia meet at the gravedigger's cottage, where they are revived by an antidote. Their plan for revenge against Claudius accomplished, Hamlet and Ophelia leave Denmark to start a new life in Verona, Italy.

Theme Connector

   Ophelia's story parallels many of the same plot situations as Shakespeare's tragedy: Prince Hamlet learns about his father's murder from the ghost of his father on the ramparts; his best friend, Horatio, witnesses the ghost and agrees to help Hamlet seek revenge. Both Hamlet and Ophelia feign madness in her story, while in Shakespeare's play, Hamlet feigns madness but does not confide in Ophelia; however, he insults her and frightens her so that she is confused and goes mad and drowns in the river. In *Dating Hamlet,* Hamlet and Ophelia are very much in love, but they show their affection for one another in private. In Shakespeare's play they are more reserved and kept apart. In both stories, Polonious forbids Ophelia to see Hamlet, and in both stories Hamlet stabs Polonious, who is eavesdropping on Hamlet's frank talk with his mother. Also, Gertrude and Claudius assign Rosencrantz and Guildenstern to spy on Hamlet, and Hamlet sets up the playlet in front of Claudius and Gertrude that ends in his duel with Laertes. In *Dating Hamlet,* Laertes, Ophelia's brother, is not an enemy of Hamlet; he participates in the revenge plot with Ophelia and Hamlet. Many situations in the plot of *Dating Hamlet* parallel Shakespeare's play, and Hamlet's melancholy character and determination to revenge his father's death are believable. However, *Dating Hamlet* does not end in tragedy. For setting, plot sequences, and character development, the novel is a good bridge to Shakespeare's tragedy; it includes all the deceit Claudius and Polonius use to foil Hamlet, and there are allusions to Hamlet's soliloquies.

BROOKS, BRUCE. *What Hearts.*

This third-person narrative is about Asa, a precocious, proud, and perceptive boy who learns at an early age to appear rational despite the continuous upheavals in his life. In the first part, six-year-old Asa eagerly runs home on the last day of school to share his excellent report card and awards with his parents. However, the house is empty, and his mother announces that she and his father are divorcing. Asa is confused and disappointed, but he says nothing to her about his report card and awards. He doesn't question or react; he calmly packs up his things. Asa's behavior is unusual, strange from a psychological point of view. He does not react when his mother tells him that she is reuniting with Dave, a former boyfriend. Within a few weeks, Asa realizes that Dave is mean and it's okay to hate him. Asa's insight and bead on his life are shared with the reader, his interaction with other people is calculated, and his interior analysis of all aspects of his life is so precise that it is difficult to believe he is a child. As he grows older, Asa's insights and intelligence make him seem different and scary to his peers. There are incidents with his mother, friends at school, teachers, and Dave that make him an enigma.

When Asa is in 7th grade, a girl in his class named Jean says, "You figure things out and you attack." She explains to him that she means he knows how to get to people. For the first time in his life, Asa connects to another human being and feels attracted to this girl. In his usual analytical manner, he tries to learn how love is supposed to feel. He listens to music but still can't figure out what he is supposed to feel. Finally he asks his mother, who explains her feelings. But in explaining love to Asa, she realizes that she is not in love with Dave and decides to divorce him and move away. Asa tells Jean that he loves her; in return, she sends him candy hearts that say, "I love you." When Asa calls Jean to say goodbye, he reaches out for the first time in his life and thanks her for the hearts. She responds, "What hearts?" Asa is canny enough to realize at that moment that his love meant nothing to Jean, and Asa, who is always in control, will not allow himself to feel any disappointment. He thinks to himself, "And if a fellow had *these* words...then surely something was in store in the future."

Theme Connector

Although Asa is much younger than Hamlet, they share certain common circumstances. Both are without a father, although Hamlet speaks to his father's ghost. Both have mothers who are so indifferent and self-centered that they neglect the emotional development of their sons. Gertrude doesn't help Hamlet when he is mourning his father's death. Asa's mother doesn't ask Asa about his feelings when she decides to divorce his father, nor does she offer emotional support during her marriage to Dave, even though they move approximately 10 times. Hamlet's mother expects him to accept her marriage to his Uncle Claudius; she treats his mourning of his father's death lightly. Both mothers do not seem to know their sons; both ignore their son's emotional needs.

Ironically, both Asa and Hamlet share some common character traits—they are masters at pretense. Their public and private personae intimidate their stepfathers, their mothers, and their peers. Although they sometimes exhibit passive behavior, there is a dark side to their nature that is capable of evil schemes. Because Asa has been neglected by most adults throughout his life, he is independent and reflective and can share his perceptions about the evil he sees in his school and home life. Unlike Hamlet, however, he does not have to sacrifice himself to gain revenge against his mother or Dave. Through his soliloquies, Hamlet shares the depth of his anguish about his father's unnatural death in the infested kingdom of Denmark and forces himself to seek revenge. Perhaps Asa will survive because he can take care of himself; in contrast, Hamlet cannot survive.

BAGDASARIAN, ADAM. *Forgotten Fire.*

Twelve-year-old Vahan Kenderian does not take life seriously; he is the youngest of six children in a very wealthy Armenian family in Bitlis, a province in Turkey. His father is one of the most prominent lawyers in the country and warns Vahan to "be steel. Steel is made strong by fire." Vahan has to repeat these words to himself often after his father is taken away, his two older brothers are shot by Turkish soldiers, and he and his remaining family are marched through the countryside with the guns of

Turkish soldiers in their faces. Vahan's mother instructs him and his brother, Sisak, to escape one night. During their journey, Sisak, who is two years older, becomes sick and dies.

For three years, Vahan is alone, using his inner resources to survive as a prisoner of a Turkish general, a street beggar, an orphan, a deaf-mute living with Turks in the mountains, and a stowaway on a barge. As he recounts his journey, he realizes that his father had warned him that he was irresponsible and needed to prepare himself for hardship. As Vahan describes the horrors of the Armenian genocide in 1915, he prepares himself to be killed. After Sisak dies, Vahan does not believe that he can survive alone. In his darkest moments he yearns for the life he had, particularly for his parents, his grandmother, and his brothers and sisters. He witnesses evil all around him until he reaches Constantinople, where Armenians are safe; by the age of 20 he arrives in the United States to start a new life.

Theme Connector

Until tragedy struck, both Vahan and Hamlet were indulged and protected by their families; neither was involved in life-or-death situations. They were unprepared for the challenges that faced them. Young Prince Hamlet, a student at Wittenberg, had few responsibilities while his father was king of Denmark. After his father's death he is treated differently by his Uncle Claudius, the new king. Claudius wants Hamlet back at Wittenberg, because Claudius does not want Hamlet involved in governing the country. And Hamlet's mother cannot understand why he is still in mourning for his father after two months. After the ghost of his father informs him about Claudius's evil deed, Hamlet has to mature very quickly and decide whether to avenge his father's murder.

Vahan was protected by his mother and siblings; only his father warned him that he was not serious enough. Suddenly Vahan is jolted when his family is destroyed. He has to call upon his inner resources to help him survive. He is surrounded by evil people—the Turks are murdering the Armenians, and he sees horrors for the first time in his life. Like Hamlet, he must make a decision to engage in the challenge facing him or to surrender. His father's words echo in his psyche as he becomes canny, alert, and adaptive to all kinds of situations. There are moments when he feels he is so alone that he is ready to give up and die.

Both Vahan and Hamlet commit to their course of action, using all of their strength and courage. While Hamlet's course of action is tragic, Vahan survives to carry on the memory of his family.

Other YAL titles that mesh with themes in *Hamlet* include the following:

Adoff, Jaime. *Names Will Never Hurt Me.* This novel shows what happens in one high school on the one-year anniversary of a school shooting, told in prose and verse, mostly from the perspectives of four teenagers, all of whom have been victims of harassment in various forms.

Alphin, Elaine Marie. *Simon Says.* Combining writing, painting, and composing music, Alphin takes us on an unusually sophisticated journey through the troubled mind of Charles Watson as he searches for a way to be himself and not the way he thinks others want him to act.

Cormier, Robert. *I Am the Cheese.* On his bicycle and in his mind, Adam Farmer searches for the truth in a corrupt society that was responsible for the death of his parents.

Crutcher, Chris. *The Crazy Horse Electric Game.* Following a disabling accident that ends his athletic career, Willie runs away to California, where his experiences in an alternative high school help turn his life around.

Delaney, Mark. *Pepperland.* After her mother's death, Star struggles to work through her anger with the help of a sensitive psychologist and John Lennon's music.

Frank, E. R. *America.* Abandoned by his mother and separated from his foster mother, a severely disturbed boy named America spends most of his youth in mental institutions, slowly making sense of his life with the help of a caring psychiatrist.

Goobie, Beth. *The Lottery.* When 15-year-old Sally Hanson is "chosen" in the Shadow Council's lottery to be shunned by her school's student body, she refuses to be a victim.

Hrdlitschka, Shelley. *Kat's Fall.* Fifteen-year-old Darcy has been taking care of his younger sister ever since their mother went to jail 10 years earlier—no easy task, especially since Kat is deaf as well as epileptic, and their father is a very poor parent—and then things get worse for Darcy.

Klass, David. *You Don't Know Me.* Although 14-year-old John says nobody knows the first thing about him, his multilayered thoughts amusingly reveal everything we need to know about his painful life—algebra class, band practice, involvements with girls, and his home life, especially his abusive stepfather.

Koertge, Ron. *The Brimstone Journals.* Using first-person poems from the points of view of 15 students, Koertge reveals the anger, hate, and longings in a suburban high school that lead to an explosive situation.

Lynch, Chris. *Freewill.* In an extremely sophisticated novel, Chris Lynch examines a lonely and disturbed teenager's efforts to make sense of his painful world.

Oates, Joyce Carol. *Big Mouth & Ugly Girl.* When Matt is accused of having said something he didn't say, Ursula defends him, but by then it's too late to stop the rumors.

Peters, Julie Anne. *Luna.* Regan's life with a preoccupied mother and a demanding, clueless father gets horribly complicated when her older transsexual brother, Liam, decides it's time to reveal to everyone that he's always felt he is a girl in a boy's body and needs to transition into his true self, Luna.

/ / /

Julius Caesar by William Shakespeare

Themes

1. Betrayal
2. Tyranny of the group
3. Sacrificing ethics for the group
4. Leaders who abuse power

Suggested YAL titles that share some of these key themes:

CORMIER, ROBERT. *The Chocolate War.*
Jerry Renault is a loner at an all-boys parochial high school. His widowed father works long hours, so Jerry is alone at home, too. His introspection about the boredom and routine of life is manifested in a poster hanging in his locker, which asks, "Do I Dare Disturb the Universe?" The opportunity to take a risk arises when the Vigils, the gang that runs the school, decide that Jerry should refuse to sell chocolates during the annual sale to raise money for the school. At first Jerry enjoys the attention that this refusal commands from the student body, but then the Vigils decide Jerry should sell chocolates. At this point, Jerry deliberates long and hard about whether it's time "to disturb the universe." Because he risks defying the Vigils' orders, Jerry is doomed. The leader of the Vigils arranges a raffle at the athletic stadium during a fight between Jerry and Emil Janza; Jerry is carried away in an ambulance.

Theme Connector

Jerry Renault and Brutus are both manipulated by the group, Jerry by the Vigils and Brutus by the conspirators. The events leading up to their tragic circumstances are parallel: Jerry is convinced not to sell chocolates and receives a lot of respect for bucking the group; however, when he agrees to fight Emil Janza in the stadium under the guise of raffling boxes of chocolates, he realizes too late that he has been betrayed. Brutus is wooed by the conspirators, particularly Cassius, in the belief that he is engaged in a noble cause—the downfall of Julius Caesar—and though he debates in his mind whether to join the conspiracy, he convinces himself that the cause is just. This decision leads to his downfall, and eventually he runs onto his own sword when defeat is imminent. Both Jerry and Brutus are surrounded by deceitful people. Despite their personal ethics, they are persuaded to engage in actions that lead to their defeat.

GILES, GAIL. *Shattering Glass.*

This tension-filled novel about conformity and popularity recounts the events of one school year that resulted in the murder of a student by his classmates. The story is narrated mainly by Young Steward, one of the participants, five years after the events occurred, with brief commentaries from other students beginning each chapter. It's obvious from the first paragraph of the book that Simon Glass is dead. But why? The most social in-group in the high school found Simon—a nerdy, pudgy, uncoordinated guy—easy to hate. Rob, the charismatic but conniving leader of the group, convinces his group of followers to agree to make Simon Glass their project. They will reshape Simon into someone like them—starting with his haircut and his clothes. They are very proud of Simon's transformation, and he becomes Senior Class Favorite. However, they use Simon in other ways—most notably for his computer hacking skills. Though Simon is pleased to be accepted by the group, he begins to act independently, and Rob can not tolerate not being in control of all decision making. Young Steward realizes that Rob's intent to reshape Simon was not altruistic; his intent was always to build Simon up and then destroy him.

Theme Connector

Group tyranny, spurred on by a calculating leader who abuses power, characterizes Cassius in *Julius Caesar* and Rob in *Shattering Glass*. Rob is a charming, extremely adept manipulator of people, not only of the willing Simon Glass, but also of his peers—Jeff, Bob, Lance, Blair, Ginger, and Alice. Like Brutus's decision to save Rome from Caesar's domination, Young Steward, who is aware of Rob's tactics, is a willing participant in the conspiracy against Glass, along with the others. But Rob's dark side is hard to see when, as Blair suggests, he shines so brightly. Rob betrays everyone, and Simon takes his revenge by betraying Rob, thereby inciting Rob's wrath. Rob never allows himself to lose. It's not until the game ends in Simon's horrible murder that Young Steward, who is serving a prison term, takes time to look back and analyze everyone's motives and unspoken needs, especially his own. When Brutus is on the battlefield with his army, he reflects on the conspiracy and realizes his motives for deposing Caesar were not honorable and that he participated in the assassination of Caesar for the wrong reasons. Young Steward realizes that the group's participation in remaking Simon Glass was self-serving; their intentions were cruel and selfish. Young Steward is the only participant who is willing to take responsibility for his actions. Brutus admits defeat when he is driven from Rome, and calls on Caesar's ghost to forgive him.

GOOBIE, BETH. *The Lottery.*

Fifteen-year-old Sally Hanson wins the secret lottery executed by the Shadow Council. But there is nothing to celebrate, because "winning" the Shadow Council lottery means that Sally will be shunned by her school's student body for the entire school year. At the same time, the winner must do whatever members of the council decree: run errands, deliver messages to other victims, and so on. The council's decision is binding; no one has ever refused an order. Sally never objected when someone else was the victim in previous years, but now she knows what it feels like. She struggles to maintain her identity when even her best friends have abandoned her, but does she have the strength and courage needed to refuse to be a victim?

Theme Connector

Group tyranny dominates this novel, with insights into the motives of the Shadow Council's key members, especially its president, Willis Cass. The members of the council need one another's support as they terrorize others; they are similar to the members of the conspiracy in *Julius Caesar,* especially when they kill Caesar's supporters. Sally shares her inner thoughts about being ostracized and about retaliation if she refuses to cooperate; Brutus shares his inner thoughts as he wrestles with his conscience about whether to join the conspiracy against Caesar. As the pranks against other students intensify, tension increases within the council. But the council rationalizes its need to exist because everyone loves a victim; they are secure within their group no matter how wrong their purpose. They lack the confidence to stand apart from the group as individuals. By the end of the novel Sally make a moral choice, aided by two other outcasts. Brutus realizes too late that his decision to join the conspiracy was unjustified. He admits to himself that Caesar was not a tyrant; he was a noble man. Goobie's novel and Shakespeare's play illustrate the power of group pressure and the abuse of power by people in leadership positions.

FLINN, ALEX. *Breaking Point.*

After his parents' divorce, Paul Richmond and his mother move to Miami, Florida, where she works at Gate-Brickell Christian High School. As a skinny sophomore over six feet tall, Paul feels completely out of place among the blond, affluent, preppy students at this private school, and the other students take every opportunity to ignore, exclude, and humiliate him. Paul is miserable until Charlie Good, a rather short, confident, and popular junior befriends him. Charlie tests Paul's loyalty by ordering him to knock down mailboxes with a baseball bat, steal bagels from a bakery at 3 A.M., break into the school's computer system to change Charlie's D in biology, and finally make a bomb from a recipe on the Internet and place it in a classroom as a prank. Because Charlie patronizes Paul (or "Einstein," as he calls him), Paul is accepted into the group. Charlie takes him to parties, flatters his ego, and convinces him that he is his best friend. Charlie's friendship guarantees Paul that his backpack, locker, and clothes won't be trashed anymore, and he won't be hassled by the jocks. Paul is dazzled by Charlie and trusts him. In a flashback, Paul recounts the relationship with Charlie from his first day at Gate-Brickell and admits that he ignored his own conscience and went along with Charlie's orders. Now, at age 17, after spending two years in juvenile prison, he takes responsibility for his own actions. Meanwhile, Charlie is protected by his affluent parents, who refuse to hold Charlie accountable for his criminal acts. In the end, Paul has learned about relationships and trust.

Theme Connector

Paul Richmond and Brutus share common character traits: they are highly intelligent, respond to flattery, and instinctively know they are engaged in evil acts but continue until their lives are out of control. Brutus is manipulated by Cassius and the members of the conspiracy; they flatter him and convince him that he should be the leader of Rome. Charlie Good preys on Paul's exclusion from the group; if Charlie brings Paul along to the gang's lunches, parties, and other activities, the group accepts Paul. What he doesn't realize or won't accept is that Charlie is insincere. Charlie is using Paul to carry out his criminal acts. As it is difficult for Brutus to recognize the conspirators' flattery and fawning, it is difficult for Paul Richmond to recognize Charlie's assurance that Paul is his best friend. Group acceptance is so important to Paul that he ignores his intuition or doubt. Both Brutus and Paul are fully developed characters who are used by a group to commit immoral acts. They are betrayed, and in the end they admit that they ignored warning signs and continued on, hoping their instincts were wrong. While Brutus's life is destroyed, Paul Richmond can start over.

Other YAL titles that mesh with themes in *Julius Caesar* include the following:

Anderson, Laurie Halse. *Speak.* Melinda describes her year of being ostracized in high school after a summer party at which she was sexually assaulted and so traumatized that she can't talk about it.

Brugman, Alyssa. *Walking Naked.* When Megan, a leader of her school's in-group, starts to associate with Perdita, "the Freak," she is forced to decide which side she's on, with tragic consequences.

Cormier, Robert. *We All Fall Down.* Buddy joins his friends in the trashing of the Jeromes' home and then later befriends one of the Jerome daughters, Jane, who eventually learns what Buddy did. The loss of Jane's friendship makes him realize the kinds of friends he chose.

Crutcher, Chris. *Running Loose.* Louie Banks makes a moral choice to stand up to his football coach and the school principal, risking everything.

DuPrau, Jeanne. *The People of Sparks.* After Lina and Doon find a way out of the City of Ember, they are joined by 400 other former residents who find temporary shelter in a nearby town of Sparks, until the local residents feel their existence is threatened by the presence of the newcomers.

Hobbs, Will. *River Thunder.* Against her better judgment, Jessie joins her friends from the previous summer's adventure (*Downriver*) for a second try at running the Colorado River, but realizes too late Troy's motives in organizing this adventure.

Klass, David. *Home of the Braves.* Eighteen-year-old Joe is frustrated when a Brazilian student joins their soccer team and starts dating the girl Joe has hoped to date, but it's violence off the playing field that threatens to destroy the school and Joe's future.

Koja, Kathe. *The Blue Mirror.* Tired of dealing with her alcoholic mother, a talented 16-year-old artist seeks solace in a downtown café, where she encounters a charismatic homeless guy named Cole, who draws her into his warped world.

Mazer, Norma Fox. *Out of Control.* After three high school friends sexually harass a girl in the hallway, one of them begins to realize how wrong his action was.

Prose, Francine. *After.* After the shootings in a nearby school, the students in Central High are subjected to increased security, random drug tests, and various restrictions that escalate until students and teachers begin to disappear.

Werlin, Nancy. *Double Helix.* Following high school graduation, Eli lands a summer job at Wyatt Transgenics to work under a legendary but amoral molecular biologist who knows secrets about Eli's birth because he betrayed the family's trust years earlier.

--- / / / ---

Lord of the Flies by William Golding

Themes

1. Loss of innocence
2. Good versus evil
3. The abuse of power by the group
4. The tyranny of the group
5. Taking a stand for one's personal beliefs
6. The need for rules to foster civilized behavior

Suggested YAL titles that share some of these key themes:

KOERTGE, RON. *The Brimstone Journals.*

The individual poems of 15 different students reveal the tension building in Brimstone High School. There is the stereotypical jock, Damon, who is not only a harasser but also a control freak with his girlfriend, Kelli; the African American, Neesha, who refuses to use standard English because it's the way white people talk; Jennifer, the religious fanatic who is charmed by Rob, who has to prove his sexual prowess; the pretty girl, Allison, whose father may be a little too affectionate with her; and the intelligent Vietnamese student, Tran, who observes on the sidelines. Then there's Lester, an overweight and not particularly bright student, tired of being harassed by fellow students; he considers bringing a gun to school to kill his tormentors, until he's recruited by Boyd and the Brotherhood, who have their own plans to blow up the school.

Theme Connector

As in *Lord of the Flies,* there are students at Brimstone High who use their power over others because they can; they intimidate and exploit weaker students who fear them. Their chief target is Lester, who is similar to Piggy in looks and personality—his weight, awkwardness, and need to be accepted make him an easy mark. But Lester chooses to seek revenge when he can't tolerate any more abuse, while Piggy tries to be a peacemaker. Both Rob and Boyd are similar to Jack—their leadership skills satisfy their need to be evil manipulators of the group. Jack is successful in convincing his "hunters" that Ralph and Piggy are evil. Jack does not want order in the community because his power would be threatened; he will not accept equality in the community. At Brimstone High each individual's poems reflect the needs and perceptions of the students and how they react to one another. Golding's novel and the journals of the Brimstone students provide an intimate look at issues of respect, belonging, ridicule, harassment, and revenge. Jack relishes picking on the weak and passive boys, just as Rob and Boyd delight in humiliating students who are unwilling to stand up to them. But as in Golding's dark novel, one student in Brimstone chooses to stand up to the group and do the right thing, thus preventing further tragedy.

HOBBS, WILL. *Downriver.*

The setting is the Grand Canyon, where a group of misfits are enrolled in an outdoor program, Discovery Unlimited. When their counselor, Al, leaves them in the van on their way to a rafting journey, they steal the van, unload the rafting equipment, and decide to go downriver on their own. Although they have spent weeks training for this adventure, the dynamics of the group, splintered leadership, and lack of shared decision making turn this journey into a life-threatening experience. Their foolhardy decision to go alone, ridicule Al's training and preparation, and ignore survival rules nearly results in a tragedy. After their experience, they begin to realize the need for order, respect, and shared decision making. Jessie, the narrator, shares her objective point of view about the members of the group and their roles in this daring adventure.

Theme Connector

Downriver shows what happens when a leader abuses his power. When Troy suggests that the group steal Al's van, he becomes the leader of the rafting expedition by default. Troy shares similar character traits with Jack, the leader of the hunters in *Lord of the Flies*. Like Jack, Troy manipulates the group, daring them to ignore authority and rules. Unlike the hunters, however, the group in *Downriver* begins to recognize the weaknesses of Troy's leadership, especially when he puts their lives in jeopardy. Troy and Jack use similar language to cajole their peers into disregarding rules and rational behaviors.

CARVELL, MARLENE. *Who Will Tell My Brother?*

Inspired by real events, this novel in verse deals with a Native American student's efforts to remove a high school's offensive Indian mascot, which results in hateful bullying and violence from officials and peers. Evan Hill, a senior not quite secure in his Mohawk Indian identity, feels ashamed when white students give war hoops and tomahawk chops and wave a banner picturing the Indian mascot. Believing he must act on his feelings about this situation, Evan approaches the school board with a request to remove this symbol of intolerance. But the school board members dismiss Evan's request, as they did the requests of his older brother before him. He returns to the school board again and again throughout the year, and the board continues to dismiss his request, with greater intolerance each time. Students begin to harass Evan, along with his family, and eventually kill their beloved dog, Butch. Eventually a few students start to understand Evan's point of view and begin to support him.

Theme Connector

The school board members and the students in Evan's school are unsympathetic and ignorant about the feelings of a Native American's view of the school's mascot symbol. When their perspective is questioned, they feel threatened and become more intolerant. The more pressure they feel, the angrier and more hateful they become, until the anger results in violence. The school board abuses its power by failing to consider Evan's point of view, and continues to reject his request. Evan is an innocent who believes he can effect change in the school's attitude, though his older brother could not. But he becomes more pessimistic after each visit to the school board, and when his brother's dog is viciously killed, he realizes that the group is unwilling to compromise.

Unlike the adults in *Lord of the Flies,* whose presence restores order to the tyrannical society that Jack has fomented on the island, the adults in charge of Evan's school system are part of the tyranny, leaders who are intolerant. Some of the students abuse their power further by creating a banner that they flaunt at the graduation ceremony. Unlike some of his peers, Evan does not allow his anger to lead to violent actions against his tormentors. He, like Ralph, has stood up with pride and dignity against the system and the students who taunted him. In the process, he earns the respect of his parents, learns about his ancestors, and finally gains the support of a few sympathetic students. There is hope for change in the future.

Other YAL titles that mesh with themes in *Lord of the Flies* include the following:

Armstrong, Jennifer, and Nancy Butcher. *Fire-Us: The Kindling.* In 2006, after a virus seems to have killed almost everyone on the planet, a small group of kids in Florida struggles to survive among the ruins.

Cormier, Robert. *The Chocolate War.* Jerry Renault finds that taking a stand for what he believes in leads to alienation and violence.

Crutcher, Chris. *Whale Talk.* Behind the triumphs of a high school swim team composed of misfits lurk painful lives and present dangers that culminate in a shocking and surprising ending.

Duncan, Lois. *Killing Mr. Griffin.* When several students decide to scare their overbearing English teacher by kidnapping him and leaving him tied to a tree in the forest, their plan backfires, with terrible consequences.

DuPrau, Jeanne. *The People of Sparks.* After Lina and Doon find a way out of the City of Ember, they are joined by 400 other former residents who find temporary shelter in a nearby town of Sparks, until the local residents feel their existence is threatened by the presence of the newcomers.

Eskilsen, Erik E. *Offsides.* Refusing to play for a manipulative soccer coach at a high school whose Indian mascot Tom opposes, he forms a ragtag team that plays against the school's varsity in a stunning climax.

Giles, Gail. *Shattering Glass.* A tension-filled story about conformity and popularity, this novel recounts the events of a school year that resulted in the murder of a classmate, told mainly from the point of view of one of the participants, with comments from other students.

Keizer, Garret. *God of Beer.* In a small town in rural Vermont, a group of high school seniors decides to challenge the status quo through an act of civil disobedience, the consequences of which are tragic.

Lowry, Lois. *Messenger.* Characters from *The Giver* and *Gathering Blue* come together in a peaceful community that's suddenly threatened with dissention until a young hero with healing powers makes the ultimate sacrifice.

Mazer, Norma Fox. *Out of Control.* After three high school friends sexually harass a girl in the hallway, one of them begins to realize how wrong his action was.

Sacher, Louis. *Holes.* Stanley Yelnats and his companions struggle daily to survive the harsh life of pointless physical labor in a youth detention facility on a dry lakebed, only slowly realizing the secret of their activity.

Spinelli, Jerry. *Wringer.* Not only is Palmer picked on by neighborhood kids, but he is also being pressured to participate in the town's annual Pigeon Day when 12-year-old kids (his age) wring the necks of birds that are only wounded by the shooters.

Strasser, Todd. *Give a Boy a Gun.* Everyone's point of view is examined and opinions expressed after two boys bring guns to school and open fire on their schoolmates in this fictional parallel to Columbine.

_____. *The Wave.* A group of students in a California high school observe the forces that control a mass movement when a teacher sets up a Nazi-type classroom and gets more student support than he expects. Based on a real experiment in a Palo Alto, California, school.

/ / /

The Odyssey by Homer

Themes

1. The journey, search, or quest to prove oneself
2. The hero returning from a challenge or test
3. The courage to face one's destiny

Suggested YAL titles that share some of these key themes:

PAULSEN, GARY. *Woodsong.*

Gary Paulsen describes his profound experiences with his sled dogs in northern Minnesota, experiences that lead to his journey—completing the Iditarod. After some friends give him four sled dogs, he learns to understand these dogs—about running and feeding them, breeding and raising them, and coming to know the "dance of the dogs." As he learns their "dance," he begins to understand the innate intelligence of the animals. In describing his journeys with the dogs, he illustrates that they have what we consider human qualities, such as courage, teamwork, perseverance, loyalty, trust, and compassion. As Paulsen lives and works with his dogs, Cookie, Wilson, Columbia, Storm, Yogi, and Olaf, the dogs change him; he decides to no longer hunt and kill for sport. As he observes their behaviors more and more, he begins to realize that the dogs—and therefore probably all animals—may be as complex as human beings. But because he has established a rapport with the dogs, he cannot stop running with them. He decides to run the Iditarod, the Alaskan sled dog race from Anchorage to Nome (1,100-plus miles). During the Iditarod he gains knowledge from the dogs about himself in relation to nature, animals, and other wonders of the universe. This autobiographical experience is poetic and insightful and conveys respect for nature.

Theme Connector

The Odyssey is the story of Odysseus's 10-year journey from Troy to Ithaka after the Trojan War. Because Odysseus has incurred the wrath of the god Poseidon after blinding his son, Polyphemos, Odysseus and his army are constantly delayed and blown off course by Poseidon. They have to combat such challenges as monsters, the Lotus Eaters, seductive women (for example, Kalypso, the Sirens, and Kirke), Apollo's sacred cattle, whirlpools, thunderbolts, gale winds, and Zeus himself. In contrast, Paulsen chooses to be challenged by the forces of nature and his own supernatural force—his mind. When Odysseus relates his journey to the Skherians, he explains the life-threatening forces that challenged him and his army at every port; but he does not reveal his own weakness for beautiful women and his determination to experience every challenge (for example, he puts wax in the crew's ears and has them lash him to the mast of the boat so he could be the first man to hear and escape the songs of the Sirens). Odysseus is unable to repress his hubris because he cannot resist a challenge.

Paulsen's challenge is different—he and his team are almost one force running in harmony, trying to coexist with nature. Unlike Odysseus, he does not have to contend with the gods. But like Odysseus, he faces life-threatening challenges, both internal and external: experiencing hallucinations caused by sleep deprivation, losing the trail, keeping the dogs fed so they remain healthy, dealing with frostbite and whiteouts, and surviving severe below-zero temperatures.

There are situations and experiences in both journeys that are comparable: the song of the Sirens and the songs of the dogs; the fear of the Kyklopes and Polyphemos by Odysseus and his men and Paulsen's fear of crossing the Alaskan mountains; Odysseus hanging on a tree while his boat and crew sail through Skylla and Kharybdis and Paulsen tied to the sled, unable to steer or stop the dogs. While Paulsen is respectful and compassionate of his dogs, Odysseus is willing to risk the lives of his men to satisfy his curiosity.

There are many other similarities between *Woodsong* and *The Odyssey*. Both journeys require similar tests or challenges. Both journeys reflect courage, tenacity, and resilience—qualities we admire in heroes. Homer's epic poem and Paulsen's autobiographical journey are strong examples of the endurance of the human spirit. The metaphorical journey, the char-acterizations, the poetic view of nature, and the individual's place in the universe provide a thoughtful reading experience for students.

FARMER, NANCY. *A Girl Named Disaster.*

Nhamo, or Disaster, lives in a Shona village in Mozambique with her grandmother, aunt, uncle, and their family. When she was very young, her mother died and her father returned to Zimbabwe. Disaster is curi-ous, intelligent, and sensitive for her 13 years, but her aunt is demand-ing and treats her with contempt. Because her family believes in spirits, they are persuaded to arrange Nhamo's marriage to the brother of the man who was killed by her father. The man is old, with many wives, and will make Nhamo a slave. In order to avoid the arranged marriage, Disas-ter's grandmother persuades her to use an old boat to run away to Zim-babwe and search for her father's family. And so Nhamo starts her journey alone, in a boat that she's never steered, headed for Zimbabwe. Using her storytelling skills, innate courage, and intelligence, Disaster faces many challenging situations on her journey until she finds her father's family.

Theme Connector

There are many touchstones in the journeys of Disaster and Odysseus as they experience the natural and supernatural world. Odysseus heeds the word of the goddess Athena, and he offers sacrifices to the gods to atone for the slaughter of Apollo's sacred cattle by his crew, his deceitful behavior with Polyphemos, and his lust for Kirke and Kalypso. Disaster is more submissive and fearful of the spirits and tries to appease the supernatural forces that surround her, such as the *njuzu* girls who appear as snakes; she summons inner courage to tolerate and respect them. After the starving Disaster lands on an island filled with vegetation, she makes an offering to the spirits to thank them for providing her with food and safety. After Odysseus's crew is destroyed and he survives alone, he too makes an offering to the gods to thank them.

Odysseus gains humility after he travels to the Land of the Shades to hear his destiny; Disaster rebuilds her boat after an accident by obeying the spirits. She regains hope by talking to the spirit of her mother and grandmother and believes she will reach Zimbabwe and find her family. After hearing his destiny, Odysseus is willing to stop defying Poseidon and make a sacrifice to him in order to rejoin his family in Ithaka.

When Disaster and Odysseus do reach land—she in Zimbabwe, he in Skheria—they are physically beaten and thus appear to be barbaric. But both regain their human characteristics when the nuns in the hospital nurse Disaster back to health and the Skherians bathe, clothe, and feed Odysseus and make him a guest in their palace.

Both Odysseus and Disaster are also amazing storytellers. She tells stories to calm her fear of the unknown; Odysseus weaves an elaborate story for the Phaiakians so that they will guess his identity and help him return to Ithaka. The epic poem and the novel describe remarkable journeys that show the ability of the human spirit to face many challenges and tests and manage to survive.

ALLENDE, ISABEL. *City of the Beasts.*

Fifteen-year-old Alexander Cold finds himself on the journey of his life when he accompanies his eccentric grandmother, Kate, to the Amazon rain forest in Brazil on a journalistic assignment for *International Geographic* to investigate reports about an enormous Beast. Traveling with a backpack, a compass, his army knife, and his flute, Alex and his grandmother join a guide and his 13-year-old daughter, Nadia; two photographers; an anthropologist; a local medical doctor; and some natives and soldiers. The humidity, mosquitoes, snakes, beetles, dampness, and primitive accommodations challenge Alex's survival skills. However, Nadia teaches him about the lore of the jungle and proceeds to confide in him about her shaman, Walibi, who protects her.

After overhearing an entrepreneur plotting against the expedition and planning to kill the Indians for the precious gems, gold, and timber in their villages, Nadia and Alex wander from the campsite and are kidnapped by the Indians called People of the Mist. Nadia and Alex establish a trusting relationship with the Indians, and when the Indians become angry or upset, Alex plays his flute to calm them and assure them that he and Nadia will help keep the *nahob* (exploiters with planes and weapons) away. The Beast, they discover, is the protector of the Indians. Huge, lumbering, with a small head and huge claws, the Beast has the capacity to leave an odor that asphyxiates humans. However, it cannot kill all the outsiders, so Nadia and Alex propose to help the natives find a peaceful way to deal with the *nahob.*

To help the People of the Mist, Alex and Nadia are sent on a heroic mission to the mountains of the gods, where they will ask the gods to save the People of the Mist. Their journey is full of challenges such as labyrinths, winged dragons, water-filled dark caves, and a meeting with many Beasts. Eventually, Nadia and Alex return to the People of the Mist with their prize—three crystal eggs—and expose the entrepreneur's plan to kill the People of the Mist. Alex's experiences with Nadia and the shaman have given him spiritual strength and courage to adapt to life-threatening circumstances.

Theme Connector

The journeys of Alex Cold and Odysseus both focus on the quest to prove oneself. Though Odysseus is a bigger-than-life hero, Alex is an ordinary kid who finds himself in circumstances that call upon his ability to be courageous, supportive, trustworthy, and tolerant. Like Odysseus, he is caught between natural and supernatural forces that test his sanity and endurance. Alex and Nadia's journey to the land of the gods parallels Odysseus's journey to the Land of the Shades. Both individuals have to seek their destiny by traveling through dark, fearful places and maintaining their equilibrium.

When Tahama, the chief of the People of the Mist, dies, Alex has to participate in the rituals of burning his corpse and making offerings to the gods. Odysseus has to return to Kirke's island to burn the corpse of his dead soldier, Elpenor, and make a sacrifice to the gods in order to continue his journey home. Other parallel situations include Walibi, the shaman, and Athena, the goddess of wisdom, both of whom advise and protect the travelers through the natural and supernatural world. The shaman recites epic poems about the Indians' past and the need to respect their gods. Odysseus mesmerizes the Phaiakians with his story of the Trojan War and his journey from Troy to Skheria. Odysseus's battle with the suitors in his palace might be compared to Nadia and Alex's attempt to save the Indians from fatal inoculations and the soldiers' guns. *City of the Beasts* and *The Odyssey* provide countless situations to examine the challenges of nature, the mysteries of the supernatural, the importance of rituals in different cultures, and the need to respect nature. Both journeys exemplify the resilience of the human spirit to continue under the most trying circumstances.

WEAVER, WILL. *Memory Boy.*

After monstrous volcanic eruptions in Washington State in 2006 have destroyed major cities and sprayed ash on eastern cities so that they are paralyzed, 16-year-old Miles Newell's family abandons their suburban Minneapolis home. Hoping to escape the crime and rioting in their city, the family sets out for their log cabin in rural Minnesota on a power-pedaled vehicle designed by Miles out of three bicycles and four lawn chairs, including a mast and sail from their boat. During their journey they encounter homeless people, scavengers, bandits, armed sentries, barricaded roads, hijackers on all-terrain vehicles, and finally squatters with rifles in their log cabin. Using his "memory book" about wilderness survival from an oral-history project with 90-year-old Hans Kurz, Miles learns to trust his senses and helps his family find shelter and relative safety.

Theme Connector

As Odysseus escaped the chaos of the Trojan War, Miles and his family seek refuge from a city in chaos. Although their land journey contrasts with Odysseus's sea journey, the Newell family's vehicle sails (literally) along the highways and back roads of Minnesota to return to their rural log cabin. Like Odysseus, they are faced with life-threatening individuals such as bandits, hijackers, and armed squatters. They have to be as canny as Odysseus is when he tricks Polyphemos into removing the boulder so he and his soldiers can escape under the sheep's bellies. As the gods manipulated Odysseus's struggle to return home, Miles listens to the "voice" of Mr. Kurz, whom he interviewed for his survival history project. As a professional warrior, Odysseus usually engaged in battles to kill his adversaries, while the Newells avoid violence by circumventing the rioters and armed guards. Odysseus has to use violence to reestablish his position in Ithaka; the Newells relocate to another area rather than confront the armed squatters in their cabin. However, both Odysseus and the Newells demonstrate personal courage, intelligence, resilience, and the triumph of the human spirit.

Other YAL titles that mesh with themes in *The Odyssey* include the following:

Bell, William. *Zack.* Zack, whose mother is black and whose father is Jewish, begins a project for his history class in Canada that leads him on a journey to his African American roots in Mississippi.

Buss, Fran Leeper. *Journey of the Sparrows.* Fourteen-year-old Maria and her family, refugees from El Salvador, journey through Mexico and try to survive in Chicago without a green card.

Gallo, Donald R., ed. *Destination Unexpected.* These 10 stories about journeys—to Europe, Cape Cod, a golf course, the racetrack, a local diner—bring unexpected insights for the teenage protagonists, from writers such as Ron Koertge, Alex Flinn, Kimberly Willis Holt, Richard Peck, and Ellen Wittlinger.

Goobie, Beth. *Flux.* By shape-shifting, 12-year-old Nellie is able to travel to parallel worlds in this frightening novel about a society where young children are abducted for science experiments.

Hobbs, Will. *Far North.* Two contemporary teenage boys, one Anglo and one Indian, fight to survive the bitter winter and find their way to safety in Canada's Northwest Territories.

_____. *Jason's Gold.* Jason's physical stamina as well as his resolve are tested during the Klondike Gold Rush, with the help of an abandoned dog and a young writer named Jack London.

_____. *Leaving Protection.* When Robbie Daniels, age 16, leaves home to work on a salmon fishing boat off the coast of southeast Alaska, he gets more adventure and suspense than he bargained for.

_____. *Wild Man Island.* In the wilderness of Admiralty Island off the coast of southern Alaska, 14-year-old Andy finds evidence of the first Americans after he is stranded during a storm in this novel with nonstop action, punctuated with information about wildlife and archaeology.

Mazer, Harry. *A Boy No More.* Adam and his mother move from Pearl Harbor, Hawaii, to Bakersfield, California, where Adam is asked to deliver a letter from his friend Davi Mori in Hawaii to Davi's father, who has been forced with other Japanese Americans into an internment camp in nearby Manzanar.

Mikaelsen, Ben. *Red Midnight.* After soldiers in Guatemala kill his family, 12-year-old Santiago escapes with his 4-year-old sister in a small boat, aiming to paddle across the Gulf of Mexico to the United States.

_____. *Touching Spirit Bear.* Because of his violent behavior, Cole is ordered to participate in a Native American Circle of Justice program on a deserted island for a year, where he is mauled by a huge white bear.

Philbrick, Rodman. *The Young Man and the Sea.* After his mother dies and his father is immobilized by grief, 12-year-old Skiff Beaman takes action by repairing their sunken boat and then setting out alone in his skiff to try to harpoon a giant tuna that he hopes to sell at a huge price.

Salisbury, Graham. *Eyes of the Emperor.* Just before the bombing of Pearl Harbor, a Hawaiian teenager of Japanese ancestry joins the U.S. army, only to find himself and his Hawaiian comrades discriminated against; they are then sent to a secret island in Mississippi, where they become the bait for training attack dogs.

Three books that provide historical background about the Trojan War are the following:

Cooney, Caroline B. *Goddess of Yesterday.* In her adventure-filled life, young Anaxandra is taken hostage from her island home, is the sole survivor of an attack by pirates, is taken in by King Menelaus of Sparta, accompanies Helen to Troy, and plays a crucial role in the first days of the Trojan War.

Geras, Adele. *Troy.* Focusing on a teenage handmaiden to Helen and another girl who looks after wounded soldiers in the Blood Room, this lengthy novel looks at the last days of the Trojan War as Aphrodite, goddess of love, stirs up some intrigue and brings the war to its bloody conclusion.

McLaren, Clemence. *Waiting for Odysseus.* McLaren retells the tale of Odysseus from the points of view of four women: Penelope, his wife; Circe, the sorceress; the goddess Pallas Athena; and Odysseus's old servant, Eurycleia.

———————————————— / / / ————————————————

Of Mice and Men by John Steinbeck

Themes

1. Exclusion from mainstream society
2. Surviving poverty, prejudice, and brutality
3. Holding on to friends who are loyal
4. The dignity of each individual

Suggested YAL titles that share some of these key themes:

GIBBONS, KAYE. *Ellen Foster.*
The narrator of this novel is a young southern girl who is abandoned by a vicious father after her mother dies. She "makes her way," staying with some "Negroes" down the road, too proud to eat their food because she is white. After finding the situation intolerable, she goes to live with her well-to-do grandmother, who abhors her. Because the narrator's mother married beneath her social class, the grandmother considers her granddaughter "poor white trash." She treats her like a Negro, sending her into the fields to pick cotton. When the grandmother dies, the girl is placed in a foster home, where she finds love and support for the first time in her life. She changes her name to Ellen Foster. Told in flashback by an adult recalling her deprived childhood, this is a richly textured story about an abandoned child who manages to survive.

Theme Connector

Ellen Foster and *Of Mice and Men* share a view of characters stuck in poverty, existing day by day. Both novels illustrate the effects of poverty on people searching for their place in society. The comments of the ranch owner in *Of Mice and Men* and of the father and grandmother in *Ellen Foster* clearly convey contempt toward these rootless characters. The castoffs manage to maintain their sense of dignity because they find friendship and trust—George and Lennie have each other; Ellen finds protection with a black family and a foster family. Both novels express the dignity of these characters and their ability to survive in an uncaring society.

PHILBRICK, RODMAN. *Freak the Mighty.*
Max, the narrator, announces, "My brain is vacant." Living with his grandparents, Gram and Grim, Max is not looking forward to his summer before 8th grade. He is clumsy, with big feet and a huge body. Sud-

denly his life changes when a yellow-haired midget named Kevin moves
into his neighborhood. Kevin is going into 8th grade too, and he and Max
become close friends. Kevin is intelligent, has an advanced vocabulary,
and is particularly interested in robots, astronomy, and Superman. He
encourages Max to learn about a variety of subjects; he makes a diction-
ary for Max so that he can improve his reading. Max, who feels excluded
from his peers and is always in learning-disabled classes, starts to gain
confidence in himself. When a gang of bullies intimidates Max and
Kevin, Kevin rides on Max's shoulders, directing him away from the
gang. As Kevin rides on Max's shoulders, he nicknames them Freak the
Mighty. They outwit the gang, and Max plans a quest for them. They
walk to the hospital, where Freak says he will become a normal-sized
8th grader through their robotics lab.

During the summer Max and Kevin have many exciting adventures;
Kevin saves Max's life when his father, alias Killer Kane, tries to kidnap
him. But when Max is in the hospital, he realizes that Freak's explanation about robotics changing him physically is a fantasy. After Freak's
death, Max writes their story, remembering their quests, dealing with
Tony D. and his gang, and escaping from his murderous father. And Max
realizes the gift that Freak left him—the confidence to believe in himself
and his memory.

Theme Connector

Like the characters Lennie and George in *Of Mice and Men,* Max and
Kevin in *Freak the Mighty* operate on the edge of society. They are
excluded by their peer group in school and intimidated by Tony D. and
his gang. However, Kevin, alias Freak, is bright enough to use many
strategies to combat these injustices. He transmits his confidence to
Max, and together they confront their enemies. Unlike George and
Lennie, Max and Kevin have families that protect them. But until Freak
comes into his life, Max avoids people and speaking in public, hides out
in his basement room, and feels he has no brain whatsoever. He relies on
Freak to guide him, just as Lenny relies on George to navigate their life
on ranches, working with all kinds of people. George weaves a fantasy
for Lennie about owning their own land and raising rabbits and growing
crops; Freak weaves a fantasy for Max about their going on a quest, slay-
ing dragons, and walking high above the world. Freak convinces Max
that anything he puts his mind to is possible. George uses his fantasy
story to help Lenny control his physical prowess and protect Lenny from
himself. But George is unable to protect Lenny after the situation with
Curley's wife, and they have to leave the ranch. George is a loyal friend
to Lenny; he treats him with dignity. In writing about his adventures
with Freak, Max learns how to deal with people, how to speak directly

to them, how to stand up for his rights, and, most importantly, the value of a loyal and trustworthy friend. Freak has taught him about the dignity of each individual.

LUBAR, DAVID. *Hidden Talents.*

Martin Anderson attends Edgeview Alternative School because everyone has given up on him—teachers, parents, Scout leader, Little League coach, everybody. It's his last chance to fit in. Martin has a problem with authority; he can't help mouthing off to adults. But he does fit in at Edgeview—he's just one of many misfits housed there. The friends he ends up with are a collection of the school's five freakiest delinquents: Torchie, who sets fire to various objects, like his textbooks; Trash, who can move objects with his mind; Lucky, who is able to find lost things; Flinch, who sees into the future; and Cheater, who can read minds. By helping them discover that their apparent problems are hidden talents, Martin and his friends battle the school bullies and help save the school from being closed down. In the process, Martin discovers that his own talent of being able to "read" people's vulnerabilities can be used for positive purposes, and he eventually is able to return to public school.

Theme Connector

The schoolboys are isolated from mainstream society in a different way than Lennie and George are isolated on the ranch, but their feelings of not belonging and of being picked on by the other boys are similar. Being ostracized from the dominant society, Martin and his five friends have no chance of ever succeeding, but their support of one another gives them some comfort, just as Lennie and George find comfort and support in each other. And just as Lennie finds it impossible to act appropriately in social situations, the boys at Edgeview can't control their impulses. Fortunately, through the wisdom of their good friend Martin, the young boys discover ways to tame those so-called talents and use them in positive ways, while Lennie is killed by his best friend, George, in order to avoid further suffering. Both novels illustrate the importance of supportive friends, the need for a more caring society, and finding dignity in each person's character.

MIKAELSEN, BEN. *Petey.*

Told in two parts, this bittersweet story is heart-wrenching and unforgettable. Born with cerebral palsy in 1920, Petey is diagnosed as an idiot and sent to spend his life in a mental institution, where few people see beyond his grunts and deformed body until 70 years later, when he is befriended by a teenager, Trevor Ladd. Petey was automatically excluded from mainstream society by the misdiagnosis of his condition. And though a couple of perceptive staff people see more behind Petey's gurgles and squeaks, none of them is able to stay around indefinitely to nurse him along. Even the brotherly bond that develops between Petey and retarded Calvin is brought to an abrupt end when the asylum is closed and both men are sent to different facilities. But Petey is brought out of his loneliness and silence by a teenage boy who reluctantly, at first, visits the old man. Once a connection is established between Petey and young Trevor, Trevor is able to bring pleasure and new experiences to Petey's life as well as to his own, even helping Petey reconnect with Calvin and a former staff member, before Petey's life ends.

Theme Connector

There are numerous indirect parallels between *Petey* and *Of Mice and Men,* including mental retardation, close friendships, prejudice, human dignity, and even furry wild creatures as pets. Most importantly, teenage readers will easily come to sympathize with Petey as well as with Lennie, since both are treated poorly by others in the dominant society. Although much of the lack of support for Petey comes from ignorance of cerebral palsy at the time, there are still individuals, along with the rules of the system, that prevent his being treated properly. Both Petey and Calvin are rather sad cases, as is Lennie, of course, but they each have at least one supporter—Trevor for Petey and George for Lennie. Both friends go to extreme lengths to protect and support their buddies, though Trevor never has to go to the extreme George does to save Lennie from further harm in the end.

And Petey has more friends than Lennie: Petey has Calvin, Joe, Cassie, and Owen. But Petey is much older than Lennie, so readers become aware of more injustices and disappointments in *Petey* than they do in *Of Mice and Men.* And the ending of *Petey* is more upbeat, even though Petey is on his deathbed. George is as loyal and supportive a friend to Lennie as anyone could be; he tries to protect Lennie at all times. And Petey's friends, until Trevor comes along, have been loyal, though unable to provide lasting support. Trevor's support of Petey is brief because Petey is 70 years old and not in good health. But Trevor's devotion to Petey is no less than George's to Lennie, and in both books we see the mistreated men nearing death with happy thoughts. Both stories should leave readers with greater understanding for people like Petey and Lennie, and maybe a greater sensitivity toward individuals like them.

Other YAL titles that mesh with themes in *Of Mice and Men* include the following:

Brugman, Alyssa. *Walking Naked.* Megan Twu is not only part of the 11th grade in-group, she leads it, until she gets put in detention with Perdita Wiguiggan, the school freak, and against every rule of her group, Megan starts to befriend Perdita.

Crutcher, Chris. *Staying Fat for Sarah Byrnes.* Outsiders Moby and Sarah have always supported each other, but when Moby makes the swimming team and begins to slim down, Sarah falls apart and is institutionalized, until Moby can help figure out what's wrong.

Hartinger, Brent. *The Last Chance Texaco.* Feisty Lucy Pitt faces new challenges—and finds acceptance—at a last-chance group home for orphans and troubled teens.

Hesse, Karen. *Phoenix Rising.* After a radiation leak in a nuclear reactor, Nyle and her grandmother show compassion for Ezra and his mother, who are outcasts in their community.

_____. *Witness.* A stunning novel in free verse about the effects of Ku Klux Klan activities on 11 narrators in a small Vermont town in the 1920s.

Holt, Kimberly Willis. *My Louisiana Sky.* Tiger Ann is embarrassed by her mentally slow parents and dominated by her strong grandmother, but when Granny dies, Aunt Dorie Kay takes over, and things begin to change for Tiger Ann.

_____. *When Zachary Beaver Came to Town.* Toby Wilson thinks nothing exciting ever happens in Antler, Texas, until his mom wins a chance to sing at the Grand Ole Opry, his best friend's brother writes home from Vietnam, and Zachary Beaver, the fattest boy in the world, comes to town.

Martin, Ann M. *A Corner of the Universe.* As Hattie turns 12, her life in a small town takes an unexpected turn when she meets her mentally disabled uncle and a carnival comes to town.

Meyer, Carolyn. *White Lilacs.* When plans are announced to raze the entire black neighborhood of Dillon, Texas, and replace it with a park, a torrent of anger and defiance erupts and the Klan gets involved. Based on a true event.

Paterson, Katherine. *Jip: His Story.* In 1855–56 Vermont, young Jip, an abandoned orphan, befriends the town lunatic, who lives in a cage, and later learns that he himself is half black and is about to be sold as a slave.

Plum-Ucci, Carol. *The Body of Christopher Creed.* When one of their schoolmates disappears, most of his peers offer insensitive opinions of why and what happened, until one of them is accused of killing him and hiding his body.

Smith, Sherri L. *Lucy the Giant.* Fed up with school and her drunken father, 15-year-old Lucy runs away and signs up as a crew member on a crab boat fishing in the Bering Sea.

Strasser, Todd. *Can't Get There from Here.* The painful stories of several homeless teenagers living (and dying) on the streets of New York City reveal their place in society and their search for some place to belong.

Wolff, Virginia Euwer. *Make Lemonade.* When 14-year-old LaVaughn babysits the two young children of a 17-year-old unmarried girl, all their lives are changed.

/ / /

Romeo and Juliet by William Shakespeare

Themes

1. Innocent love and friendship
2. Dealing with death; dealing with suicide
3. Family isolation
4. Secret relationships

Suggested YAL titles that share some of these key themes:

PECK, RICHARD. *Remembering the Good Times.*
The narrator, Buck Mendenhall, shares all the "good times" he and Kate and Travis had in high school. Their trust of and loyalty to one another is poignant, because they are each so different. Buck is witty and happy-go-lucky, Kate is wise and thoughtful, and Travis is a brilliant student. They hang around at the home of Kate's grandmother, playing cards and discussing their plans to be together. Buck and Kate, however, are not aware of Travis's relationship with his parents. Travis's subsequent suicide is devastating to Buck and Kate. Buck tries to recount the details and events that preceded the suicide; he looks for signals that he and Kate might have ignored. They mourn Travis, trying to understand. At a special meeting with members of the community, Travis's parents speak, but it is Kate's grandmother who reminds the community that it is everyone's responsibility to care about one another.

Theme Connector

As in *Romeo and Juliet,* the Kirbys assume that their son Travis is a "good, well-adjusted boy." He is a brilliant student who has friends, and his upper-class parents, like the upper-class Capulets and Montagues, presume that he will continue to demonstrate socially acceptable behavior. Although Romeo and Juliet do not plan to commit suicide, they use Juliet's "disguised death" as a solution to their problem. With the help of her nurse and Friar Laurence, Juliet takes a potion so that her family thinks she is dead. Then, when Romeo returns, he intends to meet her in the tomb, she will wake up, and they will leave Verona. Travis, who is as isolated from his parents as Romeo and Juliet are from theirs, does not have adults as confidants. He is isolated—almost estranged—from his parents and commits suicide to solve his dilemma. Juliet, in her innocence, weaves a plan involving a make-believe death, never considering death as a reality; Travis, too, weaves his plan around death, but his death is a reality.

RANDLE, KRISTEN D. *Breaking Rank.*

On one side of the social spectrum is Casey Willardson, an attractive young woman who is an honors student; on the other side is Thomas Fairbairn, more commonly known as Baby, whom everyone knows is a member of the Clan, an enigmatic group of boys who always wear black and who remain isolated and generally silent. The Clan members are feared just because they are different, though there has been no record of their ever having done anything violent or illegal. In fact, they are regarded as more than competent at the jobs they hold in the town. Because of their silence in school and their academic differences, no one believes they have much ability—until Baby makes the mistake of taking a test and scoring unusually well, at which point the school counselor decides to move Baby into the honors program and give him a tutor: Casey. During the slow process of learning to communicate, their initial dislike for one another turns into an attraction and a respect that grows stronger and stronger. When Baby thrives on what he is learning, he can no longer hide what he is doing from his brother and his peers. At the same time, Casey's peers in their letter jackets see Baby and his friends as a threat, and violence breaks out under the freeway viaduct.

Theme Connector

The similarities between *Breaking Rank* and *Romeo and Juliet* are easily recognizable: two attractive young people from opposite social groups who fall in love; the secrets kept from others, especially parents; the naïveté of the young lovers as to the problems their relationship cause when others find out about it; the street fight. Readers should be able to discuss the motivations of both Casey and Baby, and how their understanding of each other and each other's society grows as a result of their communication. The supportive role of Mr. Hall, the guidance counselor, is similar to that of Friar Laurence, though Mr. Hall manipulates only the initial situation and is there to keep it together. Casey's friend, Joanna, serving as her confidant, plays a role somewhat similar to that of Juliet's nurse. And just as Romeo has emotionally conflicting engagements with Mercutio, Baby has to fight with his brother and other Clan members who see him as a traitor to their way of life. But though there is violence at the end of *Breaking Rank* that parallels the fight between Mercutio and Tybalt, no one dies and the ending is not at all tragic, as it is in Shakespeare's play.

DRAPER, SHARON M. *Romiette and Julio.*

Romiette, an African American girl, and Julio, a Hispanic boy, meet and fall in love on the Internet, then discover they go to the same high school. But once they find each other, they are harassed and then kid-

napped by a gang—the Devildogs—that objects to their interracial relationship. The story is told through Romiette's journal entries, Internet
chat room conversations, telephone conversations, and television news
reports, as well as the omniscient author.

Theme Connector

Not only are the families of the star-crossed lovers in Sharon Draper's
novel named Cappelle and Montague—obviously similar to William
Shakespeare's two warring families—but Draper also reminds readers of
the similarities to Shakespeare's play as the characters continually refer
to Shakespeare's young lovers throughout the novel. Though not supportive of the relationship between their two teenagers, these two contemporary families do not hate one another; it's the Devildogs gang—the
outsiders—that does the hating and the damage. Fate in this novel comes
in the form of Romiette's friend, appropriately named Destiny, a self-
proclaimed psychic, who consults "The Scientific Soul Mate System" she
ordered from *Heavy Hunks* magazine, along with the recurring dreams
that Romiette has about fire and water. Unlike Romeo and Juliet, Romiette and Julio do not die in the end of this novel, though they come very
close in the climactic scene, where Romiette nearly drowns. In the end,
the families as well as the lovers are united and heading for eternal happiness.

WOODSON, JACQUELINE. *If You Come Softly.*
Because Jeremiah's Brooklyn family is wealthy and famous, he
attends a prep school in Manhattan, where he feels isolated among the
mostly white students. But his world brightens when he meets and falls
in love with Elisha, a Jewish student. As an interracial couple, they face
prejudice in school, on the street, and at home. Although Miah's mother
welcomes Ellie, Ellie's father is a racist and her older sister cautions her
against this relationship. From chapters that alternate between the
points of view of both teenagers, readers witness the characters' experiences and feelings as they struggle to maintain their special relationship.
But in a shocking ending, while joyfully running through the park, Miah
is mistaken for a fleeing robber by white policemen and is shot to death,
leaving Ellie devastated.

Theme Connector

Like the innocent and beautiful love between Romeo and Juliet, the
relationship between Jeremiah and Elisha is pure but doomed from the
beginning. Although there is no feud between their families, most of
their family members are against their relationship simply for religious

and racial reasons. Beneath it all lurks black-white prejudice on both sides. The whole society, in fact, frowns upon interracial dating because of the dangers that the teenagers face from other people's intolerance. Though there is a tragic death at the end of both stories, Miah's death is more shocking and unfair because the police assume he is guilty just because of his skin color. Miah, unlike Romeo, does not die for love, but instead pays the ultimate price for prejudice.

KORMAN, GORDON. *Son of the Mob.*

Vince Luca's first date with Angela O'Bannon proves to be a bust when he opens the trunk of his car and finds his beach blanket wrapped around a body! His father, Honest Abe Luca, is head of a crime syndicate, and somebody in the mob used Vince's car to carry out an order. Unlike his brother, Tommy, Vince is determined not to get involved in his Dad's "vending machine" business, but in trying to prove to his father that a debt can be settled in a reasonable way, he becomes too involved. Since the FBI has bugged their house, Vince and his dad can only level with one another in the basement woodshop while banging tools around.

But irony plays a role in Vince's life. Kendra Brightly, a sophomore at his high school, wants to interview Vince, and they become close friends after he rescues her from a drunk at a frat party. As they become more involved, the situation becomes more complex, because Kendra's father is the FBI agent in charge of gathering evidence against Abe Luca. Vince avoids meeting Kendra's parents, and he can't tell his parents about Kendra. At the risk of losing her, he finally tells Kendra about his father and the mob. When she says, "I don't care who your father is," Vince is elated, and their relationship becomes more intense than ever. The plot thickens with Vince trying to protect hoodlums who owe money to his father, and when he teaches his brother, Tommy, about computers, Tommy proceeds to design a computer program to take bets on horses at racetracks. This is a hilarious story that provides a new slant on star-crossed lovers.

Theme Connector

For a fresh approach to studying Shakespeare, *Son of the Mob* has a humorous bent, unlike the tragedy of *Romeo and Juliet.* Like Romeo and Juliet, Vince and Kendra hide their relationship from their parents. Though Kendra does not know why Vince avoids her parents until Vince explains his situation, Kendra is unwilling to stop seeing Vince. She is willing to be secretive about their relationship, just as Juliet meets secretly with Romeo. Eventually, Vince tells his dad about his relationship with the daughter of the FBI agent who is pursuing him, and when Kendra tapes a song over her dad's surveillance tape, their relationship seems as doomed as Romeo and Juliet's. Instead of devising a plan to escape their situation, Vince and Kendra decide to "stay cool, and never bring the folks together for a meet-and-greet."

Romeo and Juliet and *Son of the Mob* are realistic views of the stress and deception in a teenage relationship that is hidden from parents. Vince has a conscience and feels guilty about the subterfuge, but he doesn't want to risk losing Kendra. Romeo and Juliet feel that they must leave in order to hold on to their love. The feud between the Montagues and the Capulets might be compared to the Lucas and the FBI. The teenage lovers are placed in circumstances that they must work around in order to preserve their relationship.

Other YAL titles that mesh with themes in *Romeo and Juliet* include the following:

Avi. *Romeo and Juliet—Together (and Alive!) at Last.* Ed attempts to help his best friend Saltz romance Anabell by getting his fellow 8th grade classmates to produce their own version of *Romeo and Juliet,* with Saltz and Anabell as the lead characters.

Corrigan, Eireann. *You Remind Me of You.* A powerfully written memoir in poems about the author's struggle with anorexia and her boyfriend's suicide attempt.

Koja, Kathe. *The Blue Mirror.* Tired of dealing with her alcoholic mother, a talented 16-year-old artist seeks solace in a downtown café, where she encounters a charismatic homeless guy named Cole, who draws her into his warped world.

Oates, Joyce Carol. *Big Mouth & Ugly Girl.* When Matt is accused of having said something he didn't say, Ursula defends him, but by then it's too late to stop the rumors.

Pearson, Mary E. *Scribbler of Dreams.* Two California families—the Crutchfields and the Malones—have been feuding for five generations; then Kaitlin falls in love with Bram while lying about her identity.

Williams-Garcia, Rita. *Every Time a Rainbow Dies.* Thulani, 16, is able to get beyond his grief over his mother's death and his interest in doves when he becomes obsessed with Ysa, who has been raped in the alley near his home.

Wittlinger, Ellen. *Hard Love.* John and Marisol, two high school misfits, form a friendship after reading each other's zines. Priding himself on being immune to emotions, John breaks all his rules as he rediscovers his feelings through his writing.

_____. *Heart on My Sleeve.* Told entirely in e-mails, instant messages, letters, and postcards, this novel realistically examines the romantic lives of several teens, but especially the long-distance relationship between Chloe and Julian, through the final weeks of high school and into the beginning days of college.

_____. *Razzle.* Love and friendship are tested in Razzle's life when she's befriended by Ken Baker, who is attracted to Razzle's nemesis, Harley, and then Razzle's mother comes back into town with unpleasant news.

———————————————— / / / ————————————————

The Scarlet Letter by Nathaniel Hawthorne

Themes

1. Women's place in Puritan times
2. Alienation of the individual from his or her community
3. Puritan obsession with fear, guilt, and sin
4. Puritan repression of sexuality
5. The individual's courage to survive with dignity

Suggested YAL titles that share some of these key themes:

STAPLES, SUZANNE FISHER. *Shabanu: Daughter of the Wind.*
Shabanu, a Pakistani adolescent who adores her parents, is in conflict with her culture's system of arranging marriages. When she is betrothed to a 52-year-old magistrate, she is torn between her independent spirit and her culture's expectations for women. In discussing traditions and choices with her independent aunt, she realizes that she cannot bear to leave her family. Shabanu's sense of responsibility prevails eventually, and she returns to her family, realizing that no one can penetrate or destroy her inner spirit.

Theme Connector

Both Hester Prynne and Shabanu have to survive in seemingly impossible circumstances, but through personal introspection and innate intelligence, they confront their destiny. The comparison and contrast of the harshness and domination of the Puritan and Pakistani cultures illuminate the courage and strength of both female protagonists. There are many situations in both novels that exemplify Hester and Shabanu in challenging circumstances. Shabanu is a fully developed character who shares many of Hester's traits, especially a sense of self-worth and dignity. She shares Hester Prynne's indomitable inner strength, determined spirit, and canny wisdom. Her outward behavior becomes as dignified as Hester's, once she accepts her destiny. They are strong examples of gender oppression in two distinct cultures.

KERR, M. E. *Deliver Us from Evie.*

Parr Burrman, a freshman in high school, narrates the story about his 18-year-old sister, Evie, an independent and physically strong young woman who repairs equipment on the family farm, helps with planting and harvesting, and is capable of running the farm. Her father adores her, while her mother tries to make Evie more feminine at every opportunity. But Evie is too much of an individualist to be molded into a young woman interested in cosmetics and clothes. Though her mother is somewhat aware of Evie's masculine traits, she respects Evie's privacy and never discusses her sexuality openly.

When Evie's lesbian relationship with Patsy Duff, daughter of the town's richest man, becomes public gossip, she is ostracized by the townspeople and no longer accepted as a productive member of the community. Parr feels guilty about the situation because, in a moment of weakness, he participated in a prank that publicized Evie's relationship with Patsy. Evie's father is devastated when he learns that she is a lesbian and doesn't speak to her. Evie is a confident young woman who lives life on her own terms; she refuses to capitulate to the gossip and moves away to start a new life with Patsy Duff. When she and Patsy visit the following year, her father realizes that she is still his loving daughter, and he lets her know that she is welcome; he is no longer ashamed of her sexual preference.

Theme Connector

Like Hester Prynne, Evie is strong, independent, and self-reliant. She will not capitulate to town gossip and hide her lesbian relationship with Patsy Duff; she continues her work on the family farm and avoids confrontation with her family by meeting Patsy in another town. Hester lives with her daughter, Pearl, on the edge of town and walks through town with her head held high; she is not afraid to make eye contact with townspeople. However, she is stigmatized by the large red *A* that she is forced to wear on her chest.

Both Hester and Evie live their daily lives with pride, while choosing to continue their relationships in a positive way. They are not embarrassed by their circumstances and show courage and independence to rise above the gossip and cruel remarks made by the townspeople. Hester manages to earn respect from her community; Evie visits the farm and probably will reestablish a relationship with her family, but she has started a new life with her companion. Both Hester and Evie transcend the prejudice of their community.

HRDLITSCHKA, SHELLEY. *Dancing Naked.*

When Kia, a 16-year-old Canadian girl, realizes she is pregnant, she knows she has to make decisions that will determine her future life. Kia not only has to deal with the feelings of her parents (who are mostly supportive) and the judgmental members of her church youth group, but also with Derek, the irresponsible father, who insists she get an abortion. With the support of an old woman dying of cancer in a nursing home where Kia does volunteer work and the sensitive guidance of the church's youth counselor, 23-year-old Justin, Kia decides to give the expected baby up for adoption, and she gets to choose its new parents. Along the way she becomes emotionally attracted to Justin, whom she sees as being a great father for her unborn child, until she learns that Justin is gay. All of Kia's options have positive and negative sides, of course, and her decisions do not come easily. The story is told in third person, along with Kia's e-mails and journal entries, punctuated at the beginning of each chapter with week-by-week factual descriptions of the development of the fetus.

Theme Connector

The Scarlet Letter, of course, deals mostly with what happens after Hester's baby, Pearl, is born, while *Dancing Naked* focuses only on the period between conception and the birth of the baby. The main issue in either book, however, is not pregnancy itself, but the emotions and consequences attached to it. Although *Dancing Naked* contains no point-by-point parallels to pregnancy for an unmarried young woman today and how society viewed such situations in Puritan times, Kia still feels alone and alienated from her peers. Guilt isn't much of an issue for Kia, but fear and uncertainty surely are, as they were for Hester Prynne. And Kia, like Hester, is alone and must rely on her inner strength to make the right decisions and take responsibility for them. Unlike Hester, however, Kia has more options, and she gives up the baby instead of keeping her. Derek, the child's father, is no Arthur Dimmesdale, and Derek's wish to abort the fetus is not presented as an evil act. But Derek is no more helpful to Kia than Dimmesdale was to Hester. Both Hester and Kia's success depends on their own inner strength and courageous decisions that allow them to face their situations with dignity.

ANDERSON, LAURIE HALSE. *Speak.*

Ninth grader Melinda Sordino is alienated from every friend she ever had. The summer before her freshman year of high school, she and her best friend, Rachel, attend a party with upperclassmen. After drinking too much, Melinda goes outside for air and is raped by Andy Evans. She is so traumatized that she dials 911 and runs home. She doesn't tell anyone what happened with Andy, but she becomes a social outcast for calling the police. No one in school will speak to her; she is the butt of pranks in the cafeteria, and she is shoved around school as if she is an inanimate object. So she becomes silent, so alone that she interacts with no one, until a new girl, Heather, tries to develop a friendship that eventually fails. Her parents are busy with their jobs and do not realize the extent of Melinda's silence until she is flunking most of her subjects.

Melinda is on the verge of a breakdown; she bites her lips and nails until they bleed. When Andy Evans attacks her again, students come to her rescue, and she is finally able to speak about Andy's attack at the summer party. Through her art project she is able to confront her demons and start to heal. Despite her situation, Melinda refuses to wallow in self-pity; she uses every shred of courage to continue to attend school and avoid confrontation with peers, teachers, and parents. After Andy's cruelty is revealed, she realizes that she can grow from this experience and is ready to speak again.

Theme Connector

Melinda and Hester both carry their shame inside of themselves. They are silent about their situations but manage to force themselves to continue the routine of each day. While Hester has pride and dignity, Melinda hides and avoids as many social situations as possible. Both Hester and Melinda are alienated from their community and are social outcasts—Hester literally lives at the edge of town; Melinda exists outside the social groups in her school. While Hester finds refuge in tending the ill and creating stitchery for the wealthy Puritans, Melinda finds solace alone and in her art class. Melinda is treated with contempt by her peers, except for a new girl, Heather, who is desperately looking for a connection to someone at school. Hester is tolerated by the townspeople because they depend upon her in times of sickness and value her stitchery art. Both novels illustrate the hypocrisy of the townspeople in Hester's community and Melinda's peers who don't reach out to her. Yet there is a strength and courage in Hester and Melinda that helps them survive.

CARY, LORENE. *Black Ice.*

A young urban African American teenager, Lorene Cary becomes a scholarship student at a prestigious prep school in New Hampshire. In an honest voice, she describes her experiences at St. Paul's, especially her feelings of inferiority as one of the few token blacks, her anger at preppy traditions, and her own insecurity. When she returns many years later as an English teacher and member of the board of trustees, she realizes that she was responsible for her own feelings of isolation and alienation from her peers. She realizes that she missed an opportunity to teach her peers about her "black experience." This autobiography is a thoughtful analysis of being an outsider—a feeling shared by many adolescents.

Theme Connector

In contrast to Hester, Lorene as a teenager is feisty and confronts her white peers constantly. As an adult looking back and writing about her experiences at St. Paul's, she, like Hester, gains wisdom and objectivity. She realizes that she, too, imparted some knowledge to St. Paul's students: "They were up against those of us who'd lived a real life in the real world." Lorene Cary confronts racism, whereas Hester Prynne confronts hypocrisy. Both women demonstrate courage and intelligence.

Many YA novels share broader themes with *The Scarlet Letter,* such as searching for self (change and growth), coming of age, choosing to reject the hypocrisy of one's community, facing a moral choice, alienation from peers, and surviving under extreme circumstances (acting with grace under fire), including the following:

Alphin, Elaine Marie. *Simon Says.* Combining writing, painting, and composing music, Alphin takes us on an unusually sophisticated journey through the troubled mind of Charles Watson as he searches for a way to be himself and not the way he thinks others want him to act.

Avi. *Nothing but the Truth: A Documentary Novel.* After 9th grader Philip Malloy is suspended from school for humming "The Star Spangled Banner" during homeroom activities, everyone has a different version of what happened and what should be done about it, and the reader is left to decide what the truth is.

Bechard, Margaret. *Hanging on to Max.* From the present to the past (via flashbacks), high school senior Sam Pettigrew tells us how he tries to juggle schoolwork, friends, and the little baby boy that he fathered.

Brooks, Kevin. *Lucas.* Sixteen-year-old Caitlin befriends Lucas, a loner camping out on the beach and working on a nearby farm. But the town bully, Jamie Tait, is jealous of Lucas and turns the townspeople against him.

Donnelly, Jennifer. *A Northern Light.* Sixteen-year-old Mattie faces a number of moral dilemmas, both on her family farm in upstate New York in 1906 and at the resort hotel where she works for the summer, when a young unmarried woman drowns under suspicious conditions.

Flinn, Alex. *Breaking Point.* As a new student in an exclusive private school, Paul is subjected to all sorts of harassment until the charismatic Charlie steps in— but Charlie's friendship comes at a very high cost.

Lasky, Kathryn. *Memoirs of a Bookbat.* Harper finds solace in books until her parents become religious extremists, and so she decides to run away to her grandmother's house.

Miller, Mary Beth. *Aimee.* In this first-person narration about a group of friends who know each other inside and out, the narrator and her best friend, Aimee, are inseparable, but when she helps Aimee one night, she finds herself on trial for murder.

Oates, Joyce Carol. *Big Mouth & Ugly Girl.* When Matt is accused of having said something he didn't say, Ursula defends him, but by then it's too late to stop the rumors.

Peters, Julie Anne. *Luna.* Regan's life with a preoccupied mother and a demanding, clueless father gets horribly complicated when her older transsexual brother, Liam, decides it's time to reveal to everyone that he's always felt he is a girl in a boy's body and he needs to transition into his true self, Luna.

Strasser, Todd. *Give a Boy a Gun.* Everyone's point of view is examined and opinions expressed after two boys bring guns to school and open fire on their schoolmates in this fictional parallel to Columbine.

Tashjian, Janet. *The Gospel According to Larry.* After creating a hugely popular Web site that attacks commercialism in contemporary society, 17-year-old Josh Swensen becomes consumed by the greed and superficiality he has opposed and must find a way to normalcy.

_____. *Vote for Larry.* Josh Swenson, alias Larry, is alive and immersed in politics as "the outsider." He and his friend Beth mobilize young voters in his campaign for president of the United States.

Whelan, Gloria. *Homeless Bird.* In India, Koly is married at 13 to a sickly boy who promptly dies, widowing her and making her an outcast who has to find a life for herself in an uncaring society.

———————————————————— / / / ————————————————————

To Kill a Mockingbird by Harper Lee

Themes

1. Coming of age; fitting into one's community
2. Confronting racism, prejudice, and intolerance
3. Family values: compassion and tolerance
4. The innocence of children regarding prejudice

Suggested YAL titles that share some of these key themes:

CROWE, CHRIS. *Mississippi Trial, 1955.*
Sixteen-year-old Hiram Hillburn visits his grandfather in Greenwood, Mississippi, during the summer of 1955. He has fond memories of fishing and going to the fields and the courthouse with his grandfather; he doesn't understand why his father and grandfather can't get along. While fishing alone, he saves a black teenager, Emmett Till, from drowning. He had first seen Emmett at the train station when Emmett came in from Chicago. He noticed that Emmett is a northern Negro who is proud and independent. A few days later, Hiram's childhood memory of

Greenwood as a friendly, hospitable community is shattered when Emmett Till is brutally murdered. When Hiram hears his grandfather's comments against school integration and notices his participation in White Citizens' Council meetings, he finds it difficult to abstain from reacting to his grandfather's racist comments. Though his grandfather is determined to stop him, Hiram is determined to stay in Greenwood to testify in the Emmett Till case. The accused murderers are acquitted, and Hiram eventually learns that his beloved grandfather was involved in Emmett Till's murder. When Hiram returns home, he realizes that although his father loved his parents, he left Greenwood because he could not accept the prejudice and intolerance that permeated the community.

Theme Connector

Hiram's father, Hiram Sr., and Scout's father, Atticus, are strong role models for their children. Both fathers are determined to teach their children not to hate people, regardless of race or ethnic background. Atticus and Scout have a loving relationship, and Atticus patiently explains situations to his daughter so that she can begin to grasp the meaning of tolerance. Hiram, however, has an antagonistic relationship with his father until he returns from the Emmett Till trial. Hiram has to learn through experience why his father refuses to return to Mississippi. After the trial and the events leading up to it, he finally understands why his father and grandfather cannot have a civil discussion. When he returns to Arizona, he realizes that he loves and respects his father for his stand against the racism in Mississippi.

The trials in both novels demonstrate the injustice of the courts and the attitude of the segregationists in the community, who will not allow a fair trial. In *To Kill a Mockingbird*, Tom Robinson is innocent but is judged guilty by the white jury; in *Mississippi Trial, 1955*, the white men who murdered Emmett Till are exonerated by the white jury. Scout and Hiram are innocents who love the childhood adventures in their neighborhoods, but after the trials they become aware of the undercurrent of intolerance and prejudice in their communities. The trials awaken a sense of social consciousness within them that had been nurtured by their fathers.

HESSE, KAREN. *Witness.*

In a series of narrative poems set in a small Vermont town in 1924, the main characters—a 12-year-old African American girl, Leonora Sutter, and a 6-year-old Jewish girl, Esther Hirsh—interact with residents, many of whom exhibit their racism and prejudice. As the Ku Klux Klan organizes in the community, violent and hateful incidents happen to Esther's father and to Leanora and her father. A local farmer, Sara Chickering, along with the local newspaper editor and town doctor, stand up to members of the Klan, and eventually the state law drives the Klan out. Esther and her father continue to live in the town. Leanora Sutter and her father stay in the town too. It is ironic that Leonora's testimony saves the young racist Merlin from jail, even after he made racist remarks about her. Leanora and Esther are caring children who are unaware of the Klan's prejudice against blacks and Jews. Their innocence prevails in the hearts and minds of the townspeople.

Theme Connector

Scout, Leanora, and Esther are similar individuals who interact with their neighbors and peers and enjoy their experiences living in a small town. Leanora is aware of the prejudice against blacks; Mr. Field offers her his typewriter, but she knows people will think she stole it if she carries it through town. Esther is unaware of the anti-Semitism in the town, as Scout is unaware of the racism in her town. Both characters are too young to sense the hate and prejudice that surround them. The adults in their lives are strong role models—Scout's father, Atticus, and her Negro housekeeper, Calpurnia, are strict about conveying the right morals to her and her brother, Jem.

Esther's father and their friend Sara Chickering are supportive and caring and never gossip about the intolerance of some neighbors. Leanora's father never criticizes the white people; he wants Leanora to be strong and get an education. But Leanora cannot ignore Merlin's racist remarks. When she testifies in his behalf, she proves to him that she is an honest human being and manages to change his attitude about blacks and Jews. Scout, Leanora, and Esther are strong characters whose innocence and honesty protects them from the vicious intolerance that surrounds them on a daily basis.

Scout and Leanora, in particular, maintain their own sense of right and wrong under the most trying circumstances. Scout's father is called "nigger lover" for defending Tom Robinson, while Leanora hears Merlin talk about "the stink of Leanora Sutter," or one of the boys refers to her and her daddy as "cheap fuel…the smell of barbecue." Scout and Leanora learn to walk away from hate and prejudice with their self-esteem intact.

SHANGE, NTOZAKE. *Betsey Brown.*

Set in St. Louis, Missouri, in 1959, during the period of school integration, this coming-of-age novel focuses on 13-year-old Betsey Brown. Betsey is a talented student, a dreamer, who is conscious of her black community. Her parents are professionals: her father is a surgeon and her mother is a social worker. They live in the black community, trying to make sure that their children are aware of their cultural background. When Betsey is bused to a white school, she encounters intolerance, becomes confused about her black identity, and runs away. When she returns, her father and mother have to be honest with her about the prejudice she faces.

Theme Connector

Betsey and Scout share several personality traits: independence, free thinking, "hiding out" from the family when they think they have been treated unfairly, and curiosity. Greer, Betsey's father, is not as major a character as Atticus, but he shows similar concern and love for Betsey. Betsey's grandmother and brothers provide her with childhood experiences that are similar to the ones Scout describes. The attitudes of peers, neighbors, teachers, and adults in the community cause Betsey the same puzzlement and anger as described in Scout's narration. Young and impressionable, Betsey and Scout are fearless in their determination to understand their world.

Other YAL titles that mesh with themes in *To Kill a Mockingbird* include the following:

Atkins, Catherine. *Alt Ed.* Overweight 10th grader Susan Callaway ends up in an after-school special counseling class with five other problem students, one of whom is a gay male, and another a habitual harasser.

Brooks, Kevin. *Lucas.* Sixteen-year-old Caitlin befriends Lucas, a loner camping out on the beach and working on a nearby farm. But the town bully, Jamie Tait, is jealous of Lucas and turns the townspeople against him.

Brugman, Alyssa. *Walking Naked.* When Megan, a leader of her school's in-group, starts to associate with Perdita, "the Freak," she is forced to decide which side she's on, with tragic consequences.

Carvell, Marlene. *Who Will Tell My Brother?* Inspired by real events, this novel in verse deals with a high school Native American boy's efforts to remove the school's offensive Indian mascot and the hateful bullying and violence that he faces from officials and peers.

Coman, Carolyn. *Many Stones.* After her older sister is murdered in South Africa, Berry and her father travel there for a memorial service, where Berry comes to terms with her pain amid the country's struggle to deal with its own wounds.

Cormier, Robert. *Tunes for Bears to Dance To.* Young Henry learns about anti-Semitism and has to make a moral choice when he's put in a no-win situation by his bigoted boss.

Esckilsen, Erik E. *Offsides.* Refusing to play for a manipulative soccer coach at a high school whose Indian mascot Tom opposes, he forms a ragtag team that plays against the school's varsity in a stunning climax.

Gallo, Donald R., ed. *On the Fringe.* These are powerful stories about kids on the outside—the rejects, the unusual, the geeks, and the weirdos—by authors such as Nancy Werlin, Jack Gantos, Joan Bauer, M. E. Kerr, Will Weaver, and Chris Crutcher.

Giles, Gail. *Shattering Glass.* A tension-filled story about conformity and popularity, this novel recounts the events of a school year that resulted in the murder of a classmate, told mainly from the point of view of one of the participants, with comments from other students.

Krisher, Trudy. *Spite Fences.* The dull life of Maggie Pugh, a poor white girl, changes during the summer of 1960, when she gets her first camera and witnesses racial violence in her small town.

Lee, Marie G. *Finding My Voice.* High school senior Ellen Sung has to contend with pressure from her strict Korean immigrant parents, a guy she's attracted to, and racial slurs from her classmates as she prepares for college admissions.

Miklowitz, Gloria D. *The Enemy Has a Face.* When the 17-year-old brother of Israeli immigrant Netta Hoffman disappears, she is convinced that Palestinian terrorists have abducted him.

Plum-Ucci, Carol. *The Body of Christopher Creed.* When one of their schoolmates disappears, most of his peers offer insensitive opinions of why and what happened, until one of them is accused of killing him and hiding his body.

_____. *What Happened to Lani Garver.* Plum-Ucci combines leukemia, eating disorders, alcoholism, homosexuality, prejudices, and angels into this disturbing and thought-provoking story.

Santiago, Esmeralda. *When I Was Puerto Rican.* Santiago's touching memoir of her life from a childhood of poverty in Puerto Rico and her family's move to the prejudiced streets of Brooklyn to her acceptance into the New York High School for the Performing Arts and eventually her acceptance into Harvard convey her tenacity to succeed.

Spinelli, Jerry. *Stargirl.* A new student named Stargirl celebrates her uniqueness in eccentric ways that stun the students at Mica High School.

OTHER TITLES TO CONSIDER

Here are a few other titles and themes that are widely used in middle school and high school literature programs with which YA titles can be paired:

The themes of alienation and the need to belong to a community in Anne Frank's *The Diary of a Young Girl* can be found in

Anne Frank: A Hidden Life by Mirjam Pressler

Anne Frank and Me by Cherie Bennett and Jeff Gottesfeld

Before We Were Free by Julia Alvarez

Children of the River by Linda Crew

Chinese Cinderella: The True Story of an Unwanted Daughter by Adeline Yen Mah

Daniel's Story by Carol Matas

Farewell to Manzanar: A True Story of Japanese American Experience during and after the World War II Internment by Jeanne Wakatsuki Houston and James D. Houston

Forgotten Fire by Adam Bagdasarian

Homeless Bird by Gloria Whelan

The Invisible Thread: An Autobiography by Yoshiko Uchida

So Far from the Bamboo Grove by Yoka Kawashima Watkins

The themes of alienation and teenage rebellion in *The Catcher in the Rye* by J. D. Salinger are also found in the following titles:

After by Francine Prose

Big Mouth & Ugly Girl by Joyce Carol Oates

Celine by Brock Cole

Chinese Handcuffs by Chris Crutcher

Geography Club by Brent Hartinger

The Gospel According to Larry by Janet Tashjian

The Misfits by James Howe

Running Loose by Chris Crutcher

Slot Machine by Chris Lynch

Stoner & Spaz by Ron Koertge

Vote for Larry by Janet Tashjian

The theme of repression in a totalitarian society as shown in Ray Bradbury's *Fahrenheit 451* and George Orwell's *1984* can be found also in

The City of Ember by Jeanne DuPrau

The Day They Came to Arrest the Book by Nat Hentoff

Feed by M. T. Anderson

Gathering Blue by Lois Lowry

The Last Book in the Universe by Rodman Philbrick

The Last Safe Place on Earth by Richard Peck

Memoirs of a Bookbat by Kathryn Lasky

Mortal Engines: A Novel by Philip Reeve

Shade's Children by Garth Nix

The respect and joy in discovering the harmony in nature that occur in Henry David Thoreau's *Walden* are also detailed in

Caught by the Sea: My Life on Boats by Gary Paulsen

Downriver by Will Hobbs

A Girl Named Disaster by Nancy Farmer
The Island by Gary Paulsen
The Maze by Will Hobbs
The She by Carol Plum-Ucci
Wild Man Island by Will Hobbs
Woodsong by Gary Paulsen

The survival of the fittest, competition, and the devotion of animals as seen in Jack London's *The Call of the Wild* can be found also in

Jason's Gold by Will Hobbs
Puppies, Dogs, and Blue Northers by Gary Paulsen
Winterdance: The Fine Madness of Running the Iditarod by Gary Paulsen
Woodsong by Gary Paulsen

Aspects of *The Old Man and the Sea* by Ernest Hemingway can be bridged with any of the following:

Caught by the Sea: My Life on Boats by Gary Paulsen
Downriver by Will Hobbs
A Girl Named Disaster by Nancy Farmer
Red Midnight by Ben Mikaelsen
Voyage of the Frog by Gary Paulsen
The Young Man and the Sea by Rodman Philbrick

Spoon River Anthology by Edgar Lee Masters can be paired with the following:

The Brimstone Journals by Ron Koertge
Bronx Masquerade by Nikki Grimes
Out of the Dust by Karen Hesse
Split Image: A Story in Poems by Mel Glenn
Who Killed Mr. Chippendale? by Mel Glenn
Witness by Karen Hesse

One Flew over the Cuckoo's Nest by Ken Kesey and *I Never Promised You a Rose Garden* by Joanne Greenberg can be paired with

Cut by Patricia McCormick
Silent to the Bone by E. L. Konigsburg
So Much to Tell You by John Marsden

Staying Fat for Sarah Byrnes by Chris Crutcher

Stop Pretending: What Happened When My Big Sister Went Crazy by Sonya Sones

Treasure Island by Robert Louis Stevenson can be paired with

Bloody Jack: Being an Account of the Curious Adventures of Mary "Jacky" Faber, Ship's Boy by Louis A. Meyer

The Buccaneers by Iain Lawrence

Pirates! by Celia Rees

Stowaway by Karen Hesse

The True Confessions of Charlotte Doyle by Avi

The Wreckers by Iain Lawrence

The importance of family, pursuing a dream, and overcoming odds as found in *A Raisin in the Sun* by Lorraine Hansberry can also be found in

The Land by Mildred D. Taylor

Miracle's Boys by Jacqueline Woodson

Roll of Thunder, Hear My Cry by Mildred D. Taylor

Spite Fences by Trudy Krisher

Whale Talk by Chris Crutcher

The Merchant of Venice by William Shakespeare can be paired with

Daughter of Venice by Donna Jo Napoli

Shylock's Daughter by Mirjam Pressler

Othello by William Shakespeare can be paired with

Othello: A Novel by Julius Lester

The scientific experimentation in *Brave New World* by Aldous Huxley can be found in the more recent

Double Helix by Nancy Werlin

Feed by M. T. Anderson

The Giver by Lois Lowry

The House of the Scorpion by Nancy Farmer

The Last Book in the Universe by Rodman Philbrick

Shade's Children by Garth Nix

Chapter 5

WHAT ELSE? OTHER APPROACHES

THEMATIC EXTENSIONS

By linking YAL with the classics, we can see our students become developing readers, connecting, comparing, and drawing parallels about the elements of literature. And if we recommend carefully chosen YA novels and stories to our students and provide time for them to discuss the good books they have read with each other, we create a positive atmosphere that will carry over to the required reading.

Finding the right books to pair is not easy, but the more books you read yourself, the more possibilities you'll begin to see. Furthermore, you need not stop with a single pairing. Pairing one YA novel with one classic is just one way to accomplish these higher goals. A short story, a poem, a scene from a play, an article from a magazine or a newspaper, or a page from a Web site—or, better yet, several of these—can be used to introduce a unit, make comparisons, reinforce a point during the discussion, or pull loose ends together at the end.

For a more rewarding approach, select several different titles on the same theme and provide the class with four or five copies of each title, depending upon the size of the class. You may or may not include classics among the choices. Booktalk each title and let students choose in rank order the novels they will want to read independently. As students read their books, set aside time for them to meet in groups by title, so they can discuss their responses to the book. (Discussions might be more productive if students have been assigned reading logs or response journals.)

This activity should be student-directed; the teacher, rather than providing restrictive study-guide questions, should be eavesdropping among student groups, listening to students' opinions, and acting as a coach/provocateur by joining in when necessary. Students can later exchange critical opinions and interpretations about their group's book with the whole class, focusing on common themes, character motivations, or literary techniques.

The value of small-group discussion cannot be emphasized enough. The quiet students, those who do not raise their hand, and the shy, non-confident readers are not intimidated in this atmosphere. They risk their opinions and perceptions about their reading that they would not share in a whole-class discussion. As students become more enthusiastic about reading, the required titles in the literary canon do not seem as formidable, because with YA novels they begin to see the connections among different works of literature.

As you use YAL more and more in your classroom and listen to students' responses, your students will begin to make suggestions and speak with authority about particular titles and authors. Though you might disagree about some of their suggestions and opinions, it's a good idea to formulate your questions in a respectful manner so they continue to be active readers. Some students might want to form a panel and discuss their different points of view about the same title.

In this classroom, reading is valued and important—you no longer stand in front of the class with a prescribed list of questions to generate discussion. No more quizzes or tests to see who read the book. Members of their reading groups motivate each other—and very often decide on assignments. You can check on students' reading by examining their reading logs, response questions, double-entry reading journals, or response essays. They can use these same journals for reading the required classic.

This classroom organization fosters independent and confident readers who take pride in their ability to interpret and analyze literature by themselves and with peers. When assigned a more complex required novel, play, or short story, they take on the task with more self-assurance and don't hesitate to question that which is ambiguous or confusing. They aren't turned off by literature; they want to reach a higher level of understanding.

As an example, instead of dissecting Erich Maria Remarque's *All Quiet on the Western Front* or Hemingway's *A Farewell to Arms* or Crane's *The Red Badge of Courage* in and for itself, expand the concept so that the class examines literature about war, the effects of war, and how people respond to war. That enables students to examine different points of view while allowing you to incorporate a variety of literary works into the unit.

Here we provide lists of literary selections for two sample thematic units that you can pick from or use as models for designing your own units. Space is not available, unfortunately, for us to annotate each selection, but you can find information about any of the books on the Internet as well as in various published bibliographies. (Several of the titles—for example, *Fallen Angels, Shattered, Forgotten Fire, Out of the Dust,* and *A Year Down Yonder*—are annotated elsewhere in this text.)

Themed Unit—War: Its Effects and Its Aftermath

Many contemporary teenagers are more interested in the Vietnam War than in earlier wars, so before assigning a historical novel about an older war, you might want to have your high school students first read Walter Dean Myers's *Fallen Angels,* a powerful story about two young African American soldiers and their experiences in Vietnam. The novel provides numerous points for later comparison with a classical novel, especially with Remarque's *All Quiet on the Western Front:* the soldiers' anticipation of going to battle, their horrifying experiences face-to-face with the enemy, their thoughts of life back home, the role of mothers and girlfriends in their lives, and their conclusions about the meaning (and meaninglessness) of war.

Or you might prefer *Soldier X* by Don Wulffsen, which does for World War II what *All Quiet on the Western Front* does for World War I—this time focusing on a young German soldier caught behind Russian lines—or Harry Mazer's autobiographical novel *The Last Mission,* which provides students with the same kinds of insights during World War II, when a young American airman is shot down over Czechoslovakia and then captured by German soldiers.

You might also have students read Harry Mazer's short story "Furlough 1944," which shows the psychological preparation of a young soldier about to go off to war. Short stories, in fact, can provide brief and easy introductions to units. Graham Salisbury's "Waiting for the War" is another excellent possibility for World War II, as are many of the stories in Jennifer Armstrong's anthology *Shattered: Stories of Children and War,* with stories by Joseph Bruchac, David Lubar, Marilyn Singer, Suzanne Fisher Staples, and eight other authors that show how different young people are affected by and deal with war in various forms and times, including the American Civil War, World War II, and the Six-Day War in the Middle East, as well as fighting in Afghanistan and Venezuela.

Poems can also provide brief and easy ways to introduce students to the themes and issues in longer literary works. Use Wilfred Owens's "Dulce et Decorum Est" for a vivid view of being gassed during World War I, or any of the selections from Neil Philip's *War and the Pity of War,* along with black-and-white illustrations.

Illustrations of any kind, of course—duplicated from newspapers, magazines, or the Internet—will provide or reinforce impressions of real war scenes. So will many of the nonfiction books about war that are heavily illustrated, such as *Anne Frank in the World, 1929–1945,* compiled by the Anne Frank House; *Auschwitz: The Story of a Nazi Death Camp* by Clive A. Lawton; *Fields of Fury: The American Civil War* by James M. McPherson; *Fighting for Honor: Japanese Americans and World War II* by Michael L. Cooper; *Kilroy Was There* by Tony Hillerman, with photographs by Frank Kessler; *The Life and Death of Adolf Hitler* by James Cross Giblin; *Unsung Heroes of World War II: The Story of the Navajo Code Talkers* by Deanne Durrett; *Where the Action Was: Women War Correspondents in World War II* by Penny Colman; and *Shooting Under Fire: The World of the War Photographer* by Peter Howe. And don't forget picture books, such as Robert Innocenti's *Rose Blanche,* set during the Holocaust; Walter Dean Myers's *Patrol: An American Soldier in Vietnam,* about Vietnam; and Eve Bunting's moving *The Wall.*

Because many boys will prefer reading nonfiction to fiction, you will want to include a variety of choices for them, such as Barry Denenberg's *Voices from Vietnam* or Wallace Terry's *Bloods: An Oral History of the Vietnam War by Black Veterans.* From World War II there is Andrea Warren's *Surviving Hitler: A Boy in the Nazi Death Camps;* Irene Gut Opdyke's *In My Hands: Memories of a Holocaust Rescuer;* Peter Nelson's *Left for Dead: A Young Man's Search for Justice for the USS Indianapolis;* and Deanne Durrett's *Unsung Heroes of World War II: The Story of the Navajo Code Talkers.* For the American Civil War, try *When Johnny Went Marching Home: Young Americans Fight the Civil War* by G. Clifton Wisler. And for the most recent war involving Americans, Thura Al-Windawi's *Thura's Diary: My Life in Wartime Iraq* provides a firsthand account of the days leading up to the war in Iraq in 2003, the bombing, and the aftermath, recounted by a 19-year-old resident of Baghdad.

Most war books, it seems, especially the classics, focus on male characters, so you may want to balance those with stories about females in war, such as *Girl in Blue* by Ann Rinaldi; *Number the Stars* by Lois Lowry; *Tomorrow: When the War Began* and its sequels by John Marsden; *The Road Home* by Ellen Emerson White; *The Thought of High Windows* by Lynne Kositsky; *Angels of Mercy: The Army Nurses of World War II* by Betsy Kuhn; *Where the Action Was: Women War Correspondents in World War II* by Penny Colman; *The Storyteller's Beads* by Jane Kurtz; or *Tree Girl* by Ben Mikaelsen.

The lives of noncombatants trying to deal with the war at home are also worth looking at. For those, read *Girl of Kosovo* by Alice Mead; *The Journal of Ben Uchida: Citizen 13559, Mirror Lake Internment Camp, California, 1942* by Barry Denenberg; *Linger* by M. E. Kerr; *Sonny's War* by Valerie Hobbs; *Remembrance* by Theresa Breslin; *Almost Forever* by Maria Testa; or *Amaryllis* by Craig Crist-Evans.

Don't forget to examine what happens after a war. *After the Holocaust* by Howard Greenfeld contains the true accounts of the lives of several survivors of Hitler's atrocities. Some good fictional choices are *Heroes: A Novel* by Robert Cormier, *Park's Quest* by Katherine Paterson, *In Country* by Bobbie Ann Mason, and *Life History of a Star* by Kelly Easton, all of them about the Vietnam War. A look at a more recent event can be accomplished with *Teenage Refugees from Bosnia-Herzegovina Speak Out* by Valerie Tekavec.

Choose from among the following possibilities, depending on the focus you prefer and the ability level of your students:

CLASSICS

American Civil War

The Red Badge of Courage by Stephen Crane

World War I

All Quiet on the Western Front by Erich Maria Remarque
A Farewell to Arms by Ernest Hemingway

Spanish Civil War

For Whom the Bell Tolls by Ernest Hemingway

The Holocaust

Anne Frank: The Diary of a Young Girl by Anne Frank

CONTEMPORARY NOVELS

American Revolution

The Hollow Tree by Janet Lunn
The Journal of William Thomas Emerson: A Revolutionary War Patriot, Boston, Massa-chusetts, 1774 by Barry Denenberg
Just Jane: A Daughter of England Caught in the Struggle of the American Revolution by William Lavender
My Brother Sam Is Dead by James Lincoln Collier and Christopher Collier
A Stitch in Time: A Quilt Trilogy by Ann Rinaldi
The Winter of the Red Snow: The Revolutionary War Diary of Abigail Jane Stewart, Valley Forge, Pennsylvania, 1777 by Kristiana Gregory
The Year of the Hangman by Gary Blackwood

American Civil War

Amelia's War by Ann Rinaldi
Becoming Mary Mehan by Jennifer Armstrong
Before the Creeks Ran Red by Carolyn Reeder

Braving the Fire by John Severance

Bull Run by Paul Fleischman

Evvy's Civil War by Miriam Brenaman

For Love or Honor by G. Daniel Huff

Girl in Blue by Ann Rinaldi

Guerrilla Season by Pat Hughes

Hear the Wind Blow by Mary Downing Hahn

How I Found the Strong by Margaret McMullan

In My Father's House by Ann Rinaldi

The Journal of James Edmond Pease: A Civil War Union Soldier, Virginia, 1863 by Jim Murphy

The Journal of Rufus Rowe: The Battle of Fredericksburg, Bowling Green, Virginia, 1862 by Sid Hite

The Last Silk Dress by Ann Rinaldi

Letters from Vinnie by Maureen Stack Sappéy

A Light in the Storm: The Civil War Diary of Amelia Martin, Fenwick Island, Delaware, 1861 by Karen Hesse

Numbering all the Bones by Ann Rinaldi

Promises to the Dead by Mary Downing Hahn

The River between Us by Richard Peck

Shiloh by Shelby Foote

Soldier's Heart: Being the Story of the Enlistment and Due Service of the Boy Charley Goddard in the First Minnesota Volunteers by Gary Paulsen

Trembling Earth by Kim L. Siegelson

The War Within: A Novel of the Civil War by Carol Matas

Which Way Freedom? by Joyce Hansen

World War I

After the Dancing Days by Margaret I. Rostkowski

And in the Morning by John Wilson

Lord of the Nutcracker Men by Iain Lawrence

Pictures, 1918 by Jeanette Ingold

Private Peaceful by Michael Morpurgo

Remembrance by Theresa Breslin

Summer Soldiers by Susan Hart Lindquist

World War II

Aleutian Sparrow by Karen Hesse

Bat 6 by Virginia Euwer Wolff

B for Buster by Iain Lawrence

Blitzcat by Robert Westall

The Bomb by Theodore Taylor

A Boy at War: A Novel of Pearl Harbor by Harry Mazer

Burying the Sun by Gloria Whelan

Code Talker: A Novel about the Navajo Marines of World War Two by Joseph Bruchac

Don't You Know There's a War On? by Avi

Eyes of the Emperor by Graham Salisbury

For Freedom: The Story of a French Spy by Kimberly Brubaker Bradley

The Gadget by Paul Zindel

Heroes: A Novel by Robert Cormier

I Had Seen Castles by Cynthia Rylant

The Journal of Ben Uchida: Citizen 13559, Mirror Lake Internment Camp, California, 1942 by Barry Denenberg

The Journal of Scott Pendleton Collins, A World War II Soldier, Normandy, France, 1944 by Walter Dean Myers

Keep Smiling Through by Ann Rinaldi

The Last Mission by Harry Mazer

The Machine-Gunners by Robert Westall

My Secret War: The World War II Diary of Madeline Beck, Long Island, New York, 1941 by Mary Pope Osborne

No Man's Land: A Young Soldier's Story by Susan Campbell Bartoletti

Postcards from No Man's Land by Aidan Chambers

Shadows on the Sea by Joan Hiatt Harlow

Slap Your Sides by M. E. Kerr

Soldier Boys by Dean Hughes

Soldier X by Don Wulffsen

Stones in Water by Donna Jo Napoli

Under a War-Torn Sky by L. M. Elliott

Under the Blood-Red Sun by Graham Salisbury

When My Name Was Keoko by Linda Sue Park

When the War Is Over by Martha Attema

The Holocaust

After the War by Carol Matas

Anne Frank and Me by Cherie Bennett and Jeff Gottesfeld

Behind the Bedroom Wall by Laura E. Williams

Briar Rose by Jane Yolen

But Can the Phoenix Sing? by Christa Laird

The Cage by Ruth Minsky Sender

Daniel Half Human and the Good Nazi by David Chotjewitz, trans. Doris Orgel

Daniel's Story by Carol Matas

The Devil in Vienna by Doris Orgel

The Devil's Arithmetic by Jane Yolen

Gentlehands by M. E. Kerr

Good Night, Maman by Norma Fox Mazer

I Am David by Anne Holm (previously published as *North to Freedom*)

If I Should Die before I Wake by Han Nolan

In My Enemy's House by Carol Matas

The Island on Bird Street by Uri Orlev

Jacob's Rescue: A Holocaust Story by Malka Drucker

Malka by Mirjam Pressler

The Man from the Other Side by Uri Orlev

Marika by Andrea Cheng

Maus: A Survivor's Tale by Art Spiegelman (and its sequel, *Maus II*)

Milkweed by Jerry Spinelli

Number the Stars by Lois Lowry

Room in the Heart by Sonia Levitin

Run, Boy, Run by Uri Orlev, trans. Hillel Halkin

The Thought of High Windows by Lynne Kositsky

Vietnam War

Almost Forever by Maria Testa

Amaryllis by Craig Crist-Evans

A Blue-Eyed Daisy by Cynthia Rylant

The Crossing by Gary Paulsen

Fallen Angels by Walter Dean Myers

In Country by Bobbie Ann Mason

The Journal of Patrick Seamus Flaherty, United States Marine Corps, Khe Sanh, Vietnam, 1968 by Ellen Emerson White

Letters from Wolfie by Patti Sherlock

Life History of a Star by Kelly Easton

The Monument by Gary Paulsen

Park's Quest by Katherine Paterson

Pocket Change by Kathryn Jensen

The Purple Heart by Marc Talbert

The Road Home by Ellen Emerson White

Sonny's War by Valerie Hobbs

The Things They Carried by Tim O'Brien

Where Have All the Flowers Gone? The Diary of Molly MacKenzie Flaherty, Boston, Massachusetts, 1968 by Ellen Emerson White

Gulf War

Gulf by Robert Westall

Linger by M. E. Kerr

Operation Homefront by Caroline B. Cooney

Summer 1990 by Firyal Alshalabi

Iraq War

The Big Nothing by Adrian Fogelin

Fictional and Future Wars

Future Wars, ed. Martin Greenberg and Larry Segriff

How I Live Now by Meg Rosoff

Tomorrow: When the War Began and its sequels by John Marsden

Other Wars

Anson's Way by Gary D. Schmidt (war between English and Irish)

Before We Were Free by Julia Alvarez (civil war in the Dominican Republic)

Camel Bells by Janne Carlsson (Russian invasion of Afghanistan)

Forgotten Fire by Adam Bagdasarian (Armenian massacre by Turks)

Girl of Kosovo by Alice Mead (Kosovo war)

In the Time of the Butterflies by Julia Alvarez (civil war in the Dominican Republic)

The Kite Runner by Khaled Hosseini (war in Afghanistan)

Lightning Time by Douglas Rees (John Brown's raid at Harper's Ferry)

Red Midnight by Ben Mikaelsen (civil war in Guatemala)

The Storyteller's Beads by Jane Kurtz (political strife in Ethiopia)

Tree Girl by Ben Mikaelsen (civil war in Guatemala)

Under the Sun by Arthur Dorros (Balkan war)

NONFICTION

American Revolution

Come All You Brave Soldiers: Blacks in the Revolutionary War by Clinton Cox

A Young Patriot: The American Revolution as Experienced by One Boy by Jim Murphy

American Civil War

Behind Rebel Lines: The Incredible Story of Emma Edmonds, Civil War Spy by Seymour Reit

Fields of Fury: The American Civil War by James M. McPherson

Glory, Passion, and Principle: The Story of Eight Remarkable Women at the Core of the American Revolution by Melissa Lukeman Bohrer

The Long Road to Gettysburg by Jim Murphy

When Johnny Went Marching Home: Young Americans Fight the Civil War by G. Clifton Wisler

World War II

Air Raid—Pearl Harbor! The Story of December 7, 1941 by Theodore Taylor

Angels of Mercy: The Army Nurses of World War II by Betsy Kuhn

Behind Enemy Lines: The True Story of a French Jewish Spy in Nazi Germany by Marthe Cohn

The Children of Topaz: The Story of a Japanese-American Internment Camp Based on a Classroom Diary by Michael O. Tunnell and George W. Chilcoat

Eleanor's Story: An American Girl in Hitler's Germany by Eleanor Ramrath Garner

Farewell to Manzanar: A True Story of Japanese American Experience during and after the World War II Internment by Jeanne Wakatsuki Houston and James D. Houston

Fighting for Honor: Japanese Americans and World War II by Michael L. Cooper

Flags of Our Fathers: Heroes of Iwo Jima by James Bradley, with Ron Powers, adapted by Michael French

Hiroshima by John Hersey

Hiroshima: The Story of the First Atom Bomb by Clive A. Lawton

Hitler's Willing Warrior by Henry Gutsche

Hostage to War: A True Story by Tatjana Wassiljewa

I Am an American: A True Story of Japanese Internment by Jerry Stanley

The Invisible Thread: An Autobiography by Yoshiko Uchida

Japanese-American Internment in American History by David K. Fremon

Kilroy Was There by Tony Hillerman, with photographs by Frank Kessler

Left for Dead: A Young Man's Search for Justice for the USS Indianapolis by Peter Nelson

The Life and Death of Adolf Hitler by James Cross Giblin

The Lost Childhood: A World War II Memoir by Yehuda Nir

Remembering Manzanar: Life in a Japanese Relocation Camp by Michael L. Cooper

Unsung Heroes of World War II: The Story of the Navajo Code Talkers by Deanne Durrett

Where the Action Was: Women War Correspondents in World War II by Penny Colman

The Holocaust

After the Holocaust by Howard Greenfeld

Alicia: My Story by Alicia Appleman-Jurman

All but My Life: A Memoir by Gerda Weissmann Klein

Anne Frank: A Hidden Life by Miriam Pressler

Anne Frank in the World, 1929–1945, compiled by the Anne Frank House

Anne Frank Remembered by Miep Gies, with Alison Leslie Gold

Auschwitz: The Story of a Nazi Death Camp by Clive A. Lawton

Bearing Witness: Stories of the Holocaust, ed. Hazel Rochman and Darlene Z. McCampbell

Darkness over Denmark: The Danish Resistance and the Rescue of the Jews by Ellen Levine

Eleanor's Story: An American Girl in Hitler's Germany by Eleanor Ramrath Garner

Four Perfect Pebbles: A Holocaust Story by Marion Blumenthal Lazan and Lila Perl

I Am Rosemarie by Marietta D. Moskin

I Have Lived a Thousand Years: Growing Up in the Holocaust by Livia Bitton-Jackson

In My Hands: Memories of a Holocaust Rescuer by Irene Gut Opdyke, with Jennifer Armstrong

The Lost Childhood: A World War II Memoir by Yehuda Nir

Luba: The Angel of Bergen-Belsen by Luba Tryszynska-Frederick and Michelle Roehm

My Bridges of Hope: Searching for Life and Love after Auschwitz by Livia Bitton-Jackson

Never to Forget: The Jews of the Holocaust by Milton Meltzer

Night by Elie Wiesel

No Pretty Pictures: A Child of War by Anita Lobel

Rescue: The Story of How Gentiles Saved Jews in the Holocaust by Milton Meltzer

Shadow Life: A Portrait of Anne Frank and Her Family by Barry Denenberg

Smoke and Ashes: The Story of the Holocaust by Barbara Rogasky

A Special Fate: Chiune Sugihara: A Hero of the Holocaust by Alison Leslie Gold

Surviving Hitler: A Boy in the Nazi Death Camps by Andrea Warren

Torn Thread by Anne Isaacs

Upon the Head of a Goat: A Childhood in Hungary, 1939–1944 by Aranka Siegel

Witnesses to War: Eight True-Life Stories of Nazi Persecution by Michael Leapman

Korean War

I Remember Korea: Veterans Tell Their Stories of the Korean War, 1950–53 by Linda Granfield

Vietnam War

Always to Remember: The Story of the Vietnam Veterans Memorial by Brent Ashabranner

Bloods: An Oral History of the Vietnam War by Black Veterans, ed. Wallace Terry

Charlie Company: What Vietnam Did to Us by Peter Goldman and Tony Fuller

Dear America: Letters Home from Vietnam, ed. Bernard Edelman

Escape from Saigon: How a Vietnam War Orphan Became an American Boy by Andrea Warren

In the Combat Zone: An Oral History of American Women in Vietnam: 1966–1975 by Kathryn Marshall

Lost in the War by Nancy Antle

Offerings at the Wall: Artifacts from the Vietnam Veterans Memorial Collection by Thomas B. Allen

Shrapnel in the Heart: Letters and Remembrances from the Vietnam Veterans Memorial by Laura Palmer

Voices from Vietnam by Barry Denenberg

What Should We Tell Our Children about Vietnam? by Bill McCloud

Iraq War

Alia's Mission: Saving the Books of Iraq by Mark Alan Stamaty

Other and Various Wars

Ain't Gonna Study War No More: The Story of America's Peace Seekers by Milton Meltzer (various wars)

American Patriots: The Story of Blacks in the Military from the Revolution to Desert Storm by Gail Buckley (various wars)

The Black Soldier: 1492 to the Present by Catherine Clinton (various wars)

Encyclopedia of Youth and War: Young People as Participants and Victims by Victoria Sherrow (various wars)

Medal of Honor: Portraits of Valor beyond the Call of Duty by Nick Del Calzo and Peter Collier (various wars)

Out of War: True Stories from the Front Lines of the Children's Movement for Peace in Colombia by Sara Cameron (guerrilla war and drug war in Colombia)

Shooting Under Fire: The World of the War Photographer by Peter Howe (various wars)

Teenage Refugees from Bosnia-Herzegovina Speak Out by Valerie Tekavec (Bosnian war)

Thura's Diary: My Life in Wartime Iraq by Thura Al-Windawi (Iraq war)

Zlata's Diary: A Child's Life in Sarajevo by Zlata Filipovic (Bosnian war)

SHORT STORIES

"Furlough 1944" by Harry Mazer, in *Sixteen: Short Stories by Outstanding Writers for Young Adults,* ed. Donald R. Gallo (World War II)

"In the Valley of Elephants" by Terry Davis, in *On the Edge: Stories at the Brink,* ed. Lois Duncan (Vietnam War)

Shattered: Stories of Children and War, ed. Jennifer Armstrong (various wars)

"Waiting for the War" by Graham Salisbury, in *Time Capsule: Short Stories about Teenagers throughout the Twentieth Century,* ed. Donald R. Gallo (World War II)

POEMS

"Battle Won Is Lost" by Phil George, in *Zero Makes Me Hungry,* ed. Edward Lueders and Primus St. John (American Indian wars)

"The Death of the Ball Turret Gunner" by Randall Jarrell, in *The Complete Poems,* by Randall Jarrell (World War II)

"Dulce et Decorum Est" by Wilfred Owen, found in various anthologies (World War I)

"Grass" by Carl Sandburg, in *Harvest Poems: 1910–1960,* by Carl Sandburg (generic)

War and the Pity of War, ed. Neil Philip, with illustrations by Michael McCurdy (various wars)

PICTURE BOOKS

Always Remember Me: How One Family Survived World War II by Marisabina Russo (World War II)

Brundibar by Tony Kushner and Maurice Sendak (Holocaust)

The Cats in Krasinski Square by Karen Hesse (Holocaust)

The Harmonica by Tony Johnston (Holocaust)

I Never Saw Another Butterfly: Children's Drawings and Poems from Terezan Concentration Camp, 1942–1944, ed. Hana Volavkova (Holocaust)

Patrol: An American Soldier in Vietnam by Walter Dean Myers (Vietnam War)

Potatoes, Potatoes by Anita Lobel (generic)

Rose Blanche by Roberto Innocenti (Holocaust)

Sadako and the Thousand Paper Cranes by Eleanor Coerr (World War II)

The Wall by Eve Bunting (Vietnam War)

REFERENCES

The Holocaust in Literature for Youth by Edward T. Sullivan

Themed Unit—The Great Depression, Including the Dust Bowl

Choose from among the following possibilities, depending on the focus you prefer and the ability level of your students:

FICTION

All We Know of Heaven by Sue Ellen Bridgers

The Amazing Thinking Machine by Dennis Haseley

The Bread Winner by Arvella Whitmore

Bud, Not Buddy by Christopher Paul Curtis

Christmas After All: The Great Depression Diary of Minnie Swift—Indianapolis, Indiana, 1932 by Kathryn Lasky

Cissy Funk by Kim Taylor

Dust by Arthur G. Slade

Esperanza Rising by Pam Muñoz Ryan

Frenchtown Summer by Robert Cormier

The Grapes of Wrath by John Steinbeck

Hard Times for Jake Smith by Aileen Kilgore Henderson

The Journal of C.J. Jackson, A Dust Bowl Migrant, Oklahoma to California, 1935 by William Durbin

Just Imagine by Pat Lowery Collins

A Long Way from Chicago by Richard Peck

Macaroni Boy by Katherine Ayres

The Man Who Walked the Earth by Ian Wallace

The Midnight Train Home by Erika Tamar

No Promises in the Wind by Irene Hunt

Nothing to Fear by Jackie French Koller

Nowhere to Call Home by Cynthia DeFelice

Out of the Dust by Karen Hesse

A Part of the Sky by Robert Newton Peck

Roll of Thunder, Hear My Cry by Mildred D. Taylor

Saving Grace by Priscilla Cummings

Survival in the Storm: The Dust Bowl Diary of Grace Edwards, Dalhart, Texas, 1935 by Katelan Janke

Treasures in the Dust by Tracey Porter

The Truth about Sparrows by Marian Hale

Walking on Air by Kelly Easton

A Year Down Yonder by Richard Peck

NONFICTION

Causes and Consequences of the Great Depression by Ross Stewart

Driven from the Land: The Story of the Dust Bowl by Milton Meltzer

Dust to Eat: Drought and Depression in the 1930s by Michael L. Cooper

The Great Depression by John Douglas

The Great Depression by Jaqueline Farrell

The Great Depression by R.G. Grant

The Great Depression: America, 1929–1941 by Robert S. McElvaine

The Great Depression: An Eyewitness History by David F. Burg

The Great Depression in American History by David K. Fremon

Hard Times: An Oral History of the Great Depression by Studs Terkel

The Hungry Years: A Narrative History of the Great Depression in America by T.H. Watkins

Life during the Dust Bowl by Diane Yancey

Life during the Great Depression by Dennis Nishi

The Life of Woody Guthrie: There Ain't Nobody That Can Sing Like Me by Anne E. Neimark

Riding the Rails: Teenagers on the Move during the Great Depression by Errol Lincoln Uys

This Land Was Made for You and Me: The Life and Songs of Woody Guthrie by Elizabeth Partridge

We Had Everything but Money by Deb Mulvey

RESOURCES—INTERNET

The American Experience: Surviving the Dust Bowl. Included are a detailed timeline, maps, a film, and a teacher's guide from PBS.
http://www.pbs.org/wgbh/amex/dustbowl/

A Depression Art Gallery.
http://www.english.uiuc.edu/maps/depression.artgallery.htm

The Depression in the United States—An Overview.
http://www.english.uiuc.edu/maps/depression/overview.htm

Photographs of the Great Depression.
http://history1900s.about.com/library/photos/blyindexdepression.htm

In Praise of Shantytowns by Jeb Blount.
http://www.nextcity.com/main/town/2shanty.htm

Voices from the Dust Bowl: The Charles L. Todd and Robert Sonkin Migrant Worker Collection. Includes dance tunes, ballads, council meetings, storytelling ses-

sions, and personal narratives of Dust Bowl refugees who lived in camps such as Porterville, Bakersfield, and Yuba City, California.
http://memory.loc.gov/ammem/afctshtml/tshome.html

RESOURCES—NEWSPAPERS AND MAGAZINES

Copies of newspapers and magazines from the 1930s

RESOURCES—VIDEOS AND DVDS

Riding the Rails by Michael Uys and Lexy Lovell. Videocassette (1997) and DVD (2003), produced by Out of the Blue Productions, distributed by WGBH

ACTIVITIES FOR STUDENTS

Interview an old person—a member of your family, a neighbor, someone in a retirement home or your church—who lived through the Great Depression. (The person will have to be around 80 or more years old today.) Ask that person to describe his or her life during the Depression: town, home, food, clothing, school, transportation, family life, entertainment. Record and transcribe your interview. Write a report describing specific differences or similarities between that time and place and your life today.

Locate copies of newspapers and magazines from the 1930s. Note topics that relate to the economic situation of the time. Pay particular attention to advertisements for clothing, food, and household appliances. Organize a report that includes copies of photographs (food lines and so on) that reflect the Depression years.

Other Units

If you are interested in thematic approaches like these for other required works and would like more details on how to put such a unit together, there is no better resource than Joan F. Kaywell's *Adolescent Literature as a Complement to the Classics*—four volumes that provide specific lesson plans for such themes as Family Relationships, using *Death of a Salesman* and *The Runner;* Voices of African American Southern Women, using *Their Eyes Were Watching God* and *Roll of Thunder, Hear My Cry;* Individual Responsibility in Society, using *Brave New World* and *The Giver;* and Journey toward Home, using *A Raisin in the Sun* and *White Lilacs.* For additional recommendations of themed titles, see Kylene Beers's list on page 14 of the September 1999 issue of *Voices from the Middle.*

ARCHETYPES

Before or after studying a traditional classic or contemporary novel, teachers might choose to introduce the concept of archetypes in literature. Based on the Jungian theory of archetypes, we can examine a character type or an action that recurs frequently in literature and evokes a profound emotional response in readers because it resonates with an image already existing in the unconscious mind (Jung, *The Archetypes and the Collective Unconscious* 4–7). YAL offers teachers an effective way to introduce or reinforce the study of archetypes in literature by grouping a variety of titles around archetypal situations and characters.

By reading YAL that reflects archetypal patterns similar to those in classic and adult literature, students can more easily begin to understand the concept of recurring archetypes. By studying, discussing, and recognizing archetypes in literature, students build the foundation for making connections among various works of literature during the course of their reading lives; many students can begin to grasp and identify the archetypal images and patterns that appear in new forms. The study of archetypes may also help students become more conscious of authors' styles and to think about the ways in which particular writers develop characters and story lines.

For example, the situational archetype of Birth/Death/Rebirth often presents the main character in a conflicting situation with which he or she barely can cope. Through pain and suffering, the character's spirit survives the challenge or struggle, so that he or she is able to shed feelings of despair or hopelessness. Through a process of self-realization, the character is reborn. This archetypal situation is apparent in many YA novels. For example, in *Fault Line* by Janet Tashjian, when 17-year-old Becky Martin, a bright, aspiring comic, falls in love with Kip Costello, a rising star in San Francisco comedy clubs, she is slow to realize how controlling he is, until he becomes physically abusive, and then she is still uncertain because she loves him. At the same time, Kip, the son of an abusive father, is unable to control himself, in spite of a support group for abusive people. Their intertwined lives spiral down, rise up a bit, and then hit a painful bottom. Both teens need to come to terms with their needs and actions in order to be reborn and heal.

Other YA novels with similar situational archetypes are *Memory* by Margaret Mahy and *High Heat* by Carl Deuker. In *Memory*, 17-year-old Johnny Dart has managed to alienate himself from his parents because of his drunken brawls. He tortures himself trying to remember how Janine, his twin sister, died. In his search he meets up with Sophie, a bag lady suffering from Alzheimer's disease. She touches a compassionate spot in Johnny—he cleans her apartment, moves in, and becomes responsible for her, eventually calling in social services to help. During the process he finds out that Janine's death was an accident. Through his emotional struggles and his involvement with Sophie, he develops a conscience while gaining a new perspective on the possibilities within himself.

In *High Heat,* star athlete Shane Hunter's privileged and nearly perfect life is brought to a sudden end by his father's arrest for laundering drug money through his Lexus dealership and subsequent suicide. The trauma affects Shane's life in many ways, including his ability to pitch, and he ends up hitting and injuring an opposing player, Reese Robertson. Was it an accident or did he intend to hit Reese? Shane eventually faces the truth and apologizes to Reese, and the two of them begin to practice together, because not only is Shane afraid to pitch hard, but Reese is afraid to step into a pitch and hit it. Baseball promises redemption. Although the two athletes slowly work their way back into form, in the end only Shane has regained his confidence.

Birth/Death/Rebirth. Through pain and suffering the character overcomes feelings of despair, and through a process of self-realization is reborn.

YA Books

Brooks, Bruce. *Vanishing.* Eleven-year-old Alice attempts to starve herself to death instead of returning to her dysfunctional family, while another young terminal patient struggles to stay alive.

Cheripko, Jan. *Imitate the Tiger.* A popular high school football player, Chris Serbo, sees his world collapse because of his drinking.

Flinn, Alex. *Breathing Underwater.* After being ordered by the court to attend anger-management classes and write a journal because he has beaten his girlfriend, Nick has to face who he is and why he acted the way he did.

Frank, E. R. *America.* Abandoned by his mother and separated from his foster mother, a severely disturbed boy named America spends most of his youth in mental institutions, slowly making sense of his life with the help of a caring psychiatrist.

Gantos, Jack. *Hole in My Life.* The creator of Rotten Ralph and Joey Pigza details the events of his drug-running and dealing days that put him in prison in 1971 and how his incarceration helped make him a writer.

Haddix, Margaret Peterson. *Don't You Dare Read This, Mrs. Dunphrey.* When her abusive father returns home after a two-year absence and her mother leaves the children alone, Sarah's life falls apart, until she allows a caring teacher to read the journal she has been keeping all along.

Hrdlitschka, Shelley. *Dancing Naked.* Kia considers the alternatives after discovering she is pregnant—every possibility carries with it a different set of concerns about this realistic teen problem.

Koertge, Ron. *Shakespeare Bats Cleanup.* At 14, Kevin feels washed up because he has mono and can't play baseball, which he loves, or attend school, so he starts writing poems in a journal, describing his feelings about his mother's recent death, a girl he meets, and his progress back to health—all in a variety of poetic forms.

Lynch, Chris. *Freewill.* In one of the most sophisticated novels of the year, Chris Lynch examines a lonely and disturbed teenager's efforts to make sense of his painful world.

McCormick, Patricia. *Cut.* Interacting with other teens who struggle with their own problems in a residential treatment facility that the kids call Sick Minds, 15-year-old Callie tries to understand what drives her to cut herself.

Nolan, Han. *Born Blue.* Raised by drug dealers and addicts, Leshaya is determined to overcome her horrible life by singing—the only thing that makes her feel whole.

Simmons, Michael. *Pool Boy.* Brett, a spoiled, arrogant teenager whose family has lost their rich lifestyle when his father is sent to jail for insider trading, learns to cope with a "normal" lifestyle with the help of Alfie, his 70-year-old boss at a pool-cleaning operation.

Weaver, Will. *Claws.* Jed's perfect life is shattered when Laura tells him that her mother and his father are having an affair; then everything gets worse from there.

Woodson, Jacqueline. *Locomotion.* Inspired by his teacher, 11-year-old Lonnie Collins Motion uses poetry to sort out his emotions in the aftermath of a fatal fire that has killed his parents and separated him from his younger sister in foster homes.

Classical/Contemporary Tie-ins

Danticat, Edwidge. *The Farming of Bones: A Novel.*

Gaines, Ernest J. *A Lesson before Dying.*

Haruf, Kent. *Plainsong.*

Kelley, William Melvin. *A Different Drummer.*

McEwan, Ian. *Atonement: A Novel.*

The Fall; Expulsion from Eden. The main character is expelled because of an unacceptable action on his or her part.

YA Books

Anderson, Laurie Halse. *Speak.* Melinda describes her year of being ostracized in high school after a summer party at which she was sexually assaulted and so traumatized that she can't talk about it.

Atkins, Catherine. *Alt Ed.* Overweight 10th grader Susan Callaway ends up in an after-school special counseling class with five other problem students, one of whom is a gay male and another a habitual harasser.

Cormier, Robert. *Tenderness.* Lori, a 15-year-old runaway is emotionally drawn to Eric, a teenage serial killer recently released from juvenile detention, while a detective tries desperately to trap Eric before he kills again.

Hartinger, Brent. *Geography Club.* Several alienated gay and lesbian teens in a high school form a support group they call the Geography Club to hide their true purpose, but trouble lurks just outside their classroom door.

Kerr, M. E. *Deliver Us from Evie.* A midwestern teenage boy tells the story of his lesbian sister's alienation from their family.

Lubar, David. *Hidden Talents.* At Edgeview Alternative School, Martin and his odd friends discover they have special abilities that get them into trouble but, controlled, can be used for positive purposes—like handling school bullies.

Spinelli, Jerry. *Stargirl.* A new student named Stargirl celebrates her uniqueness in eccentric ways that alienate her from the students at Mica High School.

Classical/Contemporary Tie-ins

Hawthorne, Nathaniel. *The Scarlet Letter.*

Miller, Arthur. *The Crucible.*

Shakespeare, William. *King Lear.*

Sophocles. *Oedipus Rex.*

Wharton, Edith. *Ethan Frome.*

The Journey. The protagonist takes a journey, usually physical but sometimes emotional, during which he or she learns something about himself or herself or finds meaning in his or her life as well as acceptance in a community.

YA Books

Anderson, Laurie Halse. *Catalyst.* Star science student and long-distance runner Kate Malone's world is well ordered until her college of choice (MIT) does not accept her, and a fire in the neighbors' house brings her closer to her nemesis, Teri Litch.

Bauer, Joan. *Rules of the Road.* Jenna gets a job driving the owner of a chain of shoe stores from Chicago to Texas, honing her sales skills and also confronting her alcoholic father along the way.

Bell, William. *Zack.* Zack, whose mother is black and whose father is Jewish, begins a project for his history class in Canada that leads him to his African American roots in Mississippi.

Carbone, Elisa. *Stealing Freedom.* The daughter of a slave mother and a freeman father in Maryland, 13-year-old Anna Maria Weems undertakes a long journey to freedom on the Underground Railroad in 1853.

Coman, Carolyn. *Many Stones.* After her older sister is murdered in South Africa, Berry and her father travel there for a memorial service, where Berry comes to terms with her pain amid the country's struggle to deal with its own wounds.

Creech, Sharon. *Walk Two Moons.* A 13-year-old girl goes on a journey with her grandparents from Ohio to Idaho in search of her absent mother, all the while trying to understand why her mother left.

Crutcher, Chris. *The Crazy Horse Electric Game.* Following a disabling accident that ends his athletic career, Willie runs away to California, where his experiences in an alternative high school help turn his life around.

Curtis, Christopher Paul. *Bud, Not Buddy.* After his mother dies, a 10-year-old homeless boy in Flint, Michigan, escapes from his foster home during the Great Depression and sets out to find the man he believes is his father—a famous bandleader in Grand Rapids.

_____. *The Watsons Go to Birmingham—1963.* Ten-year-old Kenny and his family from Flint, Michigan, visit Kenny's grandmother in Birmingham, Alabama, just in time to experience the horror of the bombing of the Baptist church.

Cushman, Karen. *The Ballad of Lucy Whipple.* Lucy Whipple's diary describes her experiences moving from Massachusetts to the gold-mining town of Lucky Diggins, California, during the years 1849–52.

Farmer, Nancy. *A Girl Named Disaster.* Eleven-year-old Nhamo runs away from an arranged marriage in Mozambique and sets out by boat on a long and arduous journey to find her father in Zimbabwe.

Fleischman, Paul. *Whirligig.* To atone for the death of a girl he has killed accidentally, Brent travels to each corner of the country to place a whirligig in her memory.

Gallo, Donald R., ed. *Destination Unexpected.* Ten stories about journeys—to Europe, Cape Cod, a golf course, the racetrack, a local diner—that bring unexpected insights for the teenage protagonists, from writers such as Ron Koertge, Alex Flinn, Kimberly Willis Holt, Richard Peck, and Ellen Wittlinger.

Haddix, Margaret Peterson. *Takeoffs and Landings.* Lori resents her mother, who abandoned the family after Lori's father died, but a two-week cross-country trip together, along with her brother, brings out the truth behind her father's death.

Hobbs, Will. *Far North.* Two contemporary teenage boys, one Anglo and one Indian, fight to survive the bitter winter in Canada's Northwest Territories.

_____. *Jason's Gold.* Jason's physical stamina as well as his resolve are tested during the Klondike Gold Rush, with help from an abandoned dog and a young writer named Jack London.

Levine, Gail Carson. *The Two Princesses of Bamarre.* Two sisters with very different temperaments set out to find a cure for the Gray Death, fighting ogres, dragons, griffins, and other assorted monsters.

Mikaelsen, Ben. *Touching Spirit Bear.* Because of his violent behavior, Cole is ordered to participate in a Native American Circle of Justice program on a deserted island for a year, where he is mauled by a huge white bear.

Myers, Walter Dean. *Somewhere in the Darkness.* Fourteen-year-old Jimmy accompanies his estranged father, Crab, who has recently escaped from prison, on a trip to the South.

Naidoo, Beverly. *The Other Side of Truth.* After Sade and her brother are smuggled out of Nigeria after their mother's murder, they find themselves abandoned in London while they wait for their father.

Nye, Naomi Shihab. *Habibi.* When 15-year-old Liyana Abboud moves with her family from St. Louis to Jerusalem, she has to come to terms with her own cultural identity and that of an Israeli boy she meets.

Paulsen, Gary. *The Beet Fields: Memories of a Sixteenth Summer.* The earthy and true story of author Gary Paulsen's 16th year: hoeing beets, repairing farm machinery, and joining the carnival, where he meets the irresistible Ruby.

Pearsall, Shelley. *Trouble Don't Last.* A young boy and an old man, both slaves in Kentucky, escape and make their way to Canada via the Underground Railroad.

Peck, Richard. *A Year Down Yonder.* In a series of separate incidents, 15-year-old Mary Alice describes her experiences in school and with her feisty grandmother in rural Illinois in 1937.

Philbrick, Rodman. *The Journal of Douglas Allen Deeds: The Donner Party Expedition, 1846.* With the hope of finding a better life, a recently orphaned boy joins a wagon train from Missouri heading to California, but fate brings heavy snow in the mountains only 60 miles from the group's goal.

Pierce, Meredith Ann. *Treasure at the Heart of the Tanglewood.* Hannah leaves the wizard she has served and embarks on an enchanted journey to learn the story of who she is.

Rochman, Hazel, and Darlene Z. McCampbell, eds. *Leaving Home: Stories.* The main characters in these 15 short stories and excerpts from longer works explore the feelings they experience when they leave home to seek new directions for their lives.

Ryan, Pam Muñoz. *Esperanza Rising.* After her father is killed, young Esperanza and her mother leave their life of luxury in Mexico for the impoverished life in a farm labor camp in southern California during the Depression.

Spooner, Michael. *Daniel's Walk.* Hoping to locate his long-missing father, young Daniel joins a wagon train on the Oregon Trail in 1846, facing all sorts of dangers and adventures along the way.

Wittlinger, Ellen. *Zigzag.* During the summer before her senior year, Robin accompanies her aunt and two younger cousins on a drive from Iowa to California, discovering how dysfunctional her relatives are because of her uncle's recent death, and how strong her own inner resources are.

Woodson, Jacqueline. *Hush.* Because their father testified against fellow police officers, two sisters and their parents are forced to leave everything—home, relatives, friends, school, even pets—and adopt new identities in a Witness Protection Program.

Classical/Contemporary Tie-ins

Homer. *The Odyssey.*

Steinbeck, John. *Of Mice and Men.*

Twain, Mark. *The Adventures of Huckleberry Finn.*

Wright, Richard. *Black Boy.*

The Test or Trial. In the transition from one stage of life to another, the main character experiences a rite of passage through growth and change; he or she experiences a transformation.

YA Books

Alphin, Elaine Marie. *Simon Says.* Combining writing, painting, and composing music, Alphin takes us on an unusually sophisticated journey through the troubled mind of Charles Watson as he searches for a way to be himself and not the way he thinks others want him to act.

Atkins, Catherine. *When Jeff Comes Home.* Even though Jeff Hart's kidnapper has released him after two and a half years, the horror, fear, and guilt don't go away, and Jeff doesn't feel he can talk about it with anyone.

Bridgers, Sue Ellen. *Permanent Connections.* Rob rebels against his parents' middle-class values by failing in school and using drugs and alcohol, but when he is forced by circumstances to spend months caring for his uncle, aunt, and grandfather in rural North Carolina, Rob's attitude changes dramatically.

Cooney, Caroline B. *Driver's Ed.* Stealing a stop sign seems like innocent fun to Remy, Morgan, and Nickie until an unsuspecting woman drives through the intersection and is killed by a passing truck.

Deuker, Carl. *High Heat.* When Shane Hunter's privileged life is brought to a sudden end by his father's suicide after being arrested for laundering drug money, the trauma affects his ability to pitch, but baseball still promises redemption for him.

Ferris, Jean. *Bad.* After Dallas is arrested for attempted robbery, she's sentenced to six months in a rehabilitation center, where she has to decide if she's going to control her emotions or they are going to control her.

Henson, Heather. *Making the Run.* In a world with no guarantees and no protection from grief, 18-year-old Lulu can't wait to graduate from high school so she can leave her small Kentucky town to pursue her love of photography.

Hesse, Karen. *Out of the Dust.* This Newbery-winning novel is about the Oklahoma Dust Bowl told in a series of poems written by a spunky 14-year-old girl during the Depression era.

Keizer, Garret. *God of Beer.* In a small town in rural Vermont, a group of high school seniors decides to challenge the status quo through an act of civil disobedience, the consequences of which are tragic.

Marsden, John. *So Much to Tell You.* Marina has been mute for some time, and it is mainly through her journal that we discover the reason for her deformed face and her anger at her father.

Mazer, Norma Fox. *Out of Control.* Rollo Wingate thought his life was perfect because he had two best friends—the three of them were the Lethal Threesome—until joining his friends in sexually harassing a girl forces him to decide what he stands for.

McDonald, Joyce. *Swallowing Stones.* On his 17th birthday, Michael discharges his new rifle in his backyard and unknowingly kills the father of a classmate he is dating.

Myers, Walter Dean. *Fallen Angels.* Richie, a 17-year-old African American soldier in Vietnam, experiences all the fears and horrors that war brings, described in vivid and unforgettable detail.

_____. *Monster.* During his trial as an accomplice to the murder of an Asian shopkeeper, a black teenager retells his version of the event in movie-script format, with surprising results.

Plum-Ucci, Carol. *The Body of Christopher Creed.* When Christopher Creed disappears, most of his peers offer insensitive opinions of why and what happened, until one of them is accused of killing him and hiding his body.

_____. *What Happened to Lani Garver.* Claire McKenzie tells the story of her friend Lani Garver's brief stay on Hackett Island, where most of the island is trying to decide if Lani is a he or a she, but Lani—wise, sensitive, courageous—is killed by the island's rednecks.

Simmons, Michael. *Pool Boy.* Brett, a spoiled, arrogant teenager whose family has lost their rich lifestyle when his father is sent to jail for insider trading, learns to cope with a "normal" lifestyle with the help of Alfie, his 70-year-old boss at a pool-cleaning operation.

Smith, Sherri L. *Lucy the Giant.* Fed up with school and her drunken father, 15-year-old Lucy runs away and signs up as a crew member on a crab boat fishing in the Bering Sea.

Classical/Contemporary Tie-ins

Crane, Stephen. *The Red Badge of Courage.*

Golding, William. *Lord of the Flies.*

Hosseini, Khaled. *The Kite Runner.*

Morrison, Toni. *The Bluest Eye.*

Potok, Chaim. *The Chosen.*

Remarque, Erich Maria. *All Quiet on the Western Front.*

Walker, Alice. *The Color Purple.*

Wilson, August. *The Piano Lesson.*

Annihilation; Absurdity; Total Oblivion. In order to exist in an intolerable world, the main character accepts that life is absurd, ridiculous, and ironic.

YA Books

Anderson, M. T. *Feed.* In a future where teens visit the moon for the weekend and most people have computer implants in their heads that enable them to receive all sorts of audio and video feeds and communicate without speaking, Titus meets Violet, whose feed is dying.

Cameron, Sara. *Out of War: True Stories from the Front Lines of the Children's Movement for Peace.* UNICEF-sponsored, and dedicated "to all children who live with violence," these first-person narratives by nine impoverished teenagers from Columbia are heart-wrenching.

Cormier, Robert. *The Chocolate War.* When Jerry Renault decides not to sell chocolates in his Catholic school's annual fund-raising event, a gang of manipulative boys and an evil teacher make his life hellish.

_____. *The Rag and Bone Shop.* Cormier's last work places an innocent 12-year-old boy in a small room with a ruthless investigator who is determined to get a murder confession out of his subject.

Crutcher, Chris. *Whale Talk.* Behind the triumphs of a high school swim team composed of misfits lurk painful lives and present dangers that culminate in a shocking and surprising ending.

Desetta, Al, and Sybil Wolin, eds. *The Struggle to Be Strong: True Stories by Teens about Overcoming Tough Times.* Teens from the Youth Communication program in New York City, supported by advisors from Project Resilience, write about their troubled lives.

Klass, David. *You Don't Know Me.* Although 14-year-old John says nobody knows the first thing about him, his multilayered thoughts amusingly reveal everything we need to know about his painful life—algebra class, band practice, involvements with girls, and his home life, especially his abusive stepfather.

Lowry, Lois. *The Giver.* A 12-year-old boy learns the horrible truth about his seemingly perfect society from the Giver and sets out to find a better world.

Lynch, Chris. *Freewill.* In an extremely sophisticated novel, Chris Lynch examines a lonely and disturbed teenager's efforts to make sense of his painful world.

_____. *Slot Machine.* Although Elvin tries to find his niche in the Christian Brothers Academy camp for incoming freshman, he fails miserably at every sport he tries.

Classical/Contemporary Tie-ins

Beckett, Samuel. *Krapp's Last Tape.*

_____. *Waiting for Godot.*

Camus, Albert. *The Stranger.*

Chute, Nevil. *On the Beach.*

Ellison, Ralph. *The Invisible Man.*

Fougard, Athol. *"Master Harold"…and the Boys.*

Heller, Joseph. *Catch-22.*

Saramago, Jose. *Blindness.*

Vonnegut, Kurt, Jr. *Slaughterhouse-Five.*

Parental Conflicts and Relationships. The protagonist deals with parental conflict by rejecting or bonding with parents.

YA Books

Anderson, Laurie Halse. *Catalyst.* Star science student and long-distance runner Kate Malone's world is well ordered until her college of choice (MIT) does not accept her, and a fire in the neighbors' house brings her closer to her nemesis, Teri Litch.

Bauer, Joan. *Rules of the Road.* Jenna gets a job driving the owner of a chain of shoe stores from Chicago to Texas, honing her sales skills and also confronting her alcoholic father along the way.

Coman, Carolyn. *Many Stones.* After her older sister is murdered in South Africa, Berry and her father travel there for a memorial service, where Berry comes to terms with her pain among the country's struggle to deal with its own wounds.

Crutcher, Chris. *Ironman.* With his anger out of control, Bo Brewster ticks off a lot of people, mainly his domineering father and his football coach, and so is ordered to attend anger-management classes while he also trains for the Yukon Jack Triathlon and writes letters to Larry King about his life.

Frank, E.R. *America.* Abandoned by his mother and separated from his foster mother, a severely disturbed boy named America spends most of his youth in mental institutions, slowly making sense of his life with the help of a caring psychiatrist.

Glenn, Mel. *Split Image: A Story in Poems.* The school's library connects a variety of students and faculty, especially those associated with a seemingly perfect Chinese student, Laura Li, whose lifestyle conflicts with the image her parents demand.

Haddix, Margaret Peterson. *Takeoffs and Landings.* Lori resents her mother, who abandoned the family after Lori's father died, but a two-week cross-country trip together, along with her brother, brings out the truth behind her father's death.

Lasky, Kathryn. *Memoirs of a Bookbat.* Harper finds solace in books until her parents become religious extremists, and so she decides she has to escape to her grandmother's house.

Lester, Julius. *When Dad Killed Mom.* A young boy and his teenaged sister describe their feelings and actions after their father shoots and kills their mother.

Myers, Walter Dean. *Somewhere in the Darkness.* Fourteen-year-old Jimmy accompanies his estranged father, Crab, who has recently escaped from prison, on a trip to the South.

Na, An. *A Step from Heaven.* From age four to high school, a young girl describes her family's difficult experiences as they emigrate from Korea and try to adjust to life in California with a domineering father.

Powell, Randy. *Run if You Dare.* A teenage boy trying to find direction in his own life realizes that his father has none in his.

_____. *Tribute to Another Dead Rock Star.* In Seattle to attend a musical tribute to his dead mother, a former rock star, 15-year-old Grady Grennan must also deal with his retarded half-brother Louie and Louie's extremely religious mother.

Simmons, Michael. *Pool Boy.* Brett, a spoiled, arrogant teenager whose family has lost their rich lifestyle when his father is sent to jail for insider trading, learns to cope with a "normal" lifestyle with the help of Alfie, his 70-year-old boss at a pool-cleaning operation.

Thomas, Rob. *Rats Saw God.* The 100-page writing assignment that Steve York must complete in order to graduate from high school helps him sort out a number of things, including his poor relationship with his famous astronaut father.

Weaver, Will. *Claws.* Jed's perfect life is shattered when Laura tells him that her mother and his father are having an affair; then everything gets worse from there.

Wittlinger, Ellen. *Hard Love.* John and Marisol, two high school misfits, form a friendship after reading each other's zines. Priding himself on being immune to emotions, John breaks all his rules as he rediscovers his feelings through his writings.

Classical/Contemporary Tie-ins

Franzen, Jonathan. *The Corrections.*

Guest, Judith. *Ordinary People.*

Kingsolver, Barbara. *The Poisonwood Bible.*

Miller, Arthur. *Death of a Salesman.*

Shakespeare, William. *Romeo and Juliet.*

Smiley, Jane. *A Thousand Acres.*

Tan, Amy. *The Joy Luck Club.*

Williams, Tennessee. *The Glass Menagerie.*

The Wise Old Woman or Man. This figure protects or assists the main character in facing challenges.

YA Books

Bauer, Joan. *Hope Was Here.* When Hope and her guardian aunt, Addie, move to a small town in Wisconsin, where Addie cooks at a diner and Hope waitresses, they can't help but get involved in local politics in an effort to oust the corrupt mayor.

Brooks, Martha. *True Confessions of a Heartless Girl.* An angry and pregnant 17-year-old girl changes the quiet lives of several adults in a small Manitoba town: a divorced mother, two old women, and a lonely middle-aged bachelor, each with their own painful pasts.

Chambers, Aidan. *Postcards from No Man's Land.* This challenging novel alternates between the 1944 battle of Arnham in the Netherlands and present-day Amsterdam, where a 17-year-old boy has come to honor his grandfather who died there, encompassing issues of war, honor, assisted suicide, honesty, sexuality, and love.

Fleischman, Paul. *Mind's Eye.* Using a play format, Fleischman's two characters—a 16-year-old paralyzed girl and an old blind woman—employ an old guidebook to journey through 1910 Italy in their imagination.

Hrdlitschka, Shelley. *Dancing Naked.* Kia considers the alternatives after discovering she is pregnant: every possibility carries with it a different set of concerns about this realistic teen problem.

Johnson, Angela. *Toning the Sweep.* Emily accompanies her mother to her terminally ill grandmother's house in Arizona, where Emily learns about her grandmother's courage and joy for life.

Lasky, Kathryn. *Memoirs of a Bookbat.* Harper finds solace in books until her parents become religious extremists, and so she decides to run away to her grandmother's house.

Mikaelsen, Ben. *Petey.* Born with cerebral palsy in 1920, Petey is treated as an idiot and sent to spend his life in a mental institution, where few people see beyond his grunts and deformed body until, 70 years later, a teenage boy befriends him.

Park, Linda Sue. *A Single Shard.* Tree-ear, a 12-year-old orphan in twelfth-century Korea, apprentices himself to Crane-man in order to learn how to make the beautiful Celedon pottery.

Pearsall, Shelley. *Trouble Don't Last.* A young boy and an old man, both slaves in Kentucky, escape and make their way to Canada via the Underground Railroad.

Peck, Richard. *A Long Way from Chicago.* Two city kids from Chicago, Mary Alice and her younger brother, Joey, spend summers with their Grandma Dowdel in a small Illinois farm community during the Great Depression.

_____. *Remembering the Good Times.* This is the story of the close friendship among three teenagers and an old woman, brought to a tragic ending by the suicide of one of the teens.

_____. *A Year Down Yonder.* In a series of separate incidents, 15-year-old Mary Alice describes her experiences in school and with her feisty grandmother in rural Illinois in 1937.

Philbrick, Rodman. *The Last Book in the Universe.* In a future time without hope, Spaz tries to rescue his little sister with the help of Ryter and a proov (genetically perfected) girl who lives in Eden.

Simmons, Michael. *Pool Boy.* Brett, a spoiled, arrogant teenager whose family has lost their rich lifestyle when his father is sent to jail for insider trading, learns to cope with a "normal" lifestyle with the help of Alfie, his 70-year-old boss at a pool-cleaning operation.

Weaver, Will. *Memory Boy.* After volcanic eruptions change their world, 16-year-old Miles and his family leave their Minneapolis home to seek what they hope will be a safer existence in rural Minnesota, having to struggle every step of the way.

Classical/Contemporary Tie-ins

Haruf, Kent. *Plainsong.*

Lee, Harper. *To Kill a Mockingbird.*

O'Neill, Eugene. *Ah, Wilderness!*

Russo, Richard. *Empire Falls.*

Shakespeare, William. *Romeo and Juliet.*

Steinbeck, John. *The Grapes of Wrath.*

Wilder, Thornton. *Our Town.*

The Hero. The main character leaves his or her community to go on an adventure, performing deeds that bring honor to the community. (See also "The Journey.")

YA Books

Ayres, Katherine. *Stealing South: A Story of the Underground Railroad.* When 16-year-old Will seeks his fortune as a peddler in Ohio, he is asked by a runaway slave to help two other slaves in Kentucky reach safety in Canada.

Bagdasarian, Adam. *Forgotten Fire.* After the privileged life of 12-year-old Vahan Kenderian is shattered when the Turks attack Armenians and kill 1.5 million people in 1915, he uses all his strength and courage to survive during the following three years on his own.

Cameron, Sara. *Out of War: True Stories from the Front Lines of the Children's Movement for Peace.* UNICEF-sponsored, and dedicated "to all children who live with violence," these first-person narratives by nine impoverished teenagers from Columbia are heart-wrenching.

Chen, Da. *China's Son: Growing Up in the Cultural Revolution.* Da Chen not only survived the horrifying Cultural Revolution in China (1966–76) but went on to become a highly educated individual. This is his true story.

Cooney, Caroline B. *The Terrorist.* Laura, a 16-year-old American living in London, searches for the terrorist who was responsible for the bomb that killed her younger brother.

Cormier, Robert. *Heroes: A Novel.* After his face has been blown away during the war in France, young Francis returns to his hometown to seek revenge on his childhood hero for raping his girlfriend.

Crutcher, Chris. *Staying Fat for Sarah Byrnes.* Outsiders Moby and Sarah have always supported each other, but when Moby makes the swimming team and begins to slim down, Sarah falls apart and is institutionalized, until Moby can help figure out what's wrong.

Desetta, Al, and Sybil Wolin, eds. *The Struggle to Be Strong: True Stories by Teens about Overcoming Tough Times.* Teens from the Youth Communication program in New York City, supported by advisors from Project Resilience, write about their troubled lives.

DuPrau, Jeanne. *The City of Ember.* As the lights of the city of Ember are beginning to fade in the year 241, threatening everyone with the endless darkness that surrounds them, 12-year-olds Lina and Doon discover an ancient parchment that seem to provide directions to the Unknown Regions.

Fradin, Denis Brindell. *My Family Shall Be Free! The Life of Peter Still.* The inspiring story of a man who, after more than 40 years of slavery, bought his freedom for $500 in 1850; found his mother and sisters, who had escaped when he was a child; and went back to seek freedom for his wife and children.

Halliday, John. *Shooting Monarchs.* The separate lives of several teens intersect, especially those of a young serial killer, a beautiful girl in a small town, and a physically disabled boy with an interest in photography.

Hobbs, Will. *Far North.* Two contemporary teenage boys, one Anglo and one Indian, fight to survive the bitter winter in Canada's Northwest Territories.

_____. *Jason's Gold.* Jason's physical stamina as well as his resolve are tested during the Klondike Gold Rush, with help from an abandoned dog and a young writer named Jack London.

Ingold, Jeanette. *The Big Burn.* The lives of three older teens are changed forever when a massive forest fire sweeps through Idaho's Coeur D'Alene National Forest in 1910.

Jiang, Ji-Li. *Red Scarf Girl: A Memoir of the Cultural Revolution.* The autobiography of a Chinese girl from the age of 12 to 18 who resigns from the Communist Party after her parents and grandmother are humiliated by party members.

Kerr, M. E. *Slap Your Sides.* When Jubal's older brother Bud refuses to enter the army during World War II because of their family's Quaker Beliefs, Jubal has to come to terms with the uproar that results in their small Pennsylvania town.

Klass, David. *California Blue.* Finding a previously undiscovered butterfly in the forest during one of his runs, John joins an environmental group to save the area from logging—except his father is an employee of the logging company.

McNamee, Graham. *Acceleration.* Duncan's boring summer job in the lost-and-found office of the Toronto subway takes an unexpected turn when he discovers a journal written by a potential serial killer, and he must use the clues in the journal to track down the man as well as his potential victims before anyone dies.

Paulsen, Gary. *Soldier's Heart: Being the Story of the Enlistment and Due Service of the Boy Charley Goddard in the First Minnesota Volunteers.* After lying about his age and joining the army, Charley is forced to face the horrors of the American Civil War.

Philbrick, Rodman. *The Last Book in the Universe.* In a future time without hope, Spaz tries to rescue his little sister with the help of Ryter and a proov (genetically perfected) girl who lives in Eden.

Trueman, Terry. *Inside Out.* Sixteen-year-old Zach, a schizophrenic in need of his medication, is one of several hostages in the botched robbery of a coffee shop by two desperate teenagers.

Weaver, Will. *Memory Boy.* After volcanic eruptions change their world, 16-year-old Miles and his family leave their Minneapolis home to seek what they hope will be a safer existence in rural Minnesota, having to struggle every step of the way.

Wolff, Virginia Euwer. *Make Lemonade.* When 14-year-old LaVaughn babysits the two young children of a 17-year-old unmarried girl, all their lives are changed.

Classical/Contemporary Tie-ins:

Crane, Stephen. *The Red Badge of Courage.*

Dickens, Charles. *A Tale of Two Cities.*

Gaines, Ernest J. *The Autobiography of Miss Jane Pitman.*

Gardner, John. *Grendel.*

Hurston, Zora Neale. *Their Eyes Were Watching God.*

Renault, Mary. *The King Must Die.*

Rostand, Edmond. *Cyrano de Bergerac.*

Sophocles. *Antigone.*

The Sacrificial Redeemer. The protagonist is willing to die for his or her beliefs; the main character maintains a strong sense of morality.

YA Books

Carvell, Marlene. *Who Will Tell My Brother?* Though Evan has always been conscious of his Mohawk heritage, it is not until his senior year in high school that he feels the need to take a stand by asking the school board to change the offensive school Indian mascot, thereby suffering verbal attacks and physical violence against his whole family.

Cormier, Robert. *The Chocolate War.* When Jerry Renault decides not to sell chocolates in his Catholic school's annual fund-raising event, a gang of manipulative boys and an evil teacher make his life hellish.

Crutcher, Chris. *Ironman.* With his anger out of control, Bo Brewster ticks off a lot of people, mainly his domineering father and his football coach, and so is ordered to attend anger-management classes while he also trains for the Yukon Jack Triathlon and writes letters to Larry King about his life.

_____. *Whale Talk.* Behind the triumphs of a high school swim team composed of misfits lurk painful lives and present dangers that culminate in a shocking and surprising ending.

Krisher, Trudy. *Spite Fences.* The dull life of Maggie Pugh, a poor white girl, changes during the summer of 1960, when she gets her first camera and witnesses racial violence in her small town.

Miklowitz, Gloria D. *Masada: The Last Fortress.* Simon ben Eleaser, 17 years old, describes the struggle of his people to save their mountaintop fortress from the overwhelming force of the Roman army that has encircled them for months.

Paulsen, Gary. *Nightjohn.* A 12-year-old slave girl tells the story of Nightjohn, a slave who escaped from the plantation but returns, risking his life to teach the slaves to read.

_____. *Sarny: A Life Remembered.* Sarny, the slave girl whom Nightjohn taught to read, tells about her challenging life after the Civil War as she teaches other blacks to read.

Plum-Ucci, Carol. *What Happened to Lani Garver.* Claire McKenzie tells the story of her friend Lani Garver's brief stay on Hackett Island, where most of the island is trying to decide if Lani is a he or a she, but Lani—wise, sensitive, courageous—is killed by the island's rednecks.

Tashjian, Janet. *The Gospel According to Larry.* After creating a hugely popular Web site that attacks commercialism in contemporary society, 17-year-old Josh Swensen becomes consumed by the greed and superficiality he has opposed and must find a way to normalcy.

Classical/Contemporary Tie-ins

Bolt, Robert. *A Man for All Seasons: A Play in Two Acts.*

Miller, Arthur. *The Crucible.*

Morrison, Toni. *Beloved.*

O'Neill, Eugene. *Mourning Becomes Electra.*

Shakespeare, William. *Julius Caesar.*

Sophocles. *Antigone.*

Many additional titles can be grouped with these archetypal situations. Using YAL will reinforce students' understanding of these recurring patterns and make the archetypes more meaningful in their interpretations of literature.

AUTHOR PAPER

The author paper is a challenging assignment that dovetails with archetypal studies in literature. Many Advanced Placement English courses require an author paper, where students read three titles by one author and write an analytical paper that reflects their critical insights about the author's use of literary structures. In other words, students must explain how an author uses setting, character, plot, style, and theme to construct a novel. This assignment is based upon critical reading and classroom discussion of demanding classics by such authors as Bellow, Roth, Camus, Sartre, Heller, Vonnegut, Shakespeare, Morrison, and Hemingway. Through careful reading and going back into the text, the student is required to identify recurring patterns an author uses to develop plot and character as well as particular stylistic devices that make these novels distinctive. For example, a student who reads three novels by John Steinbeck begins to recognize how important setting and characters are to the story line; Steinbeck's details about setting and characters emphasize particular literary structures that are unique to his style. After reading three of his novels, students should be able to grasp these recurring patterns.

The author paper is a culmination of a yearlong course, along with the AP English test. But what about the students who don't take AP English?

Don't these students need to realize they, too, can become capable and analytical readers? And why confine an author paper to just seniors? Why not introduce the author paper in 7th or 8th grade or other grade levels so that these developing readers become more confident about their interpretative skills—only with less demanding literature? Why not engage these readers in critical analyses by having them write an author paper using some of their favorite young adult authors?

Most teens find books by YA authors accessible, manageable, and pleasurable reading, while subconsciously they begin to analyze authors' storytelling techniques. They also begin to notice that most authors write in only one genre, such as fantasy, science fiction, contemporary issues, adventure/survival, sports, or novels in verse. For example, a group of 7th graders I had one year devoured every William Sleator novel because he hit the right nerve in their reading—his relatively short novels are about boys nearly their age engaged in exciting science fiction adventures. And, since students select the author they want to read, they can begin to discriminate what is plausible, what is possible, and what is contrived.

Some authors—for example, Karen Hesse, Walter Dean Myers, and M. E. Kerr—skip back and forth among different genres, so students reading three books by one of those authors could discover fewer commonalities, thus making the assignment more challenging. But whether or not there are commonalities in the three books, studying them can make readers mini-authorities on an author. As students begin to discover hidden meanings and rely on their personal responses, they are really honing their critical-reading skills as independent readers instead of relying on prescribed assignments, teacher-directed questions and/or study guides, and duplicated quizzes and tests.

Getting Started

Before introducing the steps involved in the author paper, it's important to discuss the major elements of literature with the class. Many teachers of English and language arts review these elements at the beginning of the school year—setting, character, plot, style, and theme—anyway. Using titles that the whole class has read as a reference, the class can discuss and define some of these elements, including literary devices such as foreshadowing, flashback, metaphors, conflict, rising action, turning point, and resolution. For example, if the whole class has read required novels such as John Steinbeck's *The Pearl* or Lois Lowry's *The Giver* in a previous grade, the class could identify the elements of literature in each title by listing them on the board and giving examples from the novel to support character and plot development. Or, if there are four titles in common among the class, students could work in groups and share their findings—the more discussion the better. They then understand what they are looking for when they read their three novels by the same author.

To help students decide which author to choose, the next step is to brainstorm author names with the whole class. Which authors have they enjoyed reading? It's helpful to list authors because students need to consider their author choice carefully. Reading three books by the same author is a commitment! This process helps them to recall particular titles and authors and piggyback on each other's suggestions. You might want to ask your school librarian to participate in this process too. Of course, some students will decide right away, others will dawdle, and there will be indecisive procrastinators. Teacher and librarian have to assist the latter as soon as possible. Each student then selects an author and three books to study.

Warn students at the beginning of this project that once they choose an author and begin reading, time does not allow a switch. Someone may not like his or her choice after reading the first novel; we would not advise a change at this time. Perhaps that student can write about the characteristics of the books that did not appeal to him or her. We also do not recommend letting best friends read the same three novels, nor do we believe students should be allowed to select titles that they read in 3rd, 4th, 5th, or 6th grade classrooms. It is a good idea to put all of these rules on paper, along with authors' names and a schedule of due dates, to avoid any problems.

If possible, students should purchase copies of the novels so that as they read, they can mark the novel with a ballpoint pen, noting particular pages or passages with marks in the margins, such as S = setting; C = main character (protagonist); CA = character (antagonist); C1, C2, C3 = supporting character(s); Pl = plot; St = style; and T = theme (important passages that convey a major idea).

As students read the novel, it's a good idea for them to have a five-by-eight-inch card for each category and write down page numbers and major ideas and/or names or important passages on each card. For example, if I chose Chris Crutcher as my author and chose to read *Running Loose, Chinese Handcuffs,* and *Ironman,* I would have five cards for each title—S, C, Pl, St, and T—and a total of 15 cards after reading the three novels. I might have two C cards for characters if there are lots of important supporting characters, though notes can be on the fronts and backs of cards. Students should be encouraged to go back through each book and check their marks to make sure they have noted important passages on their note cards. Making notations in the texts and keeping note cards may seem like double work, but specific passages in the books will be easier to locate later if students have page numbers for each category on their note cards.

Perhaps some students would find it helpful to make a chart to note similarities among the three novels. For example, in Crutcher's three novels, the setting is in a high school. The protagonist in each novel is a male teenager who is smart, independent, a talented athlete, and prone to losing his temper, yet unwilling to yield to unethical behavior. These defiant young men are in conflict with a coach (*Running Loose*), a teacher/coach (*Chinese Handcuffs*), and the school principal/father (*Ironman*), and defy the authority figure. In two of the novels there are deaths that are catalysts for negative behavior by the protagonists; in the other novel the protagonist attends an anger-management class to contain his rage.

The supportive and trusting adult, evident in each book (Wise Old Man or Woman archetype), helps the character realize the absurdity of his situation and the need to learn to compromise. Crutcher uses a lot of dialogue between the protagonist and the supportive adult to explain the situation; the adult offers counsel and advice in a give-and-take that helps the protagonist to learn to compromise.

In comparing the plots of each novel, the reader could explain how Crutcher places his characters in realistic situations that test their limits. These plot situations make the story exciting and fast-paced and encourage the reader to continue reading because the story is so real. Crutcher's use of flashback and first person on the opening pages draws the reader into the story immediately. The reader feels as if the main character is having an intimate conversation with him or her and is connected to the protagonist's dilemma. Going back into the text helps students point out important passages that support their analytical comments. Students begin to shape the important points they want to include in their paper.

A critical reader will note that Crutcher's characters often sum up what they have learned from their experiences at the end of the novel— adolescents have to learn to compromise with adults who are hypocritical and resolute. There are methods to work around these authoritative figures without sacrificing one's sense of what is right and what is wrong.

It may be that your students are not yet ready to analyze theme. If they recognize similarities and differences in the author's literary devices among the three novels, they're thinking and sharpening their critical-reading skills, and maybe theme is too abstract a concept at their stage of reading. As teachers we have to accept what is possible for them to grasp or interpret even if it's only a literal summary of the plot—remember, readers in our classroom are in various stages of reading development (see chapter 3 for Carlsen's stages of literary development). Any student who reads three novels by the same author deserves the highest praise—this is an achievement!

Organizing the Paper

The younger the reader, the more you will have to structure the writing assignment. You might want to put a simple outline on the board and let students fill in the key elements of each novel. It's a good idea to write some model introductory paragraphs on the board or hand out a sheet, leaving blanks for author, titles, characters, and plot. Try to coach students individually in helping them write their introduction. Keep it simple for students who are scared. And modify the organization of the paper to suit the abilities of students—that is, if a student can write only about the main character or can't identify stylistic devices, accept what he or she can analyze.

Students having trouble getting started should visit the school or town library to read some biographical information about their authors. Some print sources, such as *Authors and Artists for Young Adults* from Gale Research; Scribner's Sons' *Writers for Young Adults,* edited by Ted Hipple; and various volumes of Scarecrow Studies in Young Adult Literature, such as *Jacqueline Woodson: The Real Thing* by Lois Thomas Stover and *Graham Salisbury: Island Boy* by David Macinnis Gill, as well as Web sites such as Authors4Teens.com and the sites of individual authors (see chapter 8 for a list of authors' Web sites), will provide students with some interesting insights about the authors that may help them understand their novels better. Students might also find an interesting quote with which to start their introductory paragraphs. You may need to present a mini-lesson about how to cite quotations in the papers and list sources in the bibliography.

An example of an introductory paragraph for the Crutcher novels might look like this:

In his novels *Running Loose, Chinese Handcuffs,* and *Ironman,* Chris Crutcher places high school athletes in frustrating situations that test their physical and psychological limits. Louie Banks, the main character in *Running Loose,* is in conflict with an abusive football coach; Dillon Hemingway, the main character in *Chinese Handcuffs,* is in conflict with a principal who intimidates and harasses him at every opportunity; while Bo Brewster, the main character in *Ironman,* is in conflict with Keith Redmon, the football coach as well as his English teacher, who taunts him until Bo loses his temper. All three characters are underdogs, trying to maintain their sense of self while suffering through the comments of these three adults. Crutcher had me rooting for Louie, Dillon, and Bo because there have been times in my life I wish I would have had the courage to stand up to unethical adults.

Encourage students to write in a personal way to show their responses to these stories and to explain how the stories and characters connected to their own lives. The paper can be less personal and more formal for juniors or seniors or honors classes.

Depending on the reader and the grade level, the process is more important than the perfect paper written in formal essay style. Allow students class time to read and take notes on each novel. That gives you time to have individual conferences to check on number of pages read, answer questions, and have personal contact to cheer students' accomplishments. There are students who might need you to plan a number of pages for them to read each day. The more time you meet with students individually, the more you can judge who needs help and who might need a longer conference during another period or after school.

Scheduling

Kids have to know where they are in this long-term assignment, so schedule due dates for completing each novel and post due dates on a bulletin board along with a schedule sheet for their notebooks. (Hand students a copy of the schedule sheet for their reference. If anyone is reading a very long novel, you can allow extra time.) Schedule due dates for the rough draft, editing groups, and final draft. You need not work on this project on a daily basis—sprinkle it between other curriculum activities. After all, it's reading—reading a favorite author—not torture.

You might want to schedule some periods for an author forum where students can give a brief oral presentation about their authors and the titles they've read. Just imagine a class of 25 students—they can hear about 75 books! This is an important opportunity for those students who are more verbal and like public speaking. A shy student might want to read from some notes—accommodate, accommodate, accommodate.

Evaluating

Evaluate the project in stages—reading the novels, marking passages (only if they own the books!), keeping their notes on cards, working on their comparison of the three novels, organizing their paper, writing the rough draft, revising the rough draft, completing the final paper, and giving the oral presentation. (Students should save all this material in a 12-by-15-inch envelope so that nothing gets lost.) Always remember to praise kids for completing their author paper even if they're seniors in high school.

Provide lots of opportunities for success. We recommend giving grades on every part of the process so that there are lots of opportunities for students to make good grades. What's wrong with everyone making an A?

By this time you might be thinking the author paper is time-consuming, complex, and a lot of work for students as well as you, the teacher. Yes, it can be. But test the waters—gauge the excitement and buzz generated by the kids. You are empowering them to read and interpret books on their own! You are a coach, a supporter, a believer in their ability to complete an assignment that tests their confidence, their understanding, and their imagination, and honors their choice in books. And, unintentionally, you are preparing them for senior AP English.

Conclusion

Yes, we know that this project can be messy and you will have to gently shove kids along and probably modify assignments to meet the abilities of some students, but it can be an important step in their reading lives. The first time around is the most difficult. After one year, you'll have model papers to share with students, and you can refine the process by having your students evaluate the author-paper project. You may learn more from your students' evaluation than from any other source. They can cut right to the problems, and they can assess what was helpful. Be sure to ask students what they learned from this project.

Most important of all, you can take pride in having launched your students on the road to becoming independent and confident readers of literature.

Chapter 6

ADOLESCENTS AND LIBRARIES: FORGING A VITAL RELATIONSHIP

Many teenagers associate school libraries with study halls, special tutoring, teacher-directed research, catching up on homework, or resting between assigned periods. How many students think their library is also a place to read for pleasure? This is a tough question to answer.

Ideally, a school library should have a special corner with shelves of YA and adult books so that when students enter the library they know where they can find a wide assortment of books that meet their needs and interests, an area away from reference materials, computer terminals, and the circulation desk. This space should encourage them to browse, read, and have lively discussions. It's a good idea for teachers and library media specialists to work together in setting up this area, because classroom teachers can describe the reading space to their students and schedule an introductory visit during a class period. Teachers and library media specialists working together present a united front to students; thus, the reading area has credibility, and students realize that the library is more than an escape from study halls, unassigned periods, or cancelled classes.

Then, if we want our students to become lifetime readers, we must develop innovative strategies to achieve this goal. The competition for their attention in this electronic age is fierce. Convincing teenagers that reading books helps them find pleasure and meaning in their lives is a formidable task. Toward that end, librarians and teachers have to forge solid links between the classroom and the public and school libraries. Teenagers have to push open the doors to those libraries and find a sanctuary, a haven, a "room of their own."

Remember the infamous Willie Sutton's response when asked why he robbed banks? "'Cause that's where the money is." Imagine teenagers responding in a similar fashion when asked why they go to libraries: "'Cause that's where the books are." This vision might be in the realm of possibility if we plant some seeds early in our students' reading lives. Let's make sure that books, all kinds of books—nonfiction, fiction, graphic novels, books on tape, and more—are included in their backpack paraphernalia, tucked right in there with their cell phone, iPod, CD player, laptop, digital camera, and other electronic gadgets.

To do that, we have to get them connected to books through diverse school and public library programs that cross the divide between what is required reading in the classroom and what they can self-select according to their interests. Specific programs that cater to teens have proved successful with all kinds of readers. When libraries are user-friendly and encourage teens to browse, socialize, and discuss books in their own reserved space, teenagers are more likely to drop in often, like they check their e-mail, rove the mall, or meet at their local pizzeria. And when there is a teen group, whether called a Teen Council, Teen Advisory Panel, or Youth Advisory Group, the programming is tailored to fit teenager's interests.

There are some exemplary school and public libraries that have created a nonthreatening atmosphere with few rules, while offering a wide range of programs to meet the interests of teenagers. Many have teen advisory boards whose members participate in all facets of decision making when it comes to teen activities, whether redesigning library space for teens, selecting books, developing programs, planning social events, or organizing community outreach projects. The success of these programs can be attributed to the respect and trust fostered by the librarians and the teen volunteers who work together to implement their plans.

MESA LIBRARY

Diane Tuccillo, the young-adult coordinator of the Mesa Library in Arizona and the author of *Library Teen Advisory Groups: A VOYA Guide,* has worked with the Young Adult Advisory Council (YAAC) to mold and develop an outstanding program for teenagers. When she started in 1980, she and the YAAC agreed that their main focus would be promoting books and reading to fellow teens. And year after year they have focused on this goal, while including other events that attract teen readers.

The Mesa YAAC and their peers are involved in a variety of programs. One group edits a newsletter titled *Open Shelf,* in which teens write reviews and recommend new and previously published books; this newsletter is distributed to local middle and high schools every month. Another program is a literary magazine for all teens titled *FRANK,* which is edited and published annually. The teen volunteers also plan poetry slams, SAT prep classes, forums with community organizations, and other activities. The teen volunteer committee publicizes, organizes, and presents these programs in the Activity Room. Another teen group, called Teen Takes, designs and writes for the library's teen Web page, while others work at the YA volunteer service desk. They also do librarian/teen partner reviews for the journal *Voice of Youth Advocates* (*VOYA*), and they participate in the Young Adult Library Services Association's (YALSA) Teen Top Ten/YA Galley Project. In 2003 they helped design Teen Realm, a new space for teenagers, complete with lounge furniture, computers, homework tables, job boards, and art gallery, as well as magazines and books.

The Mesa Library program for teens attracts new participants every year as kids graduate; it is built on a strong core of teenagers who transmit their enthusiasm to peers. The participants receive community-service points at their schools. Most important, their ideas and suggestions are considered by the library board, where they have representation, and by the librarians, who listen and respect their judgments.

(For more information about the Mesa program, go to http://mesalibrary. org/teens.)

JOHN O'CONNELL HIGH SCHOOL

At John O'Connell High School in San Francisco, librarian Kay Hones and her Teen Library Advisors (TLAs) have organized a school calendar loaded with exciting events for the diverse population of their school, which is 80 percent Latino and 13 percent African American, along with Asian and Filipino students. The TLAs plan several events monthly and tie into Black History Month, Poetry Month, and so on.

Here's a sampling of some of their monthly programs: In September the TLAs present "Open Your Mind to a Banned Book" during Banned Book Week. In early September they read with classes during a three-day National Hispanic Read-In Chain. In October the TLAs plan and coordinate Teen Read Week, "Slamming@Your Library." Using the American Library Association's Best Books for Young Adults list, they conduct a Family Literacy Workshop and booktalk many of the list's titles in classrooms. In December, they run a Winter Book Fair. In February they participate in classes for an African American Read-In during Black History Month, along with a Read-In in the faculty lunchroom. They schedule speakers from universities to speak on health, environmental, or other issues, along with authors and artists; they contact lawyers to tie into classroom curricula, such as a Brown v. Board of Education panel, and compile resource materials about Cesar Chavez. This is just a sampling of their ongoing activities.

The TLA members are self-selected: during 9th grade orientation, Hones mentions the TLA group, and students join all year long. They represent all grade levels, and many of the members are male. At a retreat in the beginning of the year, Hones organizes a "Raising a Reader Workshop," where members list their reasons for wanting to become a TLA. The responses she gets are impressive—"I want to present for parents at the Homeless Prenatal Program and at the San Francisco Public Library...I want to contribute to my community." Students brainstorm ideas for programs and develop leadership skills.

By March the group is evaluating the strengths and weaknesses of their programs at another retreat. Among the service projects they highlight are collecting toys for pregnant teens, helping in the library, sponsoring Read Aloud Week, reviewing books, and organizing a panel on AIDS. They suggest new program ideas for the following year, too, and discuss smoothing out some procedures.

The goals of the library programs at John O'Connell High School are developing and promoting habits for lifelong learning, supporting student empowerment, and collaborative teaching across the curriculum. These goals are prominent in planning by the TLAs as well as the library staff. The TLAs are an integral part of the school library and take pride in their achievements.

The John O'Connell High School library has received community grants along with grants from the Coca Cola Foundation, Grolier, and individuals. These grants enrich the scope of their programming and validate their commitment to make the school library a community that reaches out to students and families. The energy, creativity, and unrelenting support of Kay Hones translate into an extraordinary high school library program.

SEQUOYAH MIDDLE SCHOOL

At Sequoyah Middle School in Edmond, Oklahoma, the media center never sleeps, thanks to librarian Michelle Hasenfratz. When she describes the school media center, it sounds like a never-ending line of students clamoring to check out books! Here are some of the activities that enrich the Sequoyah Middle School library/literacy program.

Since the school has a large student population, Michelle can't reach classes for booktalks, so she e-mails bimonthly book reviews to all staff members. She scans covers into a Word document and reviews three or more new titles that teachers can display and/or discuss on the 32-inch teaching monitors in their classrooms. Students will often come to the library to check out these new titles quickly. She has a three-by-five-foot table parallel with her front desk in the media center on which she displays the new titles as well as her Lunch Bunch groups' recommendations, along with a wide selection of books. As students look at the books, they stop and chat with Michelle and other students browsing at the table and discuss titles with each other.

Since the school requires students to have a free-reading book with them at all times, Michelle promotes reading holidays with a variety of contests and activities, such as Beach Blanket Read-In on the front lawn of the school during National Library Week and guest readers in the Library Media Center during Read across America Week. She encourages students to share their reading lives with each other. There are Lunch Bunch groups that meet twice a semester in the library (dessert provided by Michelle) during the five lunch periods. This activity helps her to know her student population. There's a student-led fantasy/sci-fi group supervised by a teacher that meets after school. The school principal, a former language-arts teacher who loves young adult books, allocates budget money for an author visit every year and some extra money to purchase new titles during the school year. And, even more impressive, he leads the YA-YA book group, which meets monthly after school in the media center to discuss the book they've all read, and he brings the snacks.

Recently, the district adopted a semester-long course in the core curriculum for all three grades titled Reading/Writing Workshop. The students in these courses are in and out of the library constantly, checking out books. Teachers often bring in whole classes for booktalking, and students spontaneously share their favorite titles.

It's obvious that the faculty values reading and discussing books. And Michelle Hasenfratz's enthusiasm for reading permeates every corner of this middle school. By offering all kinds of reading opportunities, this school is grooming lifelong readers.

CARMEL HIGH SCHOOL

Another library media specialist, Connie Mitchell of Carmel High School in Carmel, Indiana, describes reading activities that reach across school, town, and state boundaries. With 3,700 students, this high school is busy with a multitude of reading activities that touch all students.

The Eliot Rosewater Indiana High School Book Award (Rosie) committee nominates 20-plus adult and YA book titles each year that are voted on by high school students. Carmel High uses this list of Rosie nominees and past winners as the backbone of its reading program. Adult and young adult literature is incorporated into every aspect of the curriculum. The staff introduces the Rosie program to all freshmen so they will be informed voters during the second semester. Mitchell and her colleagues have done booktalks for as many as 143 classes in one year (that's nearly four booktalks a week).

The staff is constantly pulling and/or compiling titles to link up with the required curriculum. Staff members request titles that tie into required class readings such as *The Odyssey, Romeo and Juliet,* and so on. They develop bibliographies and booktalk titles that connect to specific topics, such as bioethical issues, eating disorders, existentialism, and social justice. Or they may fill a request from journalism classes for fiction and nonfiction books by journalists. Because they do a presentation to child-development classes on reading to children, they have a solid collection of picture books. Speech teachers also use the picture books to illustrate reading in different voices for speech students. They pull titles for world-history and English teachers as they prepare their students to write children's books.

To expose students to as many titles as possible, they employ a number of interesting strategies: Lightning Round means librarians and teachers pick a title from a pile of books and talk about it in one or two sentences to make kids curious; Read Around allows students to read any of the books on the table for two minutes and then pass it on and select another title; and Reader's Theater shows students how to script a book and then perform the script in class. The staff also works with consumer-science teachers on child development and interpersonal relations and finds fiction titles related to these subjects. They also involve classes in interactive presentations about intellectual-freedom issues. As you can surmise, the school library media center is integrated into the school curriculum on many levels, which makes the library media center a hub for diverse activities.

Stump the Teachers is usually scheduled for Teen Read Week. The panel includes teachers, media specialists, public librarians, and a YA specialist from a bookstore. Students take turns describing books, and the panel tries to identify the title and author. Then the students become the panel and the adults try to stump them. There is a lot of good-natured give-and-take, and the kids win most of the time. More important, the kids hear about the books that adults and peers are reading.

An M&M Read Aloud Contest is a month-long contest to identify popular children's books and Rosies from very short excerpts read by students during school announcements. Each year 120 homerooms participate in this contest. Before voting on the Rosie nominees, the library staff schedules book discussions during homeroom, after school, or at a local coffeehouse in the evening. Before they vote, most students become familiar with nominated titles. Students develop summer reading lists with librarians during the spring semester.

The library media center sponsors WRAP, the Writers and Readers Advisory Panel. Members plan and implement various programs, such as the M&M Read Aloud Contest, book discussions during and after school, book and movie discussions, and monthly coffeehouses where students share their original music, writing, and art. They also compile, edit, and distribute *WRAP Writes,* a publication of original student art and writing; organize the Book Buddies program, where high school students read and discuss books with 1st graders for four to six meetings; organize poetry slams; prepare and perform skits, reader's theater, booktalks, and games to promote books at elementary and middle schools in the district; and attend a local university's Visiting Authors programs, where WRAP members have met Ray Bradbury, Douglas Adams, Art Spiegelman, and Naomi Shihab Nye, among others.

Mitchell and her colleagues collaborate with the Carmel Clay Public Library on many projects, such as joint book discussions, a celebration of National Poetry Month in April with WRAP members, Rosie Jeopardy based on the current Rosie books during the voting party in the spring, and a program for Banned Books Week for classes titled "Feasting on Forbidden Fruit." Both public and school libraries foster parent-student book discussions on the town-wide reading selection and a title that is required reading for all incoming freshmen. This collaboration between the high school and the public library creates an excitement and social exchange among readers of all ages. Carmel High School's library media center is percolating constantly; silence in this library is not even a consideration. It reflects the possibilities for engaging young people in reading activities that they enjoy and want to include in their busy lives. And it grooms them to consider libraries a high priority in their daily lives.

WILSON MIDDLE SCHOOL

Mary Long, a library media specialist at Wilson Middle School in Plano, Texas, organizes an author's visit every year for 7th grade students. The English teachers set aside four to six weeks so students can read at least one of the author's novels. Before the author's visit, students complete a variety of writing projects, such as newspapers or short plays based on the novels. Students are enthralled by meeting authors in person, and they generate all kinds of questions. Long involves 6th graders in the Texas Bluebonnet Award reading program, which nominates 20 titles for the award. Sixth graders must read at least six titles in order to vote. She hosts a special "Bluebonnet Party" and announces the building's favorite along with the statewide winner. She also booktalks the titles on the Texas Lone Star Reading List, and any student who reads any of the titles is enrolled in a contest for a gift certificate.

Because Long is a member of the International Reading Association (IRA), her students have read and selected the IRA's Children's Choices list. Long is also active in the American Library Association (ALA), and as chair and member of the YALSA Quick Picks for Reluctant Readers committee for four years used her students' input in formulating her preferences. Her school readers participated in the ALA/YALSA YA Galley/Teens Top Ten pilot program, in which teens vote on favorite books during Teen Read Week.

In her 11 years at Wilson Middle School, Long's accomplishments include two to three student book-discussion clubs that meet before and during school, a staff book club that reads and discusses YA novels once a month, a Library Teen Advisory Board that sponsors book drives for the community's sister city in Mexico, a picture-book drive for pre-schools serving needy children, and a paperback-book drive for the troops in Iraq, as well as raising funds for students and schools in Iraq and organizing a school fund-raiser to support an adult-literacy program held in public libraries. Mary Long's last comment to me was "I love my job!" The scope of her involvement with reading and kids reflects her commitment to instilling a love of reading in students.

All of these programs are exciting and energetic, and creatively hook kids into participating in library programs. We can perceive some common threads among the programs: encouraging a love of reading in students, helping students share their reading responses with ease among their peers, emphasizing the importance of book discussions and writing responses to gain confidence in using language among adults and peers, nurturing a love of reading for pleasure, and training young people to be involved in community service. There is also a sense of freedom offered to students—come in and browse, let's talk about books, choose what you'd like to read, offer suggestions to improve the library. These libraries have hospitable and relaxed environments without too many rules. Adults are helpful and students can be themselves.

Michelle Hasenfratz, Kay Hones, Mary Long, Connie Mitchell, and Diane Tuccillo exemplify what library media specialists can achieve when adolescents' ideas and suggestions are validated, when adolescents and librarians trust and respect one another, and when adolescents consider their school or public libraries their own turf. Notice that silence is not a prerequisite in any of these environments. Kids are encouraged to browse, lounge, talk, plan, think, and enjoy their library. Their librarians and classroom teachers help them to become independent readers and thinkers and encourage them to achieve and carry out many personal goals. Whether in high school or middle school, students' involvement in library programs helps them to interact with peers in social and learning situations. And the common denominator in most instances is reading and discussing books. These school and library programs provide a solid foundation for nurturing future lifetime readers.

ONE MORE

One other suggestion: If space permits, the adolescent reading area at the public library should be separated from the children's section. After all, teenagers are no longer little kids. They are also at a stage where they move back and forth between YA books and classics, and they might also occasionally dip into the best-seller adult book. It's a good idea to find a *neutral* space for these eclectic readers. And because many students prefer softcover books, the collection should consist of paperbacks whenever possible. (Yes, we know they don't last as long as hardcover books, but do you want the books to sit on your shelves or be read?)

Library media specialists and teachers working together are the cornerstone of any reading program for adolescents. The library media specialists' expertise and knowledge about informational books as well as fiction, along with electronic information services, and the teachers' experiences with students' idiosyncratic reading habits, create a strong partnership to ensure enthusiastic readers.

Chapter 7

OTHER BACKYARDS: USING YOUNG ADULT LITERATURE ACROSS OTHER DISCIPLINES

Please don't confine Young Adult Literature to the English/language-arts classroom. Here's an opportunity to meet and talk with colleagues to coordinate some cross-discipline projects. YAL can reinforce or introduce concepts taught in different subject areas, such as science, social studies, health, art, music, or the humanities. Combined with textbooks, many YA books (fiction and nonfiction) can help students understand complex or abstract concepts. After reading YA materials, students have some basic information to bring to their study of a text, and they begin to be more confident and comfortable with the text.

It is not unusual for English teachers and social-studies teachers to share the same groups of students in a humanities program. Many humanities classes are linked around American history and literature; this is a good fit whereby students have the opportunity to read literature that reflects a particular historical era. But what happens when a student reaches an impasse? What if the student cannot synthesize Hawthorne's *The Scarlet Letter* with his or her understanding of the Puritans in Salem, Massachusetts, during the 1600s? Depending on the assignment and the expectations of the humanities team, wouldn't it be a good idea to provide more accessible titles to students who need to ease into the Puritan era with a less demanding book—one that includes many of the historical characteristics they can recognize easily?

Usually there is only one text for a history class, with some supplementary materials; English teachers, however, have the luxury of clustering biography, poetry, drama, and fiction around a historical period. In a humanities class, where there are students of varying reading abilities, it makes sense to offer alternatives to the prescribed text. Who knows? After reading a YA novel or informational book about Puritan society in Massachusetts, students might be willing to tackle *The Scarlet Letter* with more confidence and ease. Since they are somewhat familiar with the Puritans and the Salem witch trials, Hawthorne might seem less formidable.

There are other areas where English teachers might plan interdisciplinary units. For example, numerous YA novels deal with ecological and environmental issues. Wouldn't the study of ecology in a science class become more meaningful if students read novels that portray characters involved in ecology-related situations? By planning reader-response questions, science and English teachers together could challenge students to consider the factual data they have studied in science class and consider how this information is reflected in the fiction they are reading. And switching back and forth between scientific reading and fictional reading helps students use critical reading skills. They can determine what factual information the author uses to develop the characters or plot of the novel and determine whether the author's ecological dilemma is authentic. Both teachers can evaluate the students' responses to this assignment through class discussions, oral presentations, and written essays.

YA novels have a distinct advantage: the protagonists are teenagers, the books are short enough for students to read outside the classroom, and there are enough choices in YAL to meet any student's ability level.

The advantage of an interdisciplinary approach between reading/language arts and various other disciplines is the subliminal message students receive about the importance of reading across the curriculum, along with writing. Reading and writing are not the exclusive purview of English/language-arts teachers. *All* teachers are responsible for helping students learn, and a major step in students' learning is becoming independent readers. Teachers of various disciplines working together also demonstrates the importance of collegiality and provides the opportunity to understand a variety of approaches to a discipline.

Collaboration among teachers of different disciplines inspires students to recognize the connections between multiple subject areas. When students receive credit in both disciplines, they feel their work is doubly rewarded. Using YAL in interdisciplinary projects appeals to most students—it usually means they can invent, create, and choose activities that interest them, which guarantees a successful learning experience.

The possibilities are unlimited, depending on the imagination and commitment of colleagues. Here are some representative YA titles in several content areas. This list is only selective and not exhaustive.

ART AND PHOTOGRAPHY

Alphin, Elaine Marie. *Simon Says.* Sixteen-year-old Charles Weston finally risks showing his art to peers.

Anderson, Laurie Halse. *Speak.* Melinda Sordino's art assignment relieves the emotional trauma she has repressed during her freshmen year.

Butcher, Kristin. *Zee's Way.* Zee goes from spray-painting graffiti on the wall of a strip mall to painting a mural there.

Capek, Michael. *Murals: Cave, Cathedral, to Street.* Capek examines a wide selection of murals from ancient Egypt to Hollywood—a historical journey about wall art.

Cole, Brock. *Celine.* Sixteen-year-old Celine uses her artistic talent to deal with parental neglect.

Creech, Sharon. *Heartbeat.* As she learns to draw, 12-year-old Annie deals with an overbearing coach, a deteriorating grandfather, and the birth of a new baby brother.

Frank, Hillary. *Better than Running at Night.* Ellie attends the New England College of Art and Design, where she learns a lot about art and love.

Greenberg, Jan. *Heart to Heart: New Poems Inspired by Twentieth-Century Art.* This collection of poetry is inspired by modern American art.

_____. *Romare Bearden: Collage of Memories.* The story of his life and work, with images of everyday life.

Greenberg, Jan, and Sandra Jordan. *Andy Warhol: Prince of Pop.* The story of the op-art icon who popularized art in fashion, Hollywood, business, and film.

_____. *Chuck Close: Up Close.* An analytical overview of Close's work, including full-color reproductions.

_____. *Frank O. Gehry: Outside In.* The story of Gehry's world—from his early years in Canada to the Guggenheim in Bilbao.

_____. *Runaway Girl: The Artist Louise Bourgeois.* The postmodern sculptor who used metal, hemp, and naturalistic pieces to rebel against traditional art.

_____. *Vincent Van Gogh: Portrait of an Artist.* The award-winning story of the famous Dutch painter's life and work, with color photographs.

Halliday, John. *Shooting Monarchs.* A physically disabled boy with an interest in photography is one of several teens who become involved with a serial killer.

Henson, Heather. *Making the Run.* After her mother and best friend die, Lu focuses on her photography to withdraw from her real world.

Ingold, Jeanette. *Pictures, 1918.* While she assists with the war effort, Asia has her eye on a new camera as well as on Nick.

Koja, Kathe. *The Blue Mirror.* Tired of dealing with her alcoholic mother, a talented 16-year-old artist seeks solace in a downtown café.

Mack, Tracy. *Birdland.* As 13-year-old Jed works on a documentary video of his New York neighborhood, he learns about his older brother who died from diabetes.

_____. *Drawing Lessons.* When her father leaves, Aurora buries herself in drawing, using her knowledge of light and color, perspective, and form to heal the ache.

Muhlberger, Richard. *What Makes a Degas a Degas?* Twelve reproductions help to explain Degas's use of color, composition, line and subject matter.

_____. *What Makes a Monet a Monet?* A perspective of Monet's painting style, complete with 12 reproductions.

_____. *What Makes a Rembrandt a Rembrandt?* Rembrandt's uniqueness is explained through studying 12 reproductions of his paintings.

_____. *What Makes a Van Gogh a Van Gogh?* Reproductions of 12 paintings illustrate Van Gogh's use of bold colors, patterns, and thick paint.

Normandin, Christine, ed. *Spirit of the Cedar People: More Stories and Paintings of Chief Lelooska.* The distinguished Kwakiutl storyteller and artist recounts legends of the spirits and animals. Includes a CD narrated by Chief Lelooska, with chants and drumming.

Oneal, Zibby. *In Summer Light.* A talented girl lives in the shadow of her artist father.

Partridge, Elizabeth. *Restless Spirit: The Life and Work of Dorothea Lange.* The great photographer's life, complete with images of well-known portraits.

Peck, Richard. *Unfinished Portrait of Jessica.* Jessica's uncle is a talented painter who helps her resolve her conflict.

Rubin, Susan Goldman. *Art against the Odds: From Slave Quilts to Prison Paintings.* A collection of unusual art by oppressed people shows how art helps people cope with unbearable circumstances.

Scieszka, Jon, and Lane Smith. *Seen Art?* This zany pair introduce young readers to important pieces of modern art at the MoMA—the Museum of Modern Art in New York City.

Stanley, Diane. *Michelangelo.* The great Italian sculptor's tumultuous life is documented with detailed illustrations.

Vreeland, Susan. *Girl in Hyacinth Blue.* A painting thought to be a Vermeer has been hidden for decades; the effect of the painting on the various owners' lives illustrates the mystery and beauty of the painting.

CONTEMPORARY ISSUES

Abusive Relationships among Peers and Adults

Alphin, Elaine Marie. *Simon Says.* Sixteen-year-old Charles Weston hides his artistic talent from his peers and parents to avoid ridicule.

Brooks, Kevin. *Lucas.* Caitlin describes her special relationship with Lucas, and tries to help him when the townspeople believe a bully's lies.

Cormier, Robert. *The Rag and Bone Shop.* Trent, a professional interrogator, intimidates 12-year-old Jason to make him confess to a girl's murder.

_____. *Tenderness.* Lori Cranston escapes her mother's boyfriends by joining up with Eric Poole, ignoring his dangerous reputation.

_____. *Tunes for Bears to Dance To.* When he befriends a Holocaust survivor, Henry's bigoted boss, Mr. Hairston, makes Henry perform a despicable deed.

Crutcher, Chris. *Chinese Handcuffs.* Dillon Hemingway battles his demons by training for the triathlon and trying to protect his girlfriend from sexual abuse.

_____. *The Crazy Horse Electric Game.* Willie, a star athlete, leaves town after a water-skiing accident to find acceptance and understanding elsewhere.

_____. *Ironman*. While training for a triathlon, Bo Brewster analyzes his combative relationship with his father by attending an anger-management class.

_____. *Running Loose*. Louie Banks sacrifices football and friendship for his personal code of ethics.

_____. *Staying Fat for Sarah Byrnes*. Eric Calhoun, alias Moby, keeps eating to show his loyalty to Sarah Byrnes, who is traumatized.

Flinn, Alex. *Breaking Point*. In a flashback, Paul recounts his relationship with destructive Charlie and his willingness to participate in risky behavior.

_____. *Breathing Underwater*. Nick's relationship with his violent father affects his relationship with his girlfriend, Caitlin.

_____. *Nothing to Lose*. After running away from an abusive stepfather, Michael has to decide whether to come out of hiding to help his mother, who is standing trial for the murder of her husband.

Fritz, April Young. *Praying at the Sweetwater Motel*. Sarah Jane and her mother move to a motel in an effort to escape her father's abuse.

Gallo, Donald R., ed. *On the Fringe*. Eleven short stories by various authors provide insights into the lives of teens on the outside—the rejects, the unusual, the geeks, and the weirdos.

Giles, Gail. *Shattering Glass*. When popular and manipulative Rob Hanes decides to make nerdy Simon Glass acceptable to the in-group, he fails to consider Simon's intelligence.

Greene, Bette. *The Drowning of Stephan Jones*. Two gay men are harassed by a group of churchgoing boys to the point of causing Stephan's death.

Hobbs, Valerie. *Letting Go of Bobby James, or How I Found My Self of Steam*. Abandoned by her abusive husband after only 13 weeks of marriage, 16-year-old Jody finds a new life for herself in a small town in Florida.

Jones, Patrick. *Things Change*. One of the top students in her high school class gets involved with an irresponsible senior who becomes possessive and then violent.

Klass, David. *You Don't Know Me*. John's amusing thoughts about high school life deflect the reality of his home life with an abusive stepfather.

Koertge, Ron. *Margaux with an X*. After Margaux confronts her gambling father, she stops her cruel behavior and learns compassion from Danny Riley.

Koja, Kathe. *The Blue Mirror*. Tired of dealing with her alcoholic mother, a talented 16-year-old artist seeks solace in a downtown café, where she falls for a charismatic but abusive guy.

Korman, Gordon. *Jake, Reinvented*. Jack Garrett's attempt to impress his golden girl, Didi Ray, is doomed by Todd Buckley's control of the group.

Mah, Adeline Yen. *Chinese Cinderella: The True Story of an Unwanted Daughter*. Mah's memoir reflects the plight of a Chinese daughter who is rejected by her father and stepmother.

Mazer, Norma Fox. *Out of Control*. Valerie has the courage to accuse three popular males in her high school of sexual harassment.

Moriarty, Jaclyn. *The Year of Secret Assignments*. Three close friends—Lydia, Cassie, and Emily—reveal their independence and insights in letters to their pen pals, three boys from Bookfield School; however, one pen pal is cruel, deceptive, and brutal to one of the girls.

Murray, Jaye. *Bottled Up.* Phillip Downs, alias Pip, is a burnout who skirts around his volatile alcoholic father to protect his younger brother.

Oates, Joyce Carol. *Freaky Green Eyes.* Francesca testifies against her father, famous sportscaster Reid Pierson, when she witnesses his abusive behavior toward her mother.

Philbrick, Rodman. *Max the Mighty.* Max, the hero of *Freak the Mighty,* helps a young girl escape from her abusive stepfather.

Plum-Ucci, Carol. *The Body of Christopher Creed.* After Christopher Creed disappears, Torey Adams and his friends reflect on their abusive treatment of Creed.

Rapp, Adam. *33 Snowfish.* Three homeless kids—a boy running away from sexual abuse, a girl addicted to drugs and engaged in prostitution, and a boy who has killed his parents—along with a kidnapped infant, form an unusual friendship in an extremely hostile environment.

Tashjian, Janet. *Fault Line.* When Becky Martin, an aspiring comic, meets and falls in love with Kip Costello, another comic, she overlooks his jealousy and need to control her.

Voigt, Cynthia. *When She Hollers.* Tish suffers the lies in her family life until she confronts her abusive stepfather.

Whelan, Gloria. *Homeless Bird.* After her husband dies, 13-year-old Koly is abandoned by her mother-in-law in the "widow's town" in India and has to use her ingenuity to survive.

Developmental Disabilities

Betancourt, Jeanne. *My Name Is ~~Brain~~ Brian.* Brian, who is dyslexic, gains confidence in his writing with support from his teachers and friends.

Dash, Joan. *The World at Her Fingertips: The Story of Helen Keller.* Despite blindness and an inability to speak during her early years, Helen Keller's life became an inspiration to everyone, especially people with disabilities.

Ferris, Jean. *Of Sound Mind.* Tired of being the only member of his family who isn't deaf, high school senior Theo meets very creative Ivy, who is also the only hearing member of her family.

Fleischman, Paul. *Mind's Eye.* Paralyzed in an accident, 16-year-old Courtney is taken on an imaginary journey through Italy by a blind old lady.

Frank, E.R. *America.* Fifteen-year-old America's fragile emotions barely survive a series of foster homes, but with the help of Dr. B. he finds hope in his future.

Gantos, Jack. *Joey Pigza Loses Control.* In this sequel to *Joey Pigza Swallowed the Key,* Joey spends the summer with his irresponsible father, with disastrous results.

_____. *Joey Pigza Swallowed the Key.* Joey Pigza's ADHD gets him into situations that are hilarious for readers but not so funny for Joey.

Giles, Gail. *Playing in Traffic.* Goth girl Skye Colby involves Matt Lathrop in her web of deceit and lies about her parents, revealing her emotional instability.

Halliday, John. *Shooting Monarchs.* A physically disabled boy with an interest in photography is one of several teens who become involved with a serial killer.

Harrar, George. *Not as Crazy as I Seem.* After 15-year-old Devon Brown's obsessive-compulsive behaviors get him into trouble, he begins to trust a thoughtful psychiatrist in order to learn what he's been afraid of for years.

Hautman, Pete. *Sweetblood.* Lucy Szabo used to be an excellent student, but she allows her diabetes to get out of control, and now she's on a downward spiral and has an abnormal interest in vampires.

Hesser, Terry Spencer. *Kissing Doorknobs.* Tara's obsessive-compulsive behavior affects her relationships with peers and family.

Holt, Kimberly Willis. *My Louisiana Sky.* Tiger learns the power of love when her grandma dies and she accepts the limitations of her mentally deficient parents.

Ingold, Jeanette. *The Window.* Blinded by an auto accident that killed her mother, 15-year-old Mandy realizes she can hear more than other people can.

Jenkins, A.M. *Damage.* Football hero Austin Reid no longer finds joy in the game when his depression permeates every facet of his life.

Koertge, Ron. *Stoner & Spaz.* Sixteen-year-old Ben Bancroft, who has cerebral palsy, hides out in the Rialto theater watching monster movies, until druggy Colleen Minou sits down next to him and shakes up his life forever.

Martin, Ann M. *A Corner of the Universe.* Twelve-year-old Hattie shows her compassion and love for her mentally ill uncle, Adam, when she peeks into his corner of the universe.

Mazer, Harry. *The Wild Kid.* When 12-year-old Sammy, who is slightly retarded, becomes lost in the woods, he survives with the help of antisocial Kevin.

Mazer, Norma Fox. *When She Was Good.* Em Thurkill learns to survive her sister's violent, psychotic behavior after their mother dies.

Mikaelsen, Ben. *Petey.* When Trevor Ladd meets Petey, a cerebral palsy resident in a nursing home, he discovers the spirit of friendship and loyalty.

Moore, Peter. *Blind Sighted.* Kirk begins to see new possibilities in his life when he is befriended by another misfit in the school and begins to read to a blind woman who is also an excellent cook.

Orr, Wendy. *Peeling the Onion.* A horrible car accident forces Anna to face the layers of her former self now that she is no longer the pretty, popular girl she used to be.

Philbrick, Rodman. *Freak the Mighty.* Learning-disabled Max and physically deformed Freak become the dynamic duo of their school and neighborhood.

Ross, Ramon Royal. *Harper & Moon.* Though Moon is slow and speaks one-word sentences, 13-year-old Harper appreciates Moon's hunting and hiking instincts, but Harper's loyalty is tested when Moon is accused of murder.

Slepian, Jan. *The Alfred Summer.* No one appreciates the talents of Lester, Alfred, Claire, and Myron, who have cerebral palsy, until they build a beautiful boat.

Sones, Sonya. *Stop Pretending: What Happened When My Big Sister Went Crazy.* A novel in poems written from the point of view of a girl describing her older sister's breakdown and subsequent hospitalization.

Tashjian, Janet. *Multiple Choice.* Fourteen-year-old Monica Devon's obsessive-compulsive behavior spirals out of control when she invents Multiple Choice.

Trueman, Terry. *Inside Out.* Sixteen-year-old Zach, a schizophrenic in need of his medication, is one of several hostages in the botched robbery of a coffee shop by two desperate teenagers.

_____. *Stuck in Neutral.* Handicapped by cerebral palsy, 14-year old Shawn has no way to express his thoughts and feelings, and suspects that his father wants to put him out of his misery.

Voigt, Cynthia. *Izzy, Willy-Nilly.* When popular cheerleader Izzy has her leg amputated after a horrible auto accident, her friends exclude her from their lives.

Weeks, Sarah. *So B. It.* Leaving her mentally retarded mother and agoraphobic neighbor, 12-year-old Heidi takes a bus from Reno, Nevada, to Liberty, New York, to find the truth about her mother's past and her own identity.

White, Ruth. *Memories of Summer.* Thirteen-year-old Lyric witnesses her sister Summer's descent into schizophrenia.

Wolff, Virginia Euwer. *Probably Still Nick Swansen.* When learning-disabled Nick Swansen decides to go to the prom, his life comes together for a moment, and he feels like a regular kid.

Drug and Alcohol Abuse

Carter, Alden R. *Up Country.* Carl lives on the edge, repairing stolen car radios, but when his alcoholic mother is arrested, Carl is sent to live with relatives in the country, where he learns about family.

Chbosky, Stephen. *The Perks of Being a Wallflower.* Charlie's letters chronicle his freshmen year in high school—parties with alcohol, sex, and rock and roll, with Charlie trying to make sense of the whole scene.

Cheripko, Jan. *Imitate the Tiger.* Chris Serbo loves to play football, but alcoholism is ruining every aspect of his life.

Draper, Sharon M. *Tears of a Tiger.* During a night of celebratory drinking, Rob Washington is killed in a car accident that changes the lives of all of his friends, especially Andy, who was driving the car.

Gantos, Jack. *Hole in My Life.* The author of the Joey Pigza novels tells the true story about his participation in a drug run from St. Croix to New York City and how he ends up in prison and discovers he is a writer.

Henson, Heather. *Making the Run.* When Lu's drinking buddy, Ginny, is killed in a car crash, Lu goes back to photography to make sense of her life.

Keizer, Garret. *God of Beer.* Kyle Nelson and a group of friends decide to use an act of civil disobedience to measure alcohol consumption by their peers.

Korman, Gordon. *Jake, Reinvented.* Jake Garrett's Friday night parties provide unlimited booze to the in-group at Fitzgerald High, until a fateful accident happens and he is abandoned by nearly everyone.

Moore, Peter. *Blind Sighted.* Bored with school and disgusted with his alcoholic mother, Kirk begins to see new possibilities in his life when he is befriended by another misfit in the school and begins to read to a blind woman who is also an excellent cook.

Murray, Jaye. *Bottled Up.* Pip cuts classes and smokes dope to avoid his alcoholic father's temper and volatile behavior; when ordered to attend group therapy, he begins to understand how to deal with his dilemma.

Ratcliffe, Jane. *The Free Fall.* Sixteen-year-old Violet goes on a rampage of alcohol, drugs, and sex, searching for what she calls "the shine."

Smith, Sherri L. *Lucy the Giant.* Fed up with school and her drunken father, 15-year-old Lucy runs away and signs up as a crew member on a crab boat in the Bering Sea.

Wilhelm, Doug. *Raising the Shades.* Left alone to tend to his alcoholic father, 13-year-old Casey realizes the problems are too great for him to deal with alone.

Homelessness

Fox, Paula. *Monkey Island.* When his pregnant mother abandons him in a New York City welfare hotel, 11-year-old Clay Garrity runs away and lives in a park with two homeless men who befriend him.

Frank, E. R. *America.* Fifteen-year-old America barely survives foster care, but with the help of Dr. B. he finds hope in his future.

Going, K. L. *Fat Kid Rules the World.* Contemplating suicide, a 296-pound 17-year-old boy meets a homeless teenage musician who needs a drummer for his band; their relationship helps both boys.

Hobbs, Valerie. *Letting Go of Bobby James, or How I Found My Self of Steam.* Abandoned by her abusive husband after only 13 weeks of marriage, 16-year-old Jody finds a new life for herself in a small town in Florida.

Koja, Kathe. *The Blue Mirror.* A talented 16-year-old artist falls for a charismatic homeless guy who abuses the girls who are attracted to him.

Mack, Tracy. *Birdland.* As 13-year-old Jed works on a documentary video of his New York neighborhood, he comes across a homeless girl who needs his help.

Naidoo, Beverly. *No Turning Back: A Novel of South Africa.* Sipho runs away from an abusive stepfather and becomes a street boy in Johannesburg.

Paterson, Katherine. *Jip: His Story.* Jip's harsh life at the poor farm begins to change with the help of his schoolteacher.

Rapp, Adam. *33 Snowfish.* Three homeless kids—a boy running away from sex abuse, a girl addicted to drugs and engaged in prostitution, and a boy who killed his parents—along with a kidnapped infant, form an unusual friendship in an extremely hostile environment.

Strasser, Todd. *Can't Get There from Here.* After running away from an abusive family, homeless teenager Maybe lives on the streets of New York, where she shows intelligence and compassion in helping 12-year-old Tears.

Wittlinger, Ellen. *Gracie's Girl.* Bess and Ethan volunteer at a soup kitchen, where they become involved with a homeless woman named Gracie.

School Violence

Adoff, Jaime. *Names Will Never Hurt Me.* What happens in one high school on the one-year anniversary of a school shooting, told in prose and verse mostly from the perspectives of four teenagers, all of whom have been victims of harassment in various forms.

Crutcher, Chris. *Whale Talk.* Behind the triumphs of a high school swim team composed of misfits, dangerous events culminate in a violent confrontation.

Fernley, Fran, ed. *I Wrote on All Four Walls: Teens Speak Out on Violence.* Nine teens talk candidly about their harrowing experiences with violence.

Giles, Gail. *Shattering Glass.* Rob Haynes, the manipulative student leader of the senior class, decides to give nerdy Simon Glass a makeover; however, he and his accomplices resort to violence when Simon wields his new power.

Glenn, Mel. *Who Killed Mr. Chippendale?* After a teacher is shot to death, several students and teachers react in verse.

Myers, Walter Dean. *Shooter.* After a shooting incident at Madison High School, psychologists, an FBI agent, and a sheriff forcefully interview 17-year-old Cameron Porter, the friend and unknowing accomplice of the shooter.

Prose, Francine. *After.* A shooting at a high school 50 miles away changes the environment at Central High School so much that Tom and his friends feel threatened by the authorities.

Shepard, Jim. *Project X.* Two inept, depressed, and angry 8th grade misfits decide to get back at their classmates and teachers by locking everyone in the gymnasium and shooting them.

Strasser, Todd. *Give a Boy a Gun.* When high school outcasts Gary and Brendan can no longer tolerate the brutality and ridicule of the jocks along with the teachers who ignore the situation, they arrive at a school dance with guns.

Sexual Abuse and Rape

Anderson, Laurie Halse. *Speak.* After a summer party at which she was sexually assaulted, Melinda is so traumatized she cannot speak to anyone.

Cole, Brock. *The Facts Speak for Themselves.* Thirteen-year-old Linda's confession describes her mother's boyfriend's sexual relationship with her before her stepfather murders him.

Cooley, Beth. *Ostrich Eye.* Ginger has a rich fantasy life until her younger sister is kidnapped by a man Ginger thought was the father she has never met.

Cormier, Robert. *Heroes: A Novel.* Eighteen-year-old Francis, a war hero with a disfigured face, returns home to look for his childhood hero, a youth leader who raped Francis's girlfriend.

Crutcher, Chris. *Chinese Handcuffs.* Dillon Hemingway discovers that his girlfriend's stepfather has been sexually abusing her.

Dessen, Sarah. *Dreamland.* Caitlin involves herself in a destructive and sexually abusive relationship with charismatic Rogerson.

Frank, E. R. *Friction.* Twelve-year-old Alex is confused when a new girl at school insinuates that Simon, a male teacher, has a sexual interest in her.

Johnson, Kathleen Jeffrie. *The Parallel Universe of Liars.* Surrounded by adults involved in promiscuous relationships, Robin is seduced by her "hunky" next-door neighbor, Frankie, a sexual predator.

_____. *Target*. After he is raped by two strangers, 16-year-old Grady West stops talking as well as eating, but is helped along the road to recovery by friends at his new school.

Johnston, Tim. *Never So Green*. Tex, a 12-year-old with a deformed right hand, expands his horizons when he meets his new stepfather and his two kids, the older of whom is a feisty 12-year-old girl with a dark secret.

Koertge, Ron. *Margaux with an X*. Gorgeous, sarcastic, and popular, Margaux finds herself involved with Danny Riley, a scrawny, kindhearted oddball; together they learn to share the dark secrets of their individual pasts.

Mackler, Carolyn. *The Earth, My Butt, and Other Big Round Things*. Virginia Shreves's perfect family begins to disintegrate when her older brother is accused of rape.

Turner, Ann. *Learning to Swim: A Memoir*. In a series of dark and beautiful poems, the author recalls scenes from a childhood summer when she was sexually abused.

Williams-Garcia, Rita. *Every Time a Rainbow Dies*. A relationship develops between sensitive Thulani and artistic Ysa after Ysa is raped.

Sexuality

Atkins, Catherine. *Alt Ed*. Overweight 10th grader Susan Callaway ends up in an after-school special counseling class with five other problem students, one of whom is a gay male and another a habitual harasser.

Bode, Janet. *Trust and Betrayal: Real Life Stories of Friends and Enemies*. A selection of real-life stories by teenagers about friendship, peer relations, and feelings about self, recorded by the author and shared with other teens.

Cart, Michael, ed. *Love and Sex: Ten Stories of Truth*. These stories about teen sexuality range from the hilarious "Virgin" by Joan Bauer to the thought-provoking "The Cure for Curtis" by Chris Lynch, some with explicit descriptions of heterosexual and homosexual activities.

Chbosky, Stephen. *The Perks of Being a Wallflower*. Charlie's letters describe his freshmen year in high school and his sexual awakening.

Ferris, Jean. *Eight Seconds*. After his dad signs him up for rodeo camp, John finds a competition he's good at—riding bulls; that's easy compared to the friendship he has formed with Kit, his rodeo buddy, who is gay.

Flake, Sharon G. *Who Am I without Him? Short Stories about Girls and the Boys in Their Lives*. A group of stories about black teenagers and their willingness to sacrifice their individuality in order to attract the opposite sex.

Freymann-Wehr, Garret. *My Heartbeat*. Ellen, who has always loved James, her older brother's best friend, learns there might be more to the boys' friendship than she imagined.

Hartinger, Brent. *Geography Club*. Russell Middlebrook and his gay friends start an after-school club to protect themselves from harassment and validate themselves.

Hines, Sue. *Out of the Shadows*. Love, hate, and secrets abound in this love triangle set in an Australian high school.

Homes, A.M. *Jack.* When Jack learns that his athletic father is gay, he is tortured, until he meets a girl in his high school who shares this same experience.

Kerr, M.E. *Deliver Us from Evie.* A teenage boy describes his lesbian sister's relationship and its effect on his family and their small town.

Koja, Kathe. *Talk.* When Kit Webster gets the lead in a controversial school play, he unwittingly attracts the attention of his leading lady, the teen queen of the school; however, when he tells her he's gay, she becomes vicious.

Levithan, David. *Boy Meets Boy.* High school sophomore Paul is gay and has no problems in his family, school, or community until his relationship with Noah becomes complicated in this wacky and upbeat novel.

_____. *The Realm of Possibility.* In free verse, 20 high school teenagers describe their experiences, relationships, and the endless possibilities of their lives.

Mackler, Carolyn. *Vegan Virgin Valentine.* Overachiever vegan Mara Valentine's life is turned upside down when her troubled niece—who is nearly her age but far more sexually experienced—moves in with her family.

Mastoon, Adam. *The Shared Heart: Portraits and Stories Celebrating Lesbian, Gay, and Bisexual Young People.* A collection of photographs and personal narratives by young people who share experiences with family, friends, culture, and coming out.

Matthews, Andrew. *The Flip Side.* When Rob plays the role of Rosalind in a class reading of Shakespeare, he discovers that he likes wearing girl's clothing, and then he's invited to a cross-dressing party.

Myracle, Lauren. *Kissing Kate.* The friendship between Lissa and Kate changes when they kiss at a party, and now Lissa is very confused.

Perez, Marlene. *Unexpected Development.* Megan explains the problems she's had because of her large breasts and what she did during summer vacation: had sex for the first time.

Peters, Julie Ann. *Luna.* Fifteen-year-old Regan O'Neill sacrifices her personal life in order to support her 17-year-old transgendered brother, Liam.

Plum-Ucci, Carol. *What Happened to Lani Garver.* Claire McKenzie tells the story of Lani Garver and her own conflict with the islanders, trying to decide if Lani is a he or a she.

Ryan, Sara. *Empress of the World.* A delicate narrative about a group of gifted high school students enrolled in a summer program on a college campus and two young women who are attracted to each other.

Sanchez, Alex. *Rainbow Boys.* When Jason Carillo decides to attend a meeting for gay teens, he discovers two of his classmates there and becomes involved in a triangle of love, betrayal, and friendship.

_____. *Rainbow High.* The stories of Nelson, Kyle, and Jason continue in this sequel to *Rainbow Boys,* exploring the various challenges faced by these gay adolescents.

_____. *So Hard to Say.* Told from alternative first-person points of view, Xio, a Latina 8th grader in southern California looking for her first boyfriend, falls hard for Frederick, a new Anglo student from Wisconsin, who is trying to figure out why he is more interested in boys than girls.

Taylor, William. *Jerome.* Communicating through e-mails and faxes, Marco and Katie heal after the hunting death of their friend Jerome as they piece together what they know to reveal the secrets they uncover.

Winick, Judd. *Pedro and Me: Friendship, Loss, and What I Learned.* Judd Winick's graphic portrayal of the death of his AIDS-infected roommate, Pedro, is haunting and beautiful.

Wittlinger, Ellen. *Hard Love.* His parents' divorce has convinced John he is impervious to love until he meets zine writer Marisol, who is a lesbian willing to befriend him on her terms.

_____. *Heart on My Sleeve.* Besides dealing with her own love life, Chloe tries to help her sister Genevieve break the news of her lesbian relationship to their parents.

Wolff, Virginia Euwer. *True Believer.* LaVaughn deals with her mother's new boyfriend, very religious girlfriends, and the disappointment of finding out that her romantic interest, Joey, is gay.

Young, Cathy, ed. *One Hot Second: Stories about Desire.* Stories about first love and first times by Sarah Dessen, Nancy Garden, Victor Martinez, Rachel Vail, Rich Wallace, and others.

GEOGRAPHY

Armstrong, Jennifer. *Shipwreck at the Bottom of the World: The Extraordinary True Story of Shackleton and the Endurance.* A remarkable story of the survivors of this arduous journey, complete with 40 photographs from the archives.

Hesse, Karen. *Stowaway.* Eleven-year-old Nicholas Young is a stowaway on Captain Cook's ship, the HMS *Endeavour,* on its first journey to search for an unknown continent.

Hobbs, Will. *Beardance.* In this sequel to *Bearstone,* Cloyd is on a mission when he finds two orphaned bear cubs in the Colorado Rockies that he is determined to keep alive.

_____. *Bearstone.* Fourteen-year-old Cloyd, who is part Ute and part Navajo, spends the summer on a remote ranch with an old man named Walter in a battle of survival in the Colorado mountains.

_____. *Down the Yukon.* Jason Hawthorn, from *Jason's Gold,* and his girlfriend, Jamie Dunavant, combat nature and charlatans on their 2,000 mile trip from Dawson City to Nome, Alaska.

_____. *Far North.* Fifteen-year-old Gabe and his Native American roommate, Raymond Providence, are trapped in the subarctic winter weather in the Northwest Territories.

_____. *Jason's Gold.* Fifteen-year-old Jason Hawthorn and his dog, King, join the Klondike gold rush and travel 500 miles through the Yukon, barely surviving the harsh winter.

_____. *Leaving Protection.* Sixteen-year-old Robbie Daniels is hired by Tor Torsen to work on his fishing boat during the king-salmon season, but the trip turns into a hunt for historic Russian plaques buried along the Alaskan coastline.

_____. *The Maze.* When he meets up with bird biologist Len Peregrino, 14-year-old Rick Walker learns about helping condors survive among the cliffs in Canyonlands National Park and taking responsibility for his own actions.

_____. *River Thunder.* Jessie proves her strength and judgment while rafting the rapids of the Colorado River through the Grand Canyon.

_____. *Wild Man Island.* When 14-year-old Andy Galloway steals away from his kayak group to investigate the island where his father died, a storm strands him on Admiralty Island, Alaska, where he faces wolves, bears, hunger, cold, and a mysterious hermit.

Lasky, Kathryn. *The Journal of Augustus Pelletier: The Lewis and Clark Expedition, 1804.* The fictional journal of a 14-year-old boy who accompanied the Corps of Discovery and assisted Meriwether Lewis in collecting specimens.

Murphy, Virginia Reed, with letters by James Reed, ed. Karen Zeinert. *Across the Plains in the Donner Party.* Based upon the newspaper memoir of Virginia Reed, this book covers the beginning of the journey in Illinois to the rescue of the 46 survivors, including photographs and maps.

Myers, Walter Dean. *Antarctica: Journeys to the South Pole.* Stories about the explorers who dared to investigate the South Pole.

Paulsen, Gary. *Woodsong.* A day-by-day narrative about the grueling Iditarod race and Paulsen's relationship with his beloved sled dogs.

Philbrick, Rodman. *The Journal of Douglas Allen Deeds: The Donner Party Expedition, 1846.* This fictional journal includes historical events in the Donner expedition, complete with map.

Steger, Will, and John Bowermaster. *Over the Top of the World: Explorer Will Steger's Trek across the Arctic.* In 1994 Steger and his team combatted brutal temperatures and winds to cross over the ice-covered Arctic Ocean. Full of amazing photographs and profiles of sled dogs and the team.

Wolf, Allan. *New Found Land: Lewis and Clark's Voyage of Discovery.* Told in narrative verse from different characters' points of view, Lewis and Clark's voyage comes alive with the voices of the explorers who survived the challenging journey to find the Northwest Passage.

HEALTH AND FAMILY PLANNING

Anderson, Laurie Halse. *Fever, 1793.* Through the eyes of a teenage girl, we experience the yellow-fever epidemic in Philadelphia that killed over 5,000 people in 1793.

Bechard, Margaret. *Hanging on to Max.* From the present to the past (via flashbacks), high school senior Sam Pettigrew tells us how he tries to juggle schoolwork, friends, and the little baby he fathered.

Bell, William. *Death Wind.* After Allie finds herself pregnant, she runs away from home with a skateboard champion and encounters a tornado that changes both their lives.

Bennett, Cherie. *Life in the Fat Lane.* When beauty-pageant winner, homecoming queen, popular Laura faces a metabolic disorder, she is abandoned by her former friends.

Brooks, Bruce. *Vanishing.* Alice decides to go on a hunger strike so she won't have to live with her alcoholic mother and stepfather.

Brooks, Martha. *True Confessions of a Heartless Girl.* An angry and pregnant 17-year-old girl changes the quiet lives of several people in a small Manitoba town.

Carter-Scott, Chérie. *If High School Is a Game, Here's How to Break the Rules: A Cutting Edge Guide to Becoming Yourself.* Ten "truths" for surviving your teenage years to become the person you want to be, accompanied by anecdotes about real teens and quotes from famous people.

Corrigan, Eireann. *You Remind Me of You: A Poetry Memoir.* A powerful memoir written in poems about the author's struggle with anorexia and her boyfriend's attempt at suicide.

Dessen, Sarah. *Someone Like You.* Halley becomes the caretaker of her best friend, Scarlett, who is pregnant; the child's father died in a motorcycle accident.

Drill, Esther, Heather McDonald, and Rebecca Odes. *The Looks Book: A Whole New Approach to Beauty, Body Image, and Style.* Using history, psychology, anatomy, and business, the authors provide a lively guide for girls about how they look.

Fox, Paula. *The Eagle Kite.* Despite his own anger, Liam learns to love his AIDS-infected father and accept his dad's homosexuality.

Frank, Lucy. *I Am an Artichoke.* When Sarah is hired as a summer companion to 12-year-old Emily, her own feelings of inadequacy help her to understand Emily's anorexia.

Giblin, James Cross. *When Plague Strikes: The Black Death, Smallpox, AIDS.* An overview of three of the deadliest human epidemics and the social, political, and cultural reactions to these diseases.

Hanauer, Cathi. *My Sister's Bones.* Cassie Weinstein's younger sister, Bille, tries to persuade their parents to recognize Cassie's anorexia, but they are in denial.

Hrdlitschka, Shelley. *Dancing Naked.* After she discovers she is pregnant, Kia considers the choices she has, with every possibility carrying with it a different set of concerns.

Johnson, Angela. *The First Part Last.* Bobby, a new teenaged father, tells about his life before fatherhood and his life as it is now that he has decided to raise his adorable daughter, Feather, on his own.

Johnson, Spencer. *Who Moved My Cheese? for Teens: An A-Mazing Way to Change and Win!* A parable for teenagers about dealing with change, including a teenage discussion section.

Levenkron, Steven. *The Best Little Girl in the World.* A young girl nearly dies battling anorexia.

Minchin, Adele. *The Beat Goes On.* Leyla looks up to her beautiful and popular 16-year-old cousin, Emma, until Emma becomes infected with AIDS from unprotected sex.

Morgenstern, Julie, and Jessi Morgenstern-Colon. *Organizing from the Inside Out for Teenagers: The Foolproof System for Organizing Your Room, Your Time, and Your Life.* A how-to book for teens who want to organize their space and time.

Parker, Margaret Hundley. *KISS Guide to Fitness.* A four-part guide that includes information about tools for a body workout, weight training, and nutrition.

Pedersen, Stephanie. *KISS Guide to Beauty.* A five-part guide about skin, hair, nail, and body care, including makeup fundamentals.

Sweeney, Joyce. *Waiting for June.* Sophie, a pregnant high school senior in Florida, refuses to reveal the identity of her baby's father as she wards off harassment in school and anger at home and tries to make sense of her strange dreams about whales.

Williams-Garcia, Rita. *Like Sisters on the Homefront.* When 14-year-old Gayle gets pregnant for the second time, her mother sends her down south to live with her strict aunt and uncle and straight-laced cousin Cookie.

JOURNALISM

Asher, Sandy. *Summer Smith Begins.* A student runs into trouble after writing an article in the school newspaper.

Crutcher, Chris. *Staying Fat for Sarah Byrnes.* Two students are threatened by the school administration when they start an underground newspaper.

Garden, Nancy. *The Year They Burned the Books.* Senior Jamie Crawford is at the center of a controversy in a small town over books that deal with homosexuality and sex education.

Kyi, Tanya. *Truth.* Jen, a reporter for her school paper, was partying at the house of schoolmates when a man's body was discovered, but nobody is saying who beat him to death, so she begins her own investigation.

Malmgren, Dallin. *The Ninth Issue.* A high school newspaper is censored by the school administrator.

Mazer, Norma Fox, and Harry Mazer. *Bright Days, Stupid Nights.* Four teenagers are summer interns on a summer newspaper.

Tamar, Erica. *The Things I Did Last Summer.* A teenager's summer job on a newspaper teaches him about honest journalism.

Trembath, Don. *The Popsicle Journal.* Harper gets a dream job with the town newspaper, where he has to cover his own father's campaign for mayor, except that family secrets begin to emerge.

MATHEMATICS

Enzensberger, Hans Magnus. *The Number Devil: A Mathematical Adventure.* Twelve-year-old Robert hates math and his math teacher, until he meets the Number Devil in his dreams, who teaches him about zeros and ones, infinite series, and irrational numbers.

Janeczko, Paul B., with illustrations by Jenna LaReau. *Top Secret: A Handbook of Codes, Ciphers, and Secret Writing.* An entertaining and informative explanation of how to make and break codes and ciphers, with interpretations of several historical codes and the secrets behind them.

Scieszka, Jon, and Lane Smith. *Math Curse.* A humorous story of a child's problems with math and how it pervades every part of one's life, with plenty of multiple choices.

Singh, Simon. *The Code Book: How to Make It, Break It, Hack It, Crack It.* A fascinating history of cryptography, the encoding and decoding of private information, and how it creeps into our lives.

Tang, Greg. *Math Appeal: Mind-Stretching Math Riddles.* A creative and interesting approach to math through riddles that emphasize patterns and sym-
metries in problem solving.

THE MIDDLE AGES AND ELIZABETHAN ENGLAND

Avi. *Crispin: The Cross of Lead.* In fourteenth-century England, a 13-year old
orphaned peasant boy known as Asta's Son escapes a false accusation of
murder and becomes involved in a movement to help the common people,
ultimately discovering his true identity.

Blackwood, Gary. *Shakespeare's Scribe.* Widge (from *The Shakespeare Stealer*)
becomes an actor in the Lord Chamberlain's Men when the troupe leaves
London during the Black Plague, and serves as scribe to Will Shakespeare.

_____. *Shakespeare's Spy.* Widge becomes a spy for Shakespeare's company in an
effort to learn who is stealing scripts of Shakespeare's newest play.

_____. *The Shakespeare Stealer.* Widge, a 14-year-old orphan, is ordered by his
evil employer to steal a copy of *Hamlet,* Shakespeare's latest play.

Cadnum, Michael. *The Book of the Lion.* A young apprentice metalworker
becomes a squire to a knight during the Crusades.

_____. *In a Dark Wood.* Cadnum presents a different, and very adult, view of the
story of Robin Hood versus the Sheriff of Nottingham.

Cheaney, J.B. *The Playmaker.* Richard Mallory makes his way to London in
1597, where he joins the Lord Chamberlain's Men as an apprentice and
becomes involved with mysterious strangers.

Cooper, Susan. *King of Shadows.* A contemporary American teenager acting in
A Midsummer Night's Dream is transported back in time to the original
Globe Theater production of the play.

Cushman, Karen. *Catherine, Called Birdy.* The diary of a 14-year-old daughter
of an English nobleman in 1290.

_____. *The Midwife's Apprentice.* The story of a nameless homeless girl in the
fourteenth century who becomes the apprentice of a midwife.

Garden, Nancy. *Dove and Sword: A Novel of Joan of Arc.* Gabrielle, a friend of
Joan of Arc, provides her personal perspective as she follows Joan into
battle as a medic.

Lasky, Kathryn. *Elizabeth I: Red Rose of the House of Tudor, England, 1544.* Through
diary entries, 11-year-old Elizabeth describes her life as a princess, including
the execution of her mother.

_____. *Mary, Queen of Scots: Queen without a Country, France, 1553.* The fictional
diary of 11-year-old Mary, describing the varied activities of her young life.

Meyer, Carolyn. *Beware, Princess Elizabeth.* After her father's death and her
own imprisonment, Elizabeth overcomes her enemies in her determination to become the Queen of England.

_____. *Doomed Queen Anne.* Thirteen-year-old Anne Boleyn, born with an extra
finger and a mole on her neck, swears she will one day be Queen of
England in spite of her beautiful older sister.

_____. *Mary, Bloody Mary.* Mary Tudor recounts her difficult life as the daughter
of King Henry VIII, going from princess in a magnificent castle to a maid
serving her baby stepsister.

_____. *Patience, Princess Catherine.* Catherine of Aragon describes her dramatic life, starting at age 15, and how she becomes the wife of Henry VIII.

Osborne, Mary Pope. *Favorite Medieval Tales.* Nine tales from medieval Europe, including those about Roland, King Arthur, Robin Hood, Beowulf, and Chanticleer.

Paterson, Katherine. *Parzival: The Quest of the Grail Knight.* Raised as a peasant and unaware of his royal blood, Parzival sets out on a five-year journey to find the keeper of the Holy Grail.

MUSIC

Adoff, Jaime. *The Song Shoots out of My Mouth: A Celebration of Music.* Through rhythm and images, former rock musician Jaime Adoff has created a unique poetic tribute to all kinds of music, from Mozart and jazz to hip-hop and rap.

Alphin, Elaine Marie. *Simon Says.* Sixteen-year-old Charlie is unlike his roommate, Adrian, a gifted composer who is not afraid to share his artistic talent with peers.

Armstrong, Jennifer, ed. *What a Song Can Do: 12 Riffs on the Power of Music.* An engaging assemblage of short stories by Ron Koertge, Joseph Brushac, Gail Giles, Dian Curtis Regan, and eight others in which music plays a key role.

Brooks, Bruce. *Midnight Hour Encores.* Sibilance is a talented cellist who learns about 1960s music from her father, Taxi.

Curtis, Christopher Paul. *Bud, Not Buddy.* After his mother dies, 10-year-old Bud goes on a journey to find the famous band Dusky Devastators of the Depression and finds out about the famous musicians in his family.

Delaney, Mark. *Pepperland.* After her mother's death, Star struggles to work through her anger with the help of a sensitive psychologist and John Lennon's music.

Denenberg, Barry. *All Shook Up: The Life and Death of Elvis Presley.* A realistic look at Elvis's life, from his humble beginnings to his "Hound Dog" fame.

Dessen, Sarah. *This Lullaby.* Remy is taken with Dexter, a messy, impulsive musician who reminds her of the father she never knew—the father who left her a famous song that haunts her.

Going, K. L. *Fat Kid Rules the World.* Contemplating suicide, a 296-pound 17-year-old boy meets a homeless teenage musician who needs a drummer for his band.

Haskins, James. *One Love, One Heart: A History of Reggae.* All you need to know about the history and influence of reggae, explained in a refreshing and insightful manner.

_____. *One Nation under a Groove: Rap Music and Its Roots.* A fresh, thorough, and insightful history of rap music, including a glossary and an extensive bibliography.

Hentoff, Nat. *Jazz Country.* A young white boy wants to become a jazz musician.

Hesse, Karen. *Out of the Dust.* Fourteen-year-old Billie Jo plays the piano fiercely to forget the tragedies in her life during the Dust Bowl days.

Ingold, Jeanette. *Mountain Solo.* Sixteen-year-old violin prodigy Tess leaves the pressures of the New York music world and returns to Montana to find inner peace and make a decision about her musical career.

Levine, Gail Carson. *Dave at Night.* An orphan at the Hebrew Home for Boys sneaks out at night and experiences the music and culture of the Harlem Renaissance.

Neimark, Anne E. *The Life of Woody Guthrie: There Ain't Nobody That Can Sing Like Me.* This pictorial history documents Woody Guthrie's life, from Oklahoma to New York, as a vagabond folk singer who used his music to attack political and social injustice.

Nolan, Han. *Born Blue.* Raised by drug dealers and addicts, Leshaya is determined to turn her life around by pursing a singing career.

Partridge, Elizabeth. *This Land Was Made for You and Me: The Life and Songs of Woody Guthrie.* A biography that offers a historical perspective on Guthrie—the folk songs he wrote about his family, cowboys, work, and the Depression, with reproductions of posters and family photos.

Powell, Randy. *Tribute to Another Dead Rock Star.* Fifteen-year-old Grady Grennan returns to Seattle to attend a musical tribute to his dead mother, a former rock star, and encounters conflict between his retarded brother and his stepmother.

Wittlinger, Ellen. *Heart on My Sleeve.* After meeting at a weekend college visit, high school senior Chloe e-mails Julian Casper, another senior involved in music and acting, believing they have a romantic relationship.

Wolff, Virginia Euwer. *The Mozart Season.* A young violinist discovers her inner resources while preparing for a challenging competition.

POLITICAL HISTORY

Bolden, Tonya, ed. *33 Things Every Girl Should Know about Women's History: From Suffragettes to Skirt Lengths to the E.R.A.* A compilation of historical information about women's rights, including laws, landmark demonstrations, and movements that empowered women.

Colman, Penny. *Girls: A History of Growing Up Female in America.* A chronological history of distinctive females from the early colonial period to the millennium.

Fleming, Candace. *Ben Franklin's Almanac: Being a True Account of the Good Gentleman's Life.* An illustrated biography of the inventor, statesman, and scientist, including his family album and boyhood memories.

Fradin, Dennis Brindell, and Judith Bloom Fradin. *Fight On! Mary Church Terrell's Battle for Integration.* This African American woman was an activist in her 80s, helping to integrate Washington, D.C., restaurants and theaters.

Freedman, Russell. *In Defense of Liberty: The Story of America's Bill of Rights.* Though the Bill of Rights guarantees individual freedoms, Freedman shows how court cases and social changes have impacted these rights.

McKissack, Patricia, and Arlene Zarembka. *To Establish Justice: Citizenship and the Constitution.* A historical perspective of the role of the Supreme

Court in establishing civil and equal rights for minority groups, including Native Americans, African Americans, immigrants, women, Americans with disabilities, gay men, and lesbians.

McWhorter, Diane. *A Dream of Freedom: The Civil Rights Movement from 1954 to 1968.* An illustrated history of the civil rights movement, with profiles of catalysts such as Rosa Parks and Dr. Martin Luther King Jr. and the origins of the boycotts and sit-ins that reflect African Americans' struggle for racial equality.

SCIENCE/NATURE/ECOLOGY

Ackroyd, Peter. *Voyages through Time: The Beginning.* A visual history of the universe from the beginning of the heavens to the evolution of living beings such as fish, dinosaurs, monkeys, and humans.

———. *Voyages through Time: Escape from Earth.* A complete visual history of space exploration in the twentieth century.

Aczel, Amir D. *The Riddle of the Compass: The Invention That Changed the World.* A history of the compass in Europe and how it affected trade and exploration.

Adams, Simon. *Visual Timeline of the 20th Century.* A chronological review of the key innovations that shaped our modern world, with photos and an index.

Anderson, M. T. *Feed.* A peek into a future where teenagers might travel to a party on the moon and product commercials play directly into the brain via an embedded computer chip.

Atkins, Jeannine. *Wings and Rockets: The Story of Women in Air and Space.* A history of the women who broke barriers to participate in aviation and space travel.

Ayres, Katherine. *Macaroni Boy.* During the Great Depression in Pittsburgh, 6th grader Mike Costa and his friend try to figure out what's killing rats in the neighborhood warehouse district and making his grandfather sick.

Bridgman, Roger. *1000 Inventions and Discoveries.* Historical groundbreaking inventions and discoveries from 3,000,000 B.C. to 2001, with illustrations and photographs.

Couper, Heather, and Nigel Henbest. *Black Holes.* The discovery of these mysterious objects and the scientific theories that try to explain them.

Dash, Joan. *The Longitude Prize.* In the eighteenth century, a village carpenter, John Harrison, develops a system of fixing longitude that changes navigation.

Dickinson, Peter. *Eva.* A chimp with a human brain struggles to save her companions from extinction.

Farrell, Jeanette. *Invisible Allies: Microbes That Shape Our Lives.* An entertaining explanation of how microbes are a significant part of our lives, from the making of cheese and bread to how sewage is processed in waste-treatment plants.

Goodall, Jane. *The Chimpanzees I Love: Saving Their World and Ours.* Goodall's personal narrative explains her fascination with endangered chimps and her dedication to studying them.

Hesse, Karen. *Phoenix Rising.* Nyle's peaceful life on a sheep farm is changed radically when a nuclear power plant contaminates the surrounding farms.

Hiaasen, Carl. *Hoot.* Middle school student Roy Eberhardt becomes involved in saving the nesting place for owls from a construction company.

Hobbs, Will. *Beardance.* In this sequel to *Bearstone,* Cloyd is on a spirit-finding mission when he discovers two orphaned bear cubs.

_____. *Bearstone.* Fourteen-year-old Cloyd, who is part Ute and part Navajo, spends the summer on a remote ranch in the Colorado mountains.

_____. *Jackie's Wild Seattle.* A 14-year old girl and her younger brother spend the summer working with their uncle at a wildlife rescue center near Seattle.

_____. *The Maze.* Fourteen-year-old Rick travels to Canyonlands National Park, where he learns to help fledgling condors survive in the wild.

Hoose, Phillip. *The Race to Save the Lord God Bird.* Hoose looks at 200 years of history to understand the causes of the extinction of the magnificent ivory-billed woodpecker from southern forests and swamps.

Ingold, Jeanette. *The Big Burn.* The lives of three older teens are changed forever when a massive forest fire sweeps through Idaho's Coeur D'Alene National Forest in 1910.

Kerrod, Robin. *The Way Science Works.* Scientific theories are explained in concise, clear language; a list of simple experiments to understand atoms, matter, heat, energy, color, light, sound, electricity, and magnetism is included.

Klass, David. *California Blue.* A teenage runner discovers a new butterfly species in a forest owned by a lumber company where his father works.

Lauber, Patricia. *Hurricanes: Earth's Mightiest Storms.* A history of the worst storms ever and how computers track their paths.

Lipsyte, Robert. *The Chemo Kid.* Two teenagers try to stop the pollution of the town's reservoir.

Maestro, Betsy. *The Story of Clocks and Calendars: Marking a Millennium.* A fascinating history of time over thousands of years, with vibrant illustrations.

Marsh, Carole. *Unidentified Flying Objects and Extra Terrestrial Life.* A short history of UFOs in radio, television, space travel, and people involved in "channeling."

O'Brien, Robert C. *Z For Zachariah.* The diary of a teenager who is the only survivor of a nuclear war, or so she thinks.

Patent, Dorothy Hinshaw. *Biodiversity.* In this photo essay, Patent clearly explains the concept of biodiversity and why it is important to maintain it.

Philbrick, Nathaniel. *Revenge of the Whale: The True Story of the Whaleship Essex.* After a whale attack in 1803, the survivors of the *Essex* use their ingenuity to combat hunger, thirst, and fear until their rescue off the coast of South America.

Philbrick, Rodman. *The Last Book in the Universe.* In a future time without hope, Spaz rescues his little sister with the help of Ryter and a genetically perfected girl who lives in Eden.

Platt, Richard. *Eureka! Great Inventions and How They Happened.* Aided by colorful illustrations, Platt explains the origins of cereal, frozen fish sticks, elevators, hovercrafts, the Walkman, and many other inventions.

Rinaldi, Ann. *An Acquaintance with Darkness.* While living with her uncle, a prominent physician in Washington, D.C., in 1865, 14-year-old Emily observes his suspicious behavior—and finds out about the beginning of medical autopsies.

Roach, Mary. *Stiff: The Curious Lives of Human Cadavers.* A respectful look at the afterlife of human cadavers—how scientists utilize the human body.

Scieszka, Jon, and Lane Smith. *Science Verse.* A boy is cursed with writing hilariously rhyming verses about all the topics in his science class, such as evolution, spleens, vitamins, viruses, and skeletons.

Simon, Seymour. *The Universe.* A voyage into space beyond our solar system and galaxy, with phenomenal photographs.

Sis, Peter. *The Tree of Life: A Book Depicting the Life of Charles Darwin, Naturalist, Geologist and Thinker.* Material from Darwin's diaries and detailed illustrations provide important insights into Darwin's life.

Sleator, William. *Others See Us.* A teenager falls into a toxic-waste dump and discovers he has ESP.

Spinelli, Jerry. *Night of the Whale.* A boy and his classmates try to save a pod of stranded whales.

_____. *Wringer.* Palmer LaRue is dreading his participation in the Family Fest, where he will be required to wring the necks of pigeons who have been shot by local hunters.

Thimmesh, Catherine, with illustrations by Melissa Sweet. *The Sky's the Limit: Stories of Discovery by Woman and Girls.* Brief biographies about 11 females who have studied such things as sea lizards, chimpanzees, lead poisoning, T. Rex fossils, and the surface of Mars, with colorful collage illustrations and a time line of scientific discoveries by women.

Walker, Richard. *Encyclopedia of the Human Body.* A thorough guide to the human body, including key functions of each system, with detailed illustrations, charts, time line, and glossary.

SOCIAL STUDIES/AMERICAN HISTORY

Colonial Times

Fleischman, Paul. *Saturnalia.* William, a Native American captive, describes life in Boston in 1681.

Lasky, Kathryn. *Beyond the Burning Time.* A courageous young girl is forced to deal with the Salem witch trials when her mother is accused of being a witch.

_____. *A Journey to the New World: The Diary of Remember Patience Whipple, Mayflower, 1620.* A Pilgrim girl makes the dangerous journey to the New World on the *Mayflower.*

Masoff, Joy. *Colonial Times: 1600–1700.* Life in America in the 1600s, including life on board a ship crossing from Europe to America.

Rinaldi, Ann. *A Break with Charity: A Story about the Salem Witch Trials.* Susanna knows the truth about the witches' accusers, but is sworn to secrecy in order to protect her family.

_____. *The Journal of Jasper Jonathan Pierce: A Pilgrim Boy, Plymouth, 1620.* Fourteen-year-old Jasper establishes a friendship with the Nauset Indians.

Slavery

Ayres, Katherine. *North by Night: A Story of the Underground Railroad.* Sixteen-year-old Lucy Spender helps her family operate a station of the Underground Railroad.

Barnes, Joyce Annette. *Amistad: A Junior Novel.* Based on the epic film, the true story of a group of illegally enslaved Africans who rebelled against their captors.

Carbone, Elisa. *Stealing Freedom.* A fictionalized account of Anne Marie Weems's young life as a slave in 1853 and her dramatic escape to Canada.

Fox, Paula. *The Slave Dancer.* A young musician is kidnapped and forced to play music on a slave ship.

Hamilton, Virginia. *Anthony Burns: The Defeat and Triumph of a Fugitive Slave.* The biography of an escaped slave tried under the Fugitive Slave Act of 1850, who became the symbol for the abolitionist movement in 1854.

_____. *Many Thousand Gone: African Americans from Slavery to Freedom.* Individual histories of slave experiences.

Johnson, Charles. *Soulcatcher: And Other Stories.* Tales of the effects and experiences of slaves based on historical fact.

Lasky, Kathryn. *True North: A Novel of the Underground Railroad.* Lucy Bradford, a 14-year-old Bostonian, joins the workers on the Underground Railroad and helps a slave girl, Afrika, escape to Canada.

Lester, Julius. *To Be a Slave.* The stories of African American men and women who experienced the humiliation of slavery.

McGill, Alice. *Miles' Song.* When Miles is caught looking at a book in the main house, he is banished to the fields and learns the other side of slavery.

McKissack, Patricia C. *A Picture of Freedom: The Diary of Clotee, A Slave Girl, Belmont Plantation, Virginia, 1859.* In the face of terrible hardship, a slave girl's diary reveals her hope and courage on the eve of the Civil War.

McKissack, Patricia C., and Fredrick L. McKissack. *Sojourner Truth: Ain't I a Woman?* The biography of a slave who became a spokesperson against slavery and for women's suffrage.

Moses, Sheila P. *I, Dred Scott: A Fictional Slave Narrative Based on the Life and Legal Precedent of Dred Scott.* The story of the famous slave's life and his trial for his freedom, with historical notes, illustrations, and a foreword by Scott's great-grandson.

Mosley, Walter. *47.* When a young slave, 47, living under a brutal master meets a runaway slave, Tall John, he sees the possibility of his own freedom.

Myers, Walter Dean. *Amistad: A Long Road to Freedom.* The emotional story of the mutiny of slaves on the ship *Amistad* in 1839 and their subsequent imprisonment and trial.

_____. *The Glory Field.* The saga of five generations of an African American family, from slavery to contemporary times.

Paulsen, Gary. *Nightjohn.* Sarny, a 12-year-old female slave, learns to read and write from Nightjohn, despite threats from her master.

_____. *Sarny: A Life Remembered.* Sarny, a former slave, uses her freedom and independent means to help African Americans become literate.

Pearsall, Shelley. *Trouble Don't Last.* A young boy and an old man, both slaves in Kentucky, escape and make their way to Canada via the Underground Railroad.

Rinaldi, Ann. *Hang a Thousand Trees with Ribbons: The Story of Phillis Wheatley.* Purchased by the Wheatley family in 1761, a young slave girl becomes America's first published black poet.

_____. *Wolf by the Ears.* The story of Harriet Hemings, daughter of Thomas Jefferson's slave Sally.

Westward Movement

Bruchac, Joseph. *Sacajawea: The Story of Bird Woman and the Lewis and Clark Expedition.* Sacajawea joins the historic expedition as guide, translator, caretaker, and the only woman—told in the alternating points of view of Sacajawea and William Clark.

Cushman, Karen. *The Ballad of Lucy Whipple.* Lucy Whipple's diary describes her experiences moving from Massachusetts to the gold-mining town of Lucky Diggins, California, during the years 1849–52.

Freedman, Russell. *The Life and Death of Crazy Horse.* The famous Sioux warrior's valiant fight to save the hunting grounds from General Custer in the Battle of Little Bighorn in 1876, with drawings by Amos Bad Heart Bull.

Gregory, Kristiana. *Across the Wide and Lonesome Prairie: The Oregon Trail Diary of Hattie Campbell, 1847.* A young girl describes her family's challenging journey westward.

Hall, Eleanor J. *The Lewis and Clark Expedition.* Provides information about some of the lesser-known members of the famous expedition from St. Louis to the mouth of the Columbia River.

Hardman, Ric Lynden. *Sunshine Rider: The First Vegetarian Western.* Wylie Jackson goes on a cattle drive through western territory in 1881 as a cook's assistant and then a driver.

Hobbs, Will. *Down the Yukon.* Jason Hawthorn, from *Jason's Gold,* and his girlfriend, Jamie Dunavant, combat nature and charlatans on their 2,000-mile trip from Dawson City to Nome, Alaska.

_____. *Jason's Gold.* Fifteen-year-old Jason Hawthorn and his dog, King, join the Klondike gold rush and travel 500 miles through the Yukon, barely surviving the harsh winter.

Hudson, Jan. *Sweetgrass.* Suffering from starvation and smallpox, a Blackfoot Indian tribe comes to depend on the skills of a 15-year-old girl for their survival.

Lasky, Kathryn. *Beyond the Divide.* An Amish girl travels with her father to California during the Gold Rush and learns to survive.

_____. *The Journal of Augustus Pelletier: The Lewis and Clark Expedition, 1804.* The fictional journal of a 14-year-old boy who accompanied the Corps of Discovery and assisted Meriwether Lewis in collecting specimens.

Levine, Ellen. *The Journal of Jedediah Barstow: An Emigrant on the Oregon Trail, 1848.* A young orphan makes his way to the Oregon Territory on his own.

Moss, Marissa. *Rachel's Journal: The Story of a Pioneer Girl.* Rachel and her family follow the Oregon Trail from Illinois to California.

Murphy, Jim. *West to a Land of Plenty: The Diary of Teresa Angelino Viscardi, New York to Idaho Territory, 1883.* An Italian family travels to the West to start a new life.

Murphy, Virginia Reed, with letters by James Reed, ed. Karen Zeinert. *Across the Plains in the Donner Party.* Based upon the newspaper memoir of Virginia Reed, this book covers the beginning of the journey in Illinois to the rescue of the 46 survivors, including photographs and maps.

Paulsen, Gary. *Mr. Tucket.* Fourteen-year-old Francis Tucket is captured by the Pawnees while heading west on the Oregon Trail.

Philbrick, Rodman. *The Journal of Douglas Allen Deeds: The Donner Party Expedition, 1846.* This fictional journal includes historical events in the Donner expedition, complete with map.

Spooner, Michael. *Daniel's Walk.* Hoping to locate his long-missing father, young Daniel joins a wagon train on the Oregon Trail in 1846, facing all sorts of dangers.

Wolf, Allan. *New Found Land: Lewis and Clark's Voyage of Discovery.* Told in narrative verse from different characters' points of view, Lewis and Clark's voyage comes alive with the voices of the explorers who survived the challenging journey to find the Northwest Passage.

Yep, Laurence. *Dragon's Gate.* A Chinese boy joins his father and others digging a tunnel for the transcontinental railroad through the Sierra Nevada mountains in 1867.

Immigration

Alvarez, Julia. *Before We Were Free.* Anita de la Torre's family resists the Trujillo regime in the Dominican Republic during the 1960s and escapes to New York.

Auch, Mary Jane. *Ashes of Roses.* When their family returns to Ireland, 16-year-old Rose and her younger sister have to make their own way in New York City in 1911.

Avi. *Beyond the Western Sea, Book 1: The Escape from Home.* The shipboard adventures of three Irish kids in 1851—siblings Maura and Patrick leave their life of poverty, while Sir Laurence Kirkle leaves his life of privilege to escape an evil brother.

_____. *Beyond the Western Sea, Book 2: Lord Kirkle's Money.* The three young immigrants meet up with shady characters and survive disease and hunger during their voyage to the New World.

Bitton-Jackson, Livia. *Hello, America.* Having survived Nazi death camps, Elli and her mother arrive in New York City in 1951, where Elli struggles to make a life for herself.

Danticat, Edwidge. *Behind the Mountains.* Celine and her family escape from turmoil in Haiti and join her father in Brooklyn, New York.

Gallo, Donald R., ed. *First Crossing: Stories about Teen Immigrants.* Ten stories about teens from various countries, including Mexico, Venezuela, China, Korea, and Sweden, establishing lives in the United States.

Hesse, Karen. *Letters from Rifka.* In letters to her friend back home, 12-year-old Rifka describes her difficult journey from a Jewish community in Ukraine to Ellis Island, where she is quarantined.

Moss, Marissa. *Hannah's Journal: The Story of an Immigrant Girl.* Hannah and her cousin move to New York to escape religious persecution.

Ryan, Pam Muñoz. *Esperanza Rising.* After her father dies, Esperanza and her mother must leave their Mexican ranch and become migrant workers in California.

Veciana-Suarez, Ana. *Flight to Freedom.* Yara and her family are forced to leave Cuba's political oppression in 1967 and settle in Miami, Florida.

Race/Civil Rights

Carvell, Marlene. *Who Will Tell My Brother?* Inspired by real events, this novel in verse deals with a Native American teen's efforts to remove his high school's offensive Indian mascot and the hateful bullying and violence that he faces from officials and peers.

Crowe, Chris. *Getting Away with Murder: The True Story of the Emmett Till Case.* The perfect companion piece for Crowe's *Mississippi Trial, 1955,* this carefully detailed book recounts the true events behind his historical novel and includes photographs.

_____. *Mississippi Trial, 1955.* While visiting his grandfather in Mississippi, 16-year-old Hiram meets a feisty black teen from Chicago who is murdered; Hiram begins to observe the prejudice and racism of this southern community.

Curtis, Christopher Paul. *The Watsons Go to Birmingham—1963.* While visiting his grandmother in Alabama, Kenny and his family witness the bombing of the Baptist church.

Hesse, Karen. *Witness.* A stunning novel in free verse about the effect of Ku Klux Klan activities on nine residents of a small Vermont town in the 1920s.

King, Casey, and Linda Barrett Osborne. *Oh, Freedom! Kids Talk about the Civil Rights Movement with the People Who Made It Happen.* Children interview family members, friends, and civil rights activists to understand the history of the fight for equality, with a foreword by Rosa Parks.

Krisher, Trudy. *Spite Fences.* The dull life of Maggie Pugh, a poor white girl, changes during the summer of 1960, when she gets her first camera and witnesses the racial violence in her small town.

Levine, Ellen. *Freedom's Children: Young Civil Rights Activists Tell Their Own Stories.* The true stories of 20 African Americans who participated in demonstrations against segregation in the 1950s.

McDonald, Joyce. *Devil on My Heels.* In 1959, 15-year-old Dove becomes concerned about racial violence against the migrant workers in her father's Florida orange groves.

McWhorter, Diane. *A Dream of Freedom: The Civil Rights Movement from 1954 to 1968.* An illustrated history of the civil rights movement with profiles of such catalysts as Rosa Parks and Dr. Martin Luther King Jr. and the origins of the boycotts and sit-ins that reflect African Americans' struggle for equality.

Parks, Rosa, with Jim Haskins. *Rosa Parks: My Story.* The life story of Rosa Parks, a woman of courage and tenacity.

Robinet, Harriette Gillem. *Walking to the Bus-Rider Blues.* During the 1956 bus boycott in Montgomery, Alabama, Alfa's family struggles to pay their rent, but someone is stealing their payments.

Singer, Marilyn, ed. *Face Relations: 11 Stories about Seeing beyond Color.* Short stories about race relations by such authors as Rita Williams-Garcia, Joseph Bruchac, Ron Koertge, and Ellen Wittlinger.

Walter, Mildred Pitts. *The Girl on the Outside.* Walter focuses on the experiences of two students—one white, one black—during the integration of Central High School in Little Rock, Arkansas, in 1957.

Woodson, Jacqueline. *If You Come Softly.* Miah is black and Ellie is white; they meet at their private high school and fall in love.

For books about various wars (the American Revolution, American Civil War, World War I, and so on), the Holocaust, and the Great Depression, see the thematic units on war and the Great Depression in chapter 5.

SPORTS/PHYSICAL EDUCATION

Adoff, Arnold. *The Basket Counts.* Lively, creative, attractively illustrated poems celebrate foul shots, lay-ups, and slam dunks by both girls and boys.

Bennett, James. *The Squared Circle.* Sonny Youngblood enters college as a star basketball player, but academic and emotional problems threaten to derail his promising sports career.

Bloor, Edward. *Tangerine.* Paul, who is legally blind but still manages to play soccer, lives in the shadow of his older brother, Erik, who steals the family's attention as a star football kicker.

Brooks, Bruce. *The Moves Make the Man.* Jerome tells the story of his athletic friend Bix, who refuses to make the "moves" in dealing with his stepfather.

Carter, Alden R. *Bull Catcher.* Through his baseball journal, readers can follow Bull Larsen's development both as a catcher and a human being.

Cheripko, Jan. *Imitate the Tiger.* Chris Serbo loves to play football, but alcoholism is ruining every aspect of his life.

_____. *Rat.* When 15-year-old Jeremy Chandler testifies against the basketball coach for molesting a cheerleader, his friendship with the other players is destroyed, and he is tormented by a player who seeks revenge.

Cochran, Thomas. *Roughnecks.* Travis Cody is determined to beat archrival Pineview for the state football championship after his team lost a previous game that he feels responsible for.

Crutcher, Chris. *Athletic Shorts: Six Short Stories.* Probably the best set of short stories about teenagers ever written, most of them based on characters from Crutcher's novels.

_____. *Chinese Handcuffs.* Dillon Hemingway refuses to be bullied by school authorities who threaten him.

_____. *The Crazy Horse Electric Game.* When he loses his athletic coordination, Willie leaves town to find acceptance elsewhere.

_____. *Ironman.* While training for a triathlon, Bo Brewster analyzes his combative relationship with his father.

_____. *Running Loose.* Louie Banks sacrifices football and friendship for his personal code of ethics.

_____. *Staying Fat for Sarah Byrnes.* Swimmer Eric Calhoun, alias Moby, keeps eating to show his loyalty to burn victim Sarah Byrnes.

_____. *Stotan!* A four-person swim team trains rigorously for a state meet and learns about loyalty and honesty.

_____. *Whale Talk.* Behind the triumphs of a high school swim team composed of misfits lurk painful lives and present dangers that culminate in a shocking and surprising ending.

Deuker, Carl. *Heart of a Champion.* Seth and Jimmy live and breathe baseball, but their friendship is tested by the game.

_____. *High Heat.* Shane Hunter's privileged life is brought to a sudden end when his father commits suicide after being arrested for laundering drug money, thus affecting Shane's ability to pitch.

_____. *Night Hoops.* Through nightly basketball practices, Nick develops an uneasy friendship with the bad boy across the street.

_____. *Painting the Black.* Through playing baseball, Ryan realizes he can successfully face the moral challenges in his life.

Esckilsen, Erik E. *Offsides.* A Mohawk Indian who is a star soccer player refuses to play for his new school because of their offensive Indian mascot.

Farrell, Mame. *And Sometimes Why.* Jack and Chris (a girl) have always been friends and equals in sports, but now, in the 8th grade, she has gained an advantage.

Ferris, Jean. *Eight Seconds.* After his dad signs him up for rodeo camp, John finds a competition he's good at—riding bulls; that's easy compared to the friendship he has formed with Kit, his rodeo buddy, who is gay.

Gallo, Donald R., ed. *Ultimate Sports: Short Stories by Outstanding Writers for Young Adults.* Short stories about males and females engaged in various sports, including scuba diving, basketball, racquetball, tennis, and sailing.

Glenn, Mel. *Jump Ball: A Basketball Season in Poems.* A series of poems from the perspectives of various individuals tells the story of a team's season that ends in tragedy.

Halvorson, Marilyn. *Bull Rider.* Layne wants nothing more than to enter the rodeo as a bull rider, even though his father was killed riding bulls.

Hawk, Tony, with Sean Mortimer. *Tony Hawk: Professional Skateboarder.* The autobiography of one of skateboarding's hottest professionals, with lots of black and white photos.

Jenkins, A.M. *Damage.* High school senior Austin Reid is a talented, popular football star with everything going for him, except he's seriously depressed.

Johnston, Tim. *Never So Green.* Tex, a 12-year-old with a deformed right hand, expands his horizons when he meets his new stepfather and his two kids, the older of whom is a feisty 12-year-old girl with a dark secret.

Klass, David. *Danger Zone.* Jimmy Doyle learns about prejudice and politics when he joins a teen dream team of mostly black players playing in Italy.

_____. *Home of the Braves.* Joe Brickman is the ultimate success—student leader, captain of wrestling and soccer teams, modest, and rational—but the arrival of a Brazilian soccer phenom tests the social order of the school.

_____. *Wrestling with Honor.* A teenage wrestler fails a mandatory drug test and must prove himself.

Lee, Marie G. *Necessary Roughness.* When a Korean American family moves to a small town in Minnesota, Chan must cope with racism on the football team as well as tensions at home.

Lipsyte, Robert. *The Brave.* When boxer Sonny Bear leaves the Indian reservation, he meets up with Alfred Brooks of the New York Police Department.

_____. *The Chief.* Sonny Bear is on the verge of a heavyweight championship when trouble occurs on the reservation over casino gambling.

_____. *The Contender.* Alfred Brooks escapes the ghetto by training to be a boxer.

_____. *Warrior Angel.* Sonny Bear loses his emotional stability and thus his title before regaining his sense of self through contact with a deranged teenage admirer.

Lupica, Mike. *Travel Team.* When 12-year-old Danny is cut from the basketball travel team because of his size, he starts a team of castoffs that exceeds everyone's expectations.

Lynch, Chris. *Gold Dust.* In Boston in 1975, nothing matters to Richard except baseball, and he's determined to make baseball matter to his new friend from Dominica, Napoleon Charlie Ellis.

_____. *Iceman.* A violent hockey player takes out his frustration on friends and enemies.

_____. *Shadow Boxer.* An older brother tries to discourage his younger brother from becoming a boxer after their father dies in the ring.

_____. *Slot Machine.* Elvin Bishop, an overweight incoming freshman at Christian Brothers Academy, enters their three-week summer athletic program and tries to fit in, but he's not a jock.

Macy, Sue, ed. *Girls Got Game: Sports Stories and Poems.* A collection of original stories about female athletes playing baseball, softball, soccer, basketball, stickball, football, tetherball, and so on.

McKissack, Fredrick, Jr. *Black Hoops: The History of African Americans in Basketball.* McKissack looks at the sport from its beginnings to the present stars of the NBA.

McKissack, Patricia C., and Fredrick McKissack Jr. *Black Diamond: The Story of the Negro Baseball Leagues.* A comprehensive history of baseball's famous Negro Leagues, including oral accounts from surviving players.

Myers, Walter Dean. *The Greatest: Muhammad Ali.* Myers examines the complex personality of one of the world's most famous people in light of political/historical events and the damaging effects of boxing as a career.

_____. *The Journal of Biddy Owens: The Negro Leagues—Birmingham, Alabama, 1948.* A fictional diary of a teenage boy who works for the Birmingham Black Barons describes the team's experiences, including the racism it faced throughout America.

_____. *Slam!* Greg "Slam" Harris has to get his act together off the court if he wants to escape the 'hood.

Powell, Randy. *Run if You Dare.* A teenage runner trying to find direction in his own life realizes that his father has none in his.

_____. *Three Clams and an Oyster.* Flint and his two flag-football-playing friends spend the weekend trying to find a replacement for Cade Savage, who is having a hard time dealing with a friend's death.

Ripslinger, Jon. *How I Fell in Love and Learned to Shoot Free Throws.* In his campaign to win the heart of Angel McPherson, Danny Henderson asks her to teach him how to shoot free throws, but then he discovers she has not just one secret but two.

Ritter, John H. *Choosing Up Sides.* The 13-year-old son of a small-town preacher in 1921 struggles against his left-handedness, which makes him an unusually good baseball pitcher but which his father views as evil.

_____. *Over the Wall.* Tyler needs to gain control of his temper if he ever expects to make the all-star baseball team.

Ritter, Lawrence S. *The Story of Baseball,* 3rd rev. and expanded ed. First-person oral histories of baseball players during the first 20 years of the twentieth century.

Sweeney, Joyce. *Players.* A team's basketball championship effort is jeopardized when a new player's ambition results in blackmail, tampering with another player's medication, and the discovery of a gun in a player's locker.

Trueman, Terry. *Cruise Control.* Athletic Paul tries to deal with his violent anger, especially regarding his father, who has left the family, as his brother Shawn's seizures become more severe.

Walker, Paul Robert. *Hoop Dreams.* The true story of two teenagers who see basketball as their way out of inner-city poverty.

Wallace, Rich. *Losing Is Not an Option.* Nine short stories take readers through the highlights of Ron's teenage years, most of them involving basketball and long-distance running.

_____. *Playing without the Ball: A Novel in Four Quarters.* Basketball means everything to Jay, but there are so many other things to deal with—his distant mother, his absent father, lusty Sarita, and lovely Julie.

_____. *Restless: A Ghost's Story.* After his death as a teenager, Frank describes his efforts to contact his living younger brother, Herbie, a hardworking high school senior who plays football and runs cross-country.

_____. *Shots on Goal.* The friendship between Bones Austin and his best friend, Joey, is jeopardized along with their soccer team's chance for a championship because of Bones's crush on Joey's girlfriend.

_____. *Wrestling Sturbridge.* Ben, a senior, is determined to take the top spot on the Sturbridge wrestling team so that he can escape the small town's limitations on his future.

Weaver, Will. *Farm Team.* With his father in jail, Billy has to run the family farm, but he manages to organize a baseball team of friends and migrants to play against the team from town.

_____. *Hard Ball.* Billy Baggs has to figure out how to get along with his archrival on the baseball team, and both boys try to deal with their fathers' unfair expectations.

_____. *Striking Out.* Billy Baggs is a talented pitcher, but his domineering father wants him working on their Minnesota family farm.

Wolff, Virginia Euwer. *Bat 6.* The traditional softball game in a small town in Oregon between 6th graders in 1949 turns into a brutal event that reveals hidden prejudices and discrimination.

Woodson, Jacqueline. *Hush.* Because their father testified against fellow police officers, two sisters and their parents are forced to adopt new identities in the Witness Protection Program, and running is the only constant in Toswiah's life.

Zusak, Marcus. *Fighting Ruben Wolfe.* Two brothers become boxers for money when their family's financial stability is threatened by their father's unemployment.

Chapter 8

WHAT'S NEXT: WHERE CAN I FIND MORE INFORMATION?

We have listed and described a number of books in the previous chapters that you may never have heard of before—and they represent only some of the thousands of readable, exciting, teachable books that have been published for teens during the past 40 or more years. How are teachers and librarians expected to know about so many good books? With several hundred new books being published for teens each year, reading every one is physically impossible. Even keeping *informed* about new books for teens can be exhausting. In the following pages we describe several ways that the most knowledgeable teachers and librarians use to keep themselves informed while they read as many books as time permits.

TALK WITH STUDENTS

For teachers, the best sources of information might possibly be your students, especially those who are avid readers. Consider the amount of time the average teenager spends at the local mall, where there is usually at least one major bookselling chain. Teens are sometimes more likely than some teachers to browse in bookstores or peruse the paperback racks in grocery stores and pharmacies. If your town has a good library, that may be another place where a lot of teens hang out. Sure, the kids often go there to socialize, but they also check out books.

If you're a librarian, question those kids whom you see most often hanging around your YA shelves. What kinds of books do they like best? What are their friends reading? Start a library teen advisory board; it can be one of the most valuable sources of information for you.

These student informants can tell you about the latest series book they've been reading—perhaps from the *Daughters of the Moon* series, or the *Buffy the Vampire Slayer* series, or whatever comes along to take their place. Or maybe it will be Lurlene McDaniel's latest "cryin' and dyin'" novel, or a graphic novel that might look to you like nothing more than a souped-up comic book. Along with books written for teenagers, you will see them reading the same mass-market paperbacks that are popular with adults—the latest John Grisham, Tom Clancy, or Danielle Steel. Never, *never* turn up your nose about what they are reading. Your goal should be to find out what they read, and why, not to impose your adult tastes on them.

If your school has a silent recreational reading period during which everyone is supposed to be reading something for 15 or 20 minutes, take a close look at what your students pull out of their backpacks during that reading time. (If your school doesn't have such a time set aside for pleasure reading, think about starting one.) Or, if you are "lucky" enough to be assigned to supervise a study hall, look carefully at what those captive students are reading when they are not doing homework. That's also a perfect time to chat with them one-on-one to see how they are responding to what they are reading.

In addition, at the beginning of each semester, or once or twice during the school year, distribute a brief questionnaire to your classes asking for information about their reading interests, habits, favorite authors, favorite titles, and most recent books read (for their own pleasure or information, not for school required reading).

Often when you ask a teenager if the book she or he is reading is good, you'll get a shrug of the shoulders and an unenthusiastic "It's okay." But don't give up there. Ask what the book is about and what, specifically, is good (or not good) about it. If you happen to be familiar with that book, or with another book by the same author, a dialogue will usually develop between you and the student.

Knowing what students find interesting is only the beginning of your job. You also have to be willing to read a couple of the books they recommend.

Another way to make contact with students is if they see you carrying a book or reading one during a silent reading period or study hall. Some student is likely to ask you about it. And if your book happens to look like something a teenager would ordinarily read, that's even better. She or he will want to know why you're reading one of *their* books. That will be the beginning of another dialogue.

If your dialogues are anything like those we have had with students, sooner or later one of your students is going to ask you to trade books. They will want to read your book, and they will expect you to read theirs. Even if their book turns out to be the worst thing you have ever read, you've learned something valuable about that student, while she or he has possibly found a new book or author that you were reading.

But what if you are teaching in a school where there are no free reading periods and no study halls, and it seems as if no one reads? Where can you find out about good books that teenagers might be interested in reading?

PERUSE CATALOGS

If you are a school library media specialist, you should automatically be receiving catalogs from major publishers several times a year (usually quarterly). If you aren't on the mailing list of Abrams; Candlewick; Farrar, Straus & Giroux; Front Street; Harcourt; HarperCollins; Henry Holt; Houghton Mifflin; Hyperion; Little, Brown; Orca; Peachtree; Penguin; Random House; Roaring Brook; Scholastic; Simon & Schuster; and other smaller companies that publish books for children and young adults, write them a request on your school's letterhead. Publishers' addresses are usually listed in their books as well as on the Internet.

If you are a teacher who buys a lot of books for your department or your own classroom, publishers will be happy to add you to their catalog mailing list. You can also pick up copies of catalogs by attending educational conferences where publishing companies display their wares.

In addition to catalogs from publishing houses, catalogs from paperback distributors have extensive and helpful lists of books, often by grade level, genre, and topic. So if you are interested in certain types of books—say, historical fiction or multicultural books—or a set of books on a specific theme—say, Teenagers in Turmoil or Adventure/Survival—those folks have already done much of your homework for you. (Be cautious, however: those packagers don't know your students, so some of the books on their lists may not be appropriate for your classroom or your community.) Many of those catalogs will also note which titles have won awards for quality, such as the Newbery Medal or the Coretta Scott King Award. Another positive thing about purchasing class sets of books from these distributors is that they will give you a discount of 20 or 30 percent, occasionally even more.

The largest and most popular distributors, according to most librarians and teachers, are (1) Baker and Taylor, and (2) Follett. You can reach them at

Baker and Taylor, Inc.
2907 Water Ridge Parkway
Charlotte, NC 28217
1-800-775-1800
Fax: 1-800-775-7480
www.btol.com
E-mail: btinfo@btol.com

Follett Library Resources
1340 Ridgeview Drive
McHenry, IL 60050
1-888-511-5114
Fax: 1-815-759-9831
www.follett.com
E-mail: customerservice@follett.com

Among the smaller paperback distributors throughout the country are

Adams Book Co., Inc.
537 Sackett Street
Brooklyn, NY 11217
1-800-221-0909
Fax: 1-888-229-2650
www.adamsbook.com
E-mail: customerservice@adamsbook.com

BMI Educational Services, Inc.
P.O. Box 800
Dayton, NJ 08810
1-800-222-8100
Fax: 1-800-986-9393
www.bmiedserv.com

Southwest Book Company
13003 H Murphy Road
Stafford, TX 77477
1-800-444-1228
Fax: 1-281-498-7566

Some distributors also produce their own teaching materials, the best one being Sundance. Contact them at

Sundance Publishing
P.O. Box 740
One Beeman Road
Northborough, MA 01532
1-800-343-8204
Fax: 1-800-456-2419
www.sundancepub.com

For a listing of other distributors, contact

Educational Paperback Association
P.O. Box 1399
East Hampton, NY 11937
www.edupaperback.org

If your school or library prefers paperbacks with hard covers, the most popular source is Perma-Bound Books, which carries more than 40,000 books and other media. Contact them at

Perma-Bound Books
617 East Vandalia Road
Jacksonville, IL 62650
1-800-637-6581
Fax: 1-800-511-1169
www.perma-bound.com
E-mail: books@perma-bound.com

BROWSE BOOKSTORES

Be sure to peruse the shelves at bookstores in your area. Be aware, though, that some local bookstores have an excellent selection of new and paperback books for young adults, while others have almost nothing for teens. Large chains, such as Borders and Barnes & Noble, will have an entire section devoted to YA books. You should know also that both Borders and Barnes & Noble offer teachers a discount on all books with your school identification. But in any type of store, shelf space is limited, so most stores will stock mainly those types of books that sell best—perhaps mysteries or fantasies or whatever happens to be popular at the moment—and have little space remaining for new hardcover books, with the exception of the latest award-winning titles and those by the best-known authors, like Gary Paulsen. No matter how good your local bookstore is, you'll be able to learn about more new books by reading reviews in professional journals.

SUBSCRIBE TO JOURNALS AND REVIEW SOURCES

There are publications to suit a variety of professional reader's needs and interests, some mainly for English teachers, others mainly for library media people. Admitting to personal bias here, we believe that the most useful publication—as well as the most affordable—for classroom teachers looking for good new books for teenagers is the *ALAN Review.*

ALAN stands for the Assembly on Literature for Adolescents of the National Council of Teachers of English (NCTE). If you are a teacher who is interested in specializing in books for adolescents, this is *the* resource for you. Unless you intend to become an officer in ALAN, you can join this organization and receive its journal without becoming a member of NCTE. Published three times a year, the *ALAN Review* contains several pages of reviews of new books in addition to articles by educators, librarians, and authors about using YAL in classrooms. Also, don't ignore publishers' ads in this journal or in the other journals listed below; they indicate what's new and noteworthy from the point of view of individual publishing companies. For memberships/subscriptions, contact

> *The ALAN Review*
> ALAN
> P.O. Box 10427
> Largo, FL 33773
> www.alan-ya.org
> E-mail: kaywell@tempest.coedu.usf.edu
> $20 per year; half-price for students (3 issues)

Note: All of the addresses, Web sites, and prices in this chapter were accurate when we went to press. Some addresses, and probably prices, are likely to change in time.

If you are a member of NCTE, you likely receive the *English Journal* six times a year and know that every issue contains either reviews of YA books or an article on some aspect of Young Adult Literature. Other articles in the journal occasionally focus on books in this field as well. If you teach English in high school and are not a member of NCTE, you ought to be. For memberships/subscriptions, contact

> *English Journal*
> National Council of Teachers of English
> 1111 West Kenyon Road
> Urbana, IL 61801-1096
> 1-800-369-6283
> www.ncte.org
> $65 per year for individuals; journal without membership: $25 (bimonthly)

If you teach in a middle school, you'll be more interested in *Voices from the Middle.* Each of the journal's four issues contains a section on books for middle school students, along with articles by educators and authors about using books in your classroom. Subscriptions are available as part of NCTE membership at

> *Voices from the Middle*
> National Council of Teachers of English
> 1111 West Kenyon Road
> Urbana, IL 61801-1096
> 1-800-369-6283
> www.ncte.org
> $60 per year for individuals; journal without membership: $20 (quarterly)

With NCTE membership you can get both the *English Journal* and *Voices from the Middle* for $85 a year.

As the *ALAN Review* is related to NCTE; the *SIGNAL Journal* is related to the International Reading Association (IRA). Published three times a year by the Special Interest Group—a Network on Adolescent Literature within the IRA, this journal features articles about YAL and reviews of new YA books. This is another bargain. Membership in the IRA is not required for a subscription to this journal. For subscriptions, contact

> *SIGNAL Journal*
> Patricia P. Kelly, SIGNAL Membership Chair
> Department of Teaching and Learning
> Virginia Tech University
> Blacksburg, VA 24061-0313
> $15 per year (3 issues)

Library media specialists are more likely to want information about library and media use as well as news and reviews of new books, and all of the following journals contain book reviews as well as articles and bibliographies, though each has a slightly different slant. Be aware also that most of these sources review books for children and adults as well as books for teens. Among the most popular are

> *Booklist*
> P.O. Box 607
> Mt. Morris, IL 61054-7564
> 1-888-350-0949
> www.ala.org/ala/booklist
> E-mail: blst@kable.com
> $79.95 per year (22 issues)

> *Book Links*
> P.O. Box 615
> Mt. Morris, IL 61054-7566
> 1-888-350-0950
> Fax: 1-815-734-5858
> www.ala.org/booklinks
> E-mail: blnk@kable.com
> $29.95 per year (bimonthly)

This publication, from the American Library Association (ALA), is helpful to teachers using thematic approaches and trying to make connections between books and classroom activities. Although it notes mostly books for children, middle school teachers will find the bibliographies, teaching and writing activities, and interviews with authors particularly valuable.

> *Bulletin for the Center of Children's Books*
> 50 East Daniel Street

Champaign, IL 61820
1-217-244-0324
Fax: 1-217-333-5603
www.lis.uiuc.edu/puboff/bccb
E-mail: bccb@alexia.lis.uiuc.edu
$50 per year (monthly)

The Horn Book Magazine
The Horn Book, Inc.
56 Roland Street, Suite 200
Charlestown, MA 02129
1-800-325-1170
Fax: 1-617-628-0882
www.hbook.com
$45 per year (bimonthly)

The Horn Book Guide
56 Roland Street, Suite 200
Charlestown, MA 02129
1-617-628-0225
Fax: 1-617-628-0882
www.hbook.com/guide
$47 per year (semiannually)

The *Guide* is a compilation of nearly 4,000 of the best books from the previous six months.

Kirkus Reviews
VNUeMedia
770 Broadway, 7th floor
New York, NY 10003
1-646-654-5865
Fax: 1-646-654-5518
www.kirkusreviews.com
E-mail: mhazzard@vnubspubs.com
$450 per year (semimonthly); includes online subscription

Kirkus reviews nearly 5,000 books a year. The archive database contains nearly 250,000 reviews dating back to 1933.

KLIATT Young Adult Paperback Book Guide
33 Bay State Road
Wellesley, MA 02481
1-781-237-7577
Fax: 781-237-7577
hometown.aol.com/kliatt
E-mail: kliatt@aol.com
$39 per year (6 issues)

MultiCultural Review
14497 N. Dale Mabry, Suite 205N
Tampa, FL 33618
1-800-600-4364
Fax: 1-813-264-2243
www.mcreview.com
$65 per year (quarterly)

Along with articles, bibliographies, and a teacher column, each issue provides insightful annotations of new books (organized by subject area), videos, and reference materials for educators and librarians seeking to keep up with the latest multicultural sources.

Publishers Weekly
360 Park Avenue
New York, NY 10010
1-800-278-2991
Fax: 1-818-478-4550
www.publishersweekly.com
$225 per year (weekly)

Deals with all aspects of the publishing industry.

School Library Journal
360 Park Avenue South
New York, NY 10010
1-800-728-2991
Fax: 1-818-478-4550
www.schoollibraryjournal.com
E-mail: custserv@espcomp.com
$124 per year (monthly)

Probably the most authoritative and respected journal for reviewing new books for children and adolescents.

Voice of Youth Advocates (VOYA)
15200 NBN Way
Blue Ridge Summit, PA 17214
1-800-233-1687
Fax: 717-794-3852
E-mail: tmiller@rowman.com
$42 per year (bimonthly)

VOYA is the liveliest and most teen-friendly of the professional journals. From its inception, *VOYA* has maintained its commitment to review— along with the usual realistic fiction, nonfiction, and reference materials— horror, science fiction, and fantasy that most other sources ignore. Like the *ALAN Review* and *SIGNAL*, *VOYA* focuses exclusively on books for teenage readers. All reviewed titles are rated by quality and expected popularity, along with an indication of grade level of interest.

Young Adult Library Services
50 East Huron Street
Chicago, IL 60611
1-800-545-2433 (press 5)
Fax: 1-312-944-2641
www.ala.org
$40 per year (included in YALSA membership dues) (twice yearly)

Containing no reviews of new books, the strength of this journal is in its articles about the field of YA books and in its "Update" section, which keeps readers up to date on book awards, resources, and professional conferences. (Replaces *Journal of Youth Services in Libraries*.)

READ PROFESSIONAL MAGAZINES AND JOURNALS ONLINE

Some of the aforementioned journals can be found on the Internet. They include

The ALAN Review
scholar.lib.vt.edu/ejournals
See also "Bill's Books" on www.alan-ya.org

Book Links
www.ala.org/booklinks

Booklist
www.ala.org/ala/booklist

The *Horn Book Magazine*
www.hbook.com

School Library Journal
www.schoollibraryjournal.com

CONTACT ORGANIZATIONS ONLINE

ALAN (Assembly on Literature for Adolescents)/NCTE
www.alan-ya.org

American Library Association
www.ala.org

International Reading Association
www.reading.org

National Council of Teachers of English
www.ncte.org

CONSULT BOOK AWARDS

Lists of award-winning books are always worth examining, although readers need to be aware of the selection criteria: Were the books chosen for their literary quality (as the Newbery Medal books are) or for their potential interest to teenagers as well as their literary quality (as the Best Books for Young Adults are)? Were those lists chosen by adults (as the Newbery and Best Books for Young Adults are) or were they selected by groups of teen readers themselves (as the IRA's Young Adult Choices and state book awards are)? Probably the most valuable list will be the one you compile, based on which titles appear on several awards lists. The most highly respected awards are

Michael L. Printz Award—An award established in 2000 for the best YA book of the year, presented by the Young Adult Library Services Association (YALSA) and *Booklist*. First recipient, 2000: *Monster* by Walter Dean Myers. 2001 winner: *Kit's Wilderness* by David Almond. 2002 winner: *A Step from Heaven* by An Na. 2003 winner: *Postcards from No-Man's Land* by Aidan Chambers. 2004 winner: *The First Part Last* by Angela Johnson. 2005 winner: *How I Live Now* by Meg Rosoff. Honor Books are also named.

Newbery Medal—For the best American children's book of the year, presented by the Association for Library Service to Children (ALSC) of the ALA. Recent winners: 2000: *Bud, Not Buddy* by Christopher Paul Curtis. 2001: *A Year Down Yonder* by Richard Peck. 2002: *A Single Shard* by Linda Sue Park. 2003: *Crispin: Cross of Lead* by Avi. 2004: *A Tale of Despereaux* by Kate de Camillo. 2005: *Kira-Kira* by Cynthia Kadohata.

Coretta Scott King Award—For the year's best book by an African American author. 2000 winner: *Monster* by Walter Dean Myers. 2001 winner: *Miracle's Boys* by Jacqueline Woodson. 2002 winner: *The Land* by Mildred D. Taylor. 2003 winner: *Bronx Masquerade* by Nikki Grimes. 2004 winner: *The First Part Last* by Angela Johnson. 2005 winner: *Remember the Journey to School Integration* by Toni Morrison.

National Book Award, Young People's Literature—Best book of the year, presented by a committee selected by the National Book Foundation. 2000 winner: *Homeless Bird* by Gloria Whelan. 2001 winner: *True Believer* by Virginia Euwer Wolff. 2002 winner: *The House of the Scorpion* by Nancy Farmer. 2003 winner: *The Canning Season* by Polly Horvath. 2004 winner: *Godless* by Pete Hautman.

YALSA Best Books for Young Adults—Each year a committee of young adult librarians from the ALA pick several dozen of the best books for teens, fiction as well as nonfiction, along with the Top Ten of those.

YALSA Quick Picks for Young Adults—Each year a committee of YA librarians from the ALA pick the best books for reluctant teen readers, fiction as well as nonfiction, as well as the Top Ten of those, that are guaranteed to attract reluctant readers.

Popular Paperbacks for Young Adults—Each year a committee of YA librarians from the ALA pick the best paperbacks in four categories (which vary each year). The 2004–5 categories were Fairy Tales, Heartbreak, Oddballs, and Horror.

The ALEX Awards—Given to the top 10 adult books expected to be of interest to teenagers each year, presented by YALSA and *Booklist*.

Edgar Allan Poe Award (the Edgar), Young Adult Category—Best American mystery/thriller for young adults, presented by the Mystery Writers of America. 2004 winner: *Acceleration* by Graham McNamee.

***Boston Globe–Horn Book* Award**—The best fiction, nonfiction, and illustrated book of the year. 2000 winner: *The Folk Keeper* by Franny Billingsley. 2001 winner: *Carver: A Life in Poems* by Marilyn Nelson. 2002 winner: *Lord of the Deep* by Graham Salisbury.

***Los Angeles Times* Book Prize, Young Adult Fiction Category**—Best young adult novel of the year. 2002 winner: *The Land* by Mildred D. Taylor.

Scott O'Dell Award for Historical Fiction—Best American historical novel of the year set in the New World. 2001 winner: *The Land* by Mildred D. Taylor. 2002 winner: *Trouble Don't Last* by Shelley Pearsall. 2004 winner: *The River between Us* by Richard Peck. 2005 winner: *Worth* by A. LaFaye.

Golden Kite Award—Presented by the Society of Children's Book Writers and Illustrators (SCBWI), the best book for children or young adults written by a member of the organization. 2002 winner: *True Believer* by Virginia Euwer Wolff.

Delacorte Press Prize for Best Young Adult Novel—The best submission of the year from a new writer, chosen by the editors of Delacorte Press. 2001 winner: *Cuba Fifteen* by Nancy Osa. 2002 winner: *Ostrich Eye* by Beth Cooley.

Other Lists and Awards

American Bookseller's Pick of the Lists

New York Public Library Books for the Teen Age—announced in March.

***Booklist* Editor's Choices**—January edition of *Booklist*.

***Horn Book* Fanfare Books**—December issue of the *Horn Book Magazine*.

***School Library Journal* Best Books of the Year**—December issue of *SLJ*.

Teens' Top Ten—Sponsored jointly by *VOYA* and YALSA, teens in five selected school and public libraries nationwide choose the best 10 books of the year during Teen Read Week in October.

Young Adult Choices—Best books selected by teens across the country, sponsored by the IRA, published in the November issue of the *Journal of Adolescent and Adult Literacy*.

Various State Children's Book Awards—for example, the Nutmeg Award (Connecticut), Texas Bluebonnet Award, Utah Book Award, California Young Readers Medal, Oregon Book Award, Colorado Blue Spruce Young Adult Book Award, Kentucky Bluegrass Award, and Volunteer State Young Adult Book Award.

Margaret A. Edwards Award—For lifetime achievement in writing for young adults, presented by YALSA and *School Library Journal.* Past recipients: S. E. Hinton, Richard Peck, M. E. Kerr, Robert Cormier, Lois Duncan, Walter Dean Myers, Cynthia Voigt, Judy Blume, Gary Paulsen, Madeleine L'Engle, Anne McCaffrey, Chris Crutcher, and Robert Lipsyte. 2002 recipient: Paul Zindel. 2003 recipient: Nancy Garden. 2004 recipient: Ursula K. Le Guin.

The ALAN Award—For outstanding contributions to YAL, presented by the Assembly on Literature for Adolescents of NCTE. Past recipients: Robert Cormier, Sue Ellen Bridgers, Madeleine L'Engle, Katherine Paterson, Cynthia Voigt, Richard Peck, Gary Paulsen, Chris Crutcher, Walter Dean Myers, Mildred D. Taylor, S. E. Hinton, Robert Lipsyte, M. E. Kerr, and Paul Zindel, along with librarians such as Patty Campbell and educators such as Ted Hipple, Ken Donelson, Alleen Pace Nilsen, M. Jerry Weiss, Robert Small, and Don Gallo. 2004 recipient: Jacqueline Woodson.

Note: You can find the most recent recipients of many of these awards on the Web sites of the organizations that make these awards. For example, for all YALSA book awards (for example, Best Books, Quick Picks, Alex Awards, and the Edwards Award), go to www.ala.org/yalsa.

UTILIZE RESOURCE BOOKS

Although any of the aforementioned journals will be of great value to teachers and librarians seeking information about new books, there are a number of excellent resources that provide annotated bibliographies, lists of titles for thematic approaches, approaches to booktalking, suggestions for promoting reading and library use, ways of teaching literature, and dealing with censorship.

Bibliographies and Thematic Approaches

Best Books for Young Adults, 2nd ed., by Betty B. Carter, with Sally Estes and Linda Waddle

The Best of the Latino Heritage: A Guide to the Best Juvenile Books about Latino People and Cultures by Elizabeth Schon

The Best Years of Their Lives: A Resource Guide for Teenagers in Crisis, 2nd ed., ed. Stephanie Zvirin

Book Bridges for ESL Students: Using Young Adult and Children's Literature to Teach ESL Students by Suzanne Reid

Books for You: An Annotated Booklist for Senior High, 14th ed., ed. Kylene Beers and Teri S. Lesesne

Building an ESL Collection for Young Adults: A Bibliography of Recommended Fiction and Nonfiction for Schools and Public Libraries by Laura Hibbets McCaffery

The Bully in the Book and in the Classroom by C. J. Bott

Declarations of Independence: Empowered Girls in Young Adult Literature, 1990–2001 by Joanne Brown and Nancy St. Clair

Genreflecting: A Guide to Reading Interests in Genre Fiction by Diana Tixier Herald

Growing Up Is Hard to Do, ed. Sally Estes

Hearing All the Voices: Multicultural Books for Adolescents by Mary Ann Darby and Miki Pryne

Lesbian and Gay Voices: An Annotated Bibliography and Guide to Literature for Children and Young Adults by Frances Ann Day

More than a Game: Sports Literature for Young Adults by Chris Crowe

The Mystery Readers' Advisory: The Librarian's Clues to Murder and Mayhem by John Charles, Joanna Morrison, and Candace Clark

Out of the Closet and into the Classroom: Homosexuality in Books for Young People, 2nd ed., ed. Laurel Clyde and Marjorie Lobban

Radical Change: Books for Youth in a Digital Age by Eliza T. Dresang

Radical Reads: 101 YA Novels on the Edge by Joni Richards Bodart

Readers' Advisory Guide to Genre Fiction by Joyce G. Saricks

Recasting the Past: The Middle Ages in Young Adult Literature by Rebecca Barnhouse

The Romance Readers' Advisory: The Librarian's Guide to Love in the Stacks by Ann Bouricius

The Science Fiction and Fantasy Readers' Advisory: The Librarian's Guide to Cyborgs, Aliens, and Sorcerers by Derek M. Buker

Serious about Series: Evaluations and Annotations of Teen Fiction in Paperback Series by Silk Makowski

Using Picture Books to Teach Literary Devices: Recommended Books for Children and Young Adults, vol. 3, by Susan Hall

Using Young Adult Literature: Thematic Activities Based on Gardner's Multiple Intelligences by Jacqueline N. Glasgow

Your Reading: An Annotated Booklist for Middle School and Junior High, 11th ed., ed. Jean E. Brown and Elaine C. Stephens

Booktalking

Booktalk!, 5 vols., by Joni Richards Bodart

Booktalking the Award Winners, 4 vols., by Joni Richards Bodart

Booktalks and More: Motivating Teens to Read by Lucy Schall

Talk It Up! Book Discussion Programs for Young People, ed. Ann Brouse

Teen Book Discussion Groups @ the Library by Constance B. Dickerson

Dealing with Censorship

At the Schoolhouse Gate: Lessons in Intellectual Freedom by Gloria Pipkin and Releah Lent

Censorship and Selection: Issues and Answers for Schools, 3rd ed., by Henry Reichman

Censorship and the School Library Media Center by Nancy Kravitz

Hit List for Young Adults 2: Frequently Challenged Books by Teri S. Lesesne and Rosemary Chance

Rationales for Teaching Young Adult Literature, ed. Louann Reid, with Jamie Hayes Neufeld

Library Promotion and Development

Connecting Young Adults and Libraries: A How-To-Do-It Manual, 3rd ed., by Patrick Jones, Michele Gorman, and Tricia Suellentrop

A Core Collection for Young Adults by Patrick Jones, Patricia Taylor, and Kirsten Edwards

Library Teen Advisory Groups: A VOYA Guide by Diane Tuccillo

New Directions for Library Service to Young Adults by Young Adult Library Services Association (YALSA) and Patrick Jones

Teaching Reading and Literature

Adolescent Literature as a Complement to the Classics, 4 vols., ed. Joan F. Kaywell

Adolescents Talk about Reading: Exploring Resistance to and Engagement with Text by Anne R. Reeves

Against Borders: Promoting Books for a Multicultural World by Hazel Rochman

Authors' Insights: Turning Teenagers into Readers and Writers, ed. Donald R. Gallo

Better than Life by Daniel Pennac

Book Bridges for ESL Students: Using Young Adult Literature and Children's Literature to Teach ESL by Suzanne Reid

Books and Beyond: Thematic Approaches to Teaching Literature in High School, ed. Gail P. Gregg and Pamela S. Carroll

Conflict and Connection: The Psychology of Young Adult Literature by Sharon A. Stringer

Even Hockey Players Read: Boys, Literacy, and Learning by David Booth

Exploding the Myths: The Truth about Teenagers and Reading by Marc Aronson

Heirs to Shakespeare: Reinventing the Bard in Young Adult Literature by Megan Lynn Isaac

Into Focus: Understanding and Creating Middle School Readers, ed. Kylene Beers and Barbara G. Samuels

I Won't Read and You Can't Make Me: Reaching Reluctant Teen Readers by Marilyn Reynolds

Literature for Today's Young Adults, 7th ed., by Kenneth L. Donelson and Alleen Pace Nilsen

Making the Match: The Right Book for the Right Reader and the Right Time by Teri S. Lesesne

Radical Reads: 101 YA Novels on the Edge by Joni Richards Bodart

Reaching Reluctant Young Adult Readers: A Handbook for Librarians and Teachers by Edward T. Sullivan

Reading Their World: The Young Adult Novel in the Classroom, 2nd ed., ed. Virginia R. Monseau and Gary M. Salvner

Teaching Multicultural Literature in Grades 9–12: Moving beyond the Canon, ed. Arlette Ingram Willis

Teaching Reading in High School English Classes, ed. Bonnie O. Ericson

United in Diversity: Using Multicultural Young Adult Literature in the Classroom, ed. Jean E. Brown and Elaine C. Stephens

Using Literature to Help Troubled Teenagers Cope with Family Issues, ed. Joan F. Kaywell

Using Literature to Help Troubled Teenagers Cope with Health Issues, ed. Cynthia Ann Bowman

Using Literature to Help Troubled Teenagers Cope with Identity Issues, ed. Jeffrey S. Kaplan

Using Literature to Help Troubled Teenagers Cope with Societal Issues, ed. Pamela S. Carroll

Using Young Adult Literature in the English Classroom, 2nd ed, by John H. Bushman and Kay Parks Bushman

When Kids Can't Read—What Teachers Can Do: A Guide for Teachers, 6–12 by Kylene Beers

Young Adult Literature in the Classroom: Reading it, Teaching It, Loving It, ed. Joan B. Elliott and Mary M. Dupuis

Young Adult Literature: The Heart of the Middle School Curriculum by Lois T. Stover

EXAMINE AUTHOR BIOGRAPHIES

For teachers and students seeking more information about favorite authors than dust-jacket blurbs provide, there are several sources. The most extensive (and expensive) print information is found in the *Something about the Author* (*SATA*) series published by Thomson Gale. Those are also available on the Internet at Gale Virtual Reference Library (www.gale.com/eBooks).

The St. James Press in 1999 published a very large one-volume edition of the *St. James Guide to Young Adult Writers* that contains biographical, bibliographical, and critical information on nearly 500 authors of fiction, drama, and poetry for teenagers, from Richard Adams to Paul Zindel.

In 1997 Scribner's published a reader-friendly three volume set of *Writers for Young Adults,* edited by Ted Hipple, and followed that with an additional volume (*Writers for Young Adults, Supplement I*) in 2000.

Author Talk, compiled and edited by Leonard S. Marcus, published in 2000, features conversations with 15 authors, including Judy Blume, Bruce Books, Lois Lowry, Gary Paulsen, and Seymour Simon. With lots of white space and selected photographs, it is the most attractive of the print sources of information about YA authors.

The most extensive critical information about selected authors and their books can be found in the *Presenting . . .* series (as in *Presenting Walter Dean Myers*), published originally by Twayne and then by Scarecrow Press.

Print information about authors and their books, however, is unfortunately out of date by the time it is published. The Internet, on the other hand, allows readers to locate the latest information about authors and their books. You can search the Web sites of major publishers for information about their authors (be aware, though, that some publishers do not update their information as regularly as they should, and many authors publish books with more than one company). Most authors have their own Web site, some more elaborate than others. The most valuable site for accurate and up-to-date information about YA authors is Authors4Teens.com, where publications and awards are updated continually and you can find the most extensive interviews of the most famous authors who write for teens. (You'll also find a variety of photographs of each author, a list of places where the authors will be appearing in the near future, news about the YA publishing world, and links to numerous other sources.)

DISCOVER WEB SITES

You can go to Amazon.com or any of the other online booksellers to find reviews of recently published books by any author. And many organizations have Web sites that provide reviews of new books and opportunities for teens to review and chat with others about books they've been reading. All of the sites are free except where noted below.

Amazon.com Pages for Teens

www.amazon.com (click on "Teens" on the Books menu)
Recommended new books, articles, author interviews, and so on for teens.

Author and Illustrator Links

www.cbcbooks.org/html/aboutauthors.htm

Locate information about authors and illustrators through the Children's Book Council.

www.scbwi.org/member.htm

Locate the sites of members of the Society of Children's Book Writers and Illustrators.

Author Interviews, Bibliographies, Awards, Photos, and Appearances

www.Authors4Teens.com

By subscription only, but it includes the most up-to-date information and the most extensive interviews *anywhere* (conducted by Don Gallo) and is updated frequently, with new authors added continually.

Booklists for Young Adults

www.seemore.mi.org/booklists

A place to find all sorts of lists of books for teens, including biographies, best books, Harry Potter read-alikes, and fiction categorized by topic (from abuse to war), compiled by Maggie Rohde. (Not updated recently.)

Book Rap

www.discover.tased.edu.au/ec/teachers/websites/webprojects/book_raps/book_raps.htm

A site where teens (singly or in groups) can discuss books scheduled on the site's calendar.

Books for Boys

www.guysread.com

A site developed by author Jon Scieszka to encourage boys to read.

Children's Literature Resources

www.cynthialeitichsmith.com/youngadult.htm

Resources and recommended books for children and teens from Cynthia Leitich Smith.

The Children's Literature Web Guide

www.acs.ucalgary.ca/~dkbrown/index.html

Internet resources about books for children and young adults, with lots of lists (award-winning books, banned books, books about specific subjects). Contains discussion boards and links to various authors' Web sites.

Connecting Young Adults and Libraries

www.connectingya.com/index2.html

Librarian/author Patrick Jones's site, offering subject lists and links to other sites about books for teens.

Cooperative Children's Book Center

www.soemadison.wisc.edu/ccbc

Reviews of new books and discussions of related topics from the University of Wisconsin–Madison.

Free Speech and Harry Potter Lovers

www.kidspeakonline.org

A place to find information about free speech for kids, including efforts to ban Harry Potter books.

Index to YA Sites in Libraries

yahelp.suffolk.lib.ny.us/virtual.html

A directory of sites, with links, at public libraries that have their own Web pages for teens.

Kay E. Vandergrift's Young Adult Literature Page

www.scils.rutgers.edu/~kvander/YoungAdult/index.html

The famous Rutgers educator's site, with commentary by Vandergrift about her personal favorite books for teens.

No Flying, No Tights

sidekicks.noflyingnotights.com

A lively Web site by librarian Robin Brenner that reviews graphic novels for teens; includes a Core List, Top Ten List, Best of the Rest, and For Middle Schoolers.

Publishers' Home Pages

www.cbcbooks.org/about/members.html

This Children's Book Council site will get you to a listing of all major publishers of books for children and young adults. Click on "online list of current CBC members."

Reading Rants!

tln.lib.mi.us/~amutch/jen

One of the liveliest sites on the Net for teens as well as teachers and librarians, featuring no-nonsense reviews of new books written by YA librarian Jennifer Hubert, with lots of lists of recommended titles.

Richie's Picks: Great Books for Children and Young Adults

www.richiespicks.com

Richie Partington, one of the most prolific readers of books for teens, provides dozens of honest and enthusiastic reviews of new books and includes lists of the best books from previous years.

Smartwriters

www.smartwriters.com

A site for anyone who reads, writes, or teaches literature for kids.

Teen Genreflecting

www.genrefluent.com

The world of genre fiction reviewed by Diana Tixier Herald.

Teen Reading

www.ala.org/ala/yalsa/teenreading/teenreading.htm

Information about Teen Read Week, book awards, and recommended reading.

YALSA

www.ala.org/yalsa

Home page of the Young Adult Library Services Association of the ALA, with lists of YALSA book awards (Best Books for Young Adults, Quick Picks, and so on).

Some YA Author Web Sites

Elaine Marie Alphin—www.elainemariealphin.com

Laurie Halse Anderson—www.writerlady.com

Sandy Asher—www.usawrites4kids.drury.edu/author/asher

Avi—www.avi-writer.com

T. A. Baron—www.tabarron.com

Joan Bauer—www.joanbauer.com

William Bell—www.orillia.org/williambell

James W. Bennett—www.jameswbennett.com

Gary L. Blackwood—www.mowrites4kids.drury.edu/authors/blackwood

Judy Blume—www.judyblume.com

Joseph Bruchac—www.josephbruchac.com

Meg Cabot —www.megcabot.com

Elisa Carbone—www.elisacarbone.com

Alden R. Carter—www.aldencarter.com

Aidan Chambers—www.aidanchambers.co.uk

Bruce Coville—www.brucecoville.com

Sharon Creech—www.sharoncreech.com

Chris Crowe—www.chriscrowe.com

Chris Crutcher—www.chriscrutcher.com

Terry Davis—www.terrydavis.net

Charles deLint—www.charlesdelint.com

Sarah Dessen—www.sarahdessen.com

Peter Dickinson—www.peterdickinson.com

Sharon Draper—www.sharondraper.com

Alex Flinn—www.alexflinn.com

Jack Gantos—www.jackgantos.com

Nancy Garden—www.nancygarden.com

Jean Craighead George—www.jeancraigheadgeorge.com

Gail Giles—www.gailgiles.com

Mel Glenn—www.melglenn.com

Bette Greene—www.bettegreene.com

Nikki Grimes—www.nikkigrimes.com

Mary Downing Hahn—www.childrensbookguild.org/hahn.html

Virginia Hamilton—www.virginiahamilton.com

Brent Hartinger—www.brenthartinger.com

Daniel Hayes—www.danielhayes.com

Linda Oatman High—www.lindaoatmanhigh.com

S. E. Hinton—www.sehinton.com

Will Hobbs—www.willhobbsauthor.com

Kimberly Willis Holt—www.kimberlyholt.com

Jeanette Ingold—www.jeanetteingold.com

Brian Jacques—www.redwall.org

M. E. Kerr—www.mekerr.com

Jackie French Koller—www.jackiefrenchkoller.com

Kathleen Krull—www.kathleenkrull.com

Francess Lantz—www.silcom.com/~writer

Kathryn Lasky—www.kathrynlasky.com/newfilm/homelsk.htm

Madeleine L'Engle—www.madeleinelengle.com

Sonia Levitin—www.bol.ucla.edu/~slevitin

Robert Lipsyte—www.robertlipsyte.com

Janet Taylor Lisle—www.janettaylorlisle.com

David Lubar—www.davidlubar.com

Kevin Major—www4.newcomm.net/kmajor

John Marsden—www.panmacmillan.com.au/johnmarsden

Elsa Marston—www.elsamarston.com.

Lurlene McDaniel—www.eclectics.com/lurlenemcdaniel

Joyce McDonald—www.joycemcdonald.net

Robin McKinley—www.robinmckinley.com

Carolyn Meyer—www.readcarolyn.com

Ben Mikaelsen—www.benmikaelsen.com

Lensey Namioka—www.lensey.com

Donna Jo Napoli—www.donnajonapoli.com

John Neufeld—www.johnneufeld.com

Lesléa Newman—www.lesleakids.com

Garth Nix—eidolon.net/homesite.html?author=garth_nix or www.garthnix.co.uk

Katherine Paterson—www.terabithia.com

Gary Paulsen—www.garypaulsen.com

Shelley Pearsall—www.shelleypearsall.com

Richard Peck—www.richardpeck.smartwriters.com

Rodman Philbrick—www.rodmanphilbrick.com

Meredith Ann Pierce—www.moonandunicorn.com

Tamora Pierce—www.tamora-pierce.com (see also www.sheroescentral.com)

Randy Powell—www.randypowell.com

Marsha Qualey—www.marshaqualey.com

Dian Curtis Regan—www.diancurtisregan.com

John H. Ritter—www.johnhritter.com

Willo Davis Roberts—www.willodavisroberts.com

Sara Ryan—www.sararyan.com

Graham Salisbury—www.grahamsalisbury.com

Neal Shusterman—www.storyman.com

Gloria Skurzynski—www.gloriabooks.com

Arthur Slade—www.arthurslade.com

Zilpha Keatley Snyder—www.zksnyder.com

Sonya Sones—www.sonyasones.com

Gary Soto—www.garysoto.com

Jerry Spinelli—www.jerryspinelli.com

Todd Strasser—www.toddstrasser.com

Rob Thomas—www.hieran.com/rob

Terry Trueman—www.truemannews.com

Will Weaver—www.intraart.com/willweaver

Rosemary Wells—www.rosemarywells.com

Nancy Werlin—www.nancywerlin.com

Rita Williams-Garcia—www.ritawg.com

Ellen Wittlinger—www.ellenwittlinger.com

Jane Yolen—www.janeyolen.com

Note: All these sites were accurate at the time of publication.

ATTEND CONFERENCES AND WORKSHOPS

One of the most exciting aspects of developing an interest in YA books is that the authors in this field are *alive*. Not only can you read their works, but you can also write to them (and get a response), hear them speak at conferences, invite them to visit your school and/or library, and talk with them face-to-face as they autograph books for you in the exhibit hall of the convention center.

Part of the program of every national conference of NCTE, the IRA, and the ALA includes appearances by authors of YA books. The same is often true of regional and state conferences of affiliates of those organizations, though with smaller numbers of authors participating. In addition to author appearances, other conference sessions are likely to focus on specific aspects of books for teenagers (for example, new multicultural books for middle school classrooms, or new short-story and poetry anthologies for teens), and booksellers and paperback distributors usually exhibit the latest titles of interest to young readers.

The most extensive experience you can get in this field is by attending the two-day ALAN Workshop, part of the annual convention of NCTE, held the Monday and Tuesday before Thanksgiving. For two solid days you can listen to famous authors and panels of experts talk about writing books for teenagers and teaching literature in grades 6–12. In addition, each participant receives a hefty package of books, usually one book from each of the 20 or more authors on the program. A relaxing wine and cheese party also accompanies the workshop, where you can chat personally with the authors and other workshop participants—perhaps Richard Peck, Jack Gantos, Joan Bauer, M. E. Kerr, Walter Dean Myers, or some of the newer writers in the field. You will go home loaded with books, filled with new ideas, and invigorated by the possibilities.

You don't have to be a member of the sponsoring organizations in order to attend these conferences and workshops, though registration fees are usually lower for members. And since it is through the journals, newsletters, and organizational mailings that these conferences are announced, it pays to be a member.

COMMUNICATE WITH COLLEAGUES

Although resources listed in textbooks are usually limited to published materials and Web sites, we believe that the most valuable resource of all is the colleagues with whom we share common interests. If such people are in your building, so much the better. But they may even be on the other side of the country. The important thing is that you communicate with each other: through phone calls, through e-mails, through letters. What have you read lately? What do you think of so-and-so's latest book? What books seem to be the most popular in your school right now? What books are you teaching with the greatest success this year?

Almost every time we, the authors of this book, send an e-mail or talk with each other or with our closest colleagues, one of us is likely to say, "Have you read such-and-such yet?" When we correspond with friends and colleagues across the country, we almost always mention our responses to books they had recommended earlier, then suggest good books we've read recently. Sometimes we even swap copies of new books when we can't wait another day to read the latest from Chris Crutcher, Will Hobbs, Laurie Halse Anderson, or some hot new writer a publisher has just introduced to one of us.

If you don't yet have any friends who have discovered the joys of YAL, be sure to attend one of the conferences we noted above; talk with people there and find a new friend willing to correspond with you a few times a year. Or register for a course on YAL or literature for adolescents at your local college or university (assuming that such a course focuses on contemporary books and not on *Ivanhoe, Little Women,* and *Great Expectations*), and then team up with someone from that class who is willing to continue the dialogue started in class.

If you can find several people within easy driving range of some central location (like your home or local library), you might consider starting a YA book discussion group that meets once a month to share responses to some agreed-upon title and hear about whatever books members are reading. A discussion over snacks or a meal is even better.

As more schools expand their online facilities, you and your students can communicate with other teachers and students across the country, discussing books you all have read, exchanging responses and recommendations. Your future sources of information can be worldwide and shared instantly.

WORKS CITED

For each of the titles below, we have indicated the most recent paperback publisher, if a paperback edition is available; for the newest titles, only the hardcover was available at the time of this writing. The date following each title indicates the year the book was first published in the United States. For modern classics (e.g., *Walden*), we note the most popular paperback edition. No publisher is listed for older classics (e.g., *The Odyssey, Jane Eyre, Julius Caesar*), since several editions are available.

MAJOR LITERARY WORKS

Ackroyd, Peter. *Voyages through Time: The Beginning*. DK, 2003.
_____. *Voyages through Time: Escape from Earth*. DK, 2004.
Aczel, Amir D. *The Riddle of the Compass: The Invention that Changed the World*. Harvest Books, 2001.
Adams, Simon. *Visual Timeline of the 20th Century*. DK, 1996.
Adoff, Arnold. *The Basket Counts*. Simon & Schuster, 2000.
Adoff, Jaime. *Names Will Never Hurt Me*. Dutton, 2004.
_____. *The Song Shoots out of My Mouth: A Celebration of Music*. Dutton, 2002.
Allen, Thomas B. *Offerings at the Wall: Artifacts from the Vietnam Veterans Memorial Collection*. Turner Publishing, 1995.
Allende, Isabel. *City of the Beasts*. HarperCollins, 2002.
Almond, David. *Kit's Wilderness*. Laurel-Leaf, 2000.
Alphin, Elaine Marie. *Simon Says*. Harcourt, 2002.

Alshalabi, Firyal. *Summer 1990*. Aunt Strawberry Books, 1999.

Alvarez, Julia. *Before We Were Free*. Laurel-Leaf, 2002.

_____. *In the Time of the Butterflies*. Plume, 1994.

Al-Windawi, Thura. *Thura's Diary: My Life in Wartime Iraq*. Viking, 2004.

Anderson, Laurie Halse. *Catalyst*. Viking, 2002.

_____. *Fever, 1793*. Aladdin, 2000.

_____. *Speak*. Speak, 1999.

Anderson, M. T. *Feed*. Candlewick, 2002.

The Anne Frank House. *Anne Frank in the World, 1929–1945*. Knopf, 2001.

Antle, Nancy. *Lost in the War*. Puffin, 2000.

Appleman-Jurman, Alicia. *Alicia: My Story*. Bantam, 1988.

Armstrong, Jennifer. *Becoming Mary Mehan*. Laurel-Leaf, 1996, 1997.

_____, ed. *Shattered: Stories of Children and War*. Laurel-Leaf, 2002.

_____. *Shipwreck at the Bottom of the World: The Extraordinary True Story of Shackleton and the Endurance*. Crown, 1998.

_____, ed. *What a Song Can Do: 12 Riffs on the Power of Music*. Knopf, 2004.

Armstrong, Jennifer, and Nancy Butcher. *Fire-Us: The Kindling*. HarperCollins, 2002.

Ashabranner, Brent. *Always to Remember: The Story of the Vietnam Veterans Memorial*. Scholastic, 1988.

Asher, Sandy. *Summer Smith Begins*. Bantam, 1986.

Atkins, Catherine. *Alt Ed*. Speak, 2003.

_____. *When Jeff Comes Home*. Puffin, 1999.

Atkins, Jeannine. *Wings and Rockets: The Story of Women in Air and Space*. Farrar, Straus & Giroux, 2003.

Attema, Martha. *When the War Is Over*. Orca, 2003.

Auch, Mary Jane. *Ashes of Roses*. Laurel-Leaf, 2002.

Avi. *Beyond the Western Sea, Book 1: The Escape from Home*. HarperTrophy, 1996.

_____. *Beyond the Western Sea, Book 2: Lord Kirkle's Money*. HarperTrophy, 1996.

_____. *Crispin: The Cross of Lead*. Hyperion, 2002.

_____. *Don't You Know There's a War On?* HarperTrophy, 2001.

_____. *Nothing but the Truth: A Documentary Novel*. HarperTrophy, 1991.

_____. *Romeo and Juliet—Together (and Alive!) at Last*. HarperTrophy, 1987.

_____. *The True Confessions of Charlotte Doyle*. HarperTrophy, 1990.

Ayres, Katherine. *Macaroni Boy*. Delacorte, 2003.

_____. *North by Night: A Story of the Underground Railroad*. Dell Yearling, 1998.

_____. *Stealing South: A Story of the Underground Railroad*. Dell Yearling, 2001.

Bagdasarian, Adam. *Forgotten Fire*. Laurel-Leaf, 2000.

Barnes, Joyce Annette. *Amistad: A Junior Novel*. Puffin, 1997.

Barrett, William E. *Lilies of the Field*. Warner Books, 1962.

Bartoletti, Susan Campbell. *No Man's Land: A Young Soldier's Story*. Blue Sky Press, 1999.

Bauer, Joan. *Hope Was Here*. Puffin, 2000.

_____. *Rules of the Road*. G. P. Putnam's Sons, 1998.

Bechard, Margaret. *Hanging on to Max*. Roaring Brook Press, 2002.

Beckett, Samuel. *Krapp's Last Tape and Other Dramatic Pieces*. Grove Press, 1970.

_____. *Waiting for Godot*. Grove Press, 1954.

Bell, William. *Death Wind*. Orca Soundings, 2002.

_____. *Zack*. Simon Pulse, 1999.

Bennett, Cherie. *Life in the Fat Lane*. Laurel-Leaf, 1998.

Bennett, Cherie, and Jeff Gottesfeld. *Anne Frank and Me*. Puffin, 2001.

Bennett, James. *The Squared Circle*. Scholastic Signature, 1995.

Betancourt, Jeanne. *My Name Is ~~Brain~~ Brian*. Scholastic, 1993.

Billingsley, Franny. *The Folk Keeper*. Aladdin, 1999.

Bitton-Jackson, Livia. *I Have Lived a Thousand Years: Growing Up in the Holocaust*. Aladdin, 1997.

_____. *Hello, America*. Simon & Schuster, 2005.

_____. *My Bridges of Hope: Searching for Life and Love after Auschwitz*. Simon Pulse, 1999.

Blackwood, Gary. *Shakespeare's Scribe*. Puffin, 2000.

_____. *Shakespeare's Spy*. Puffin, 2003.

_____. *The Shakespeare Stealer*. Puffin, 1998.

_____. *The Year of the Hangman*. Speak, 2002.

Bloor, Edward. *Tangerine*. Scholastic, 1997.

Bode, Janet. *Trust and Betrayal: Real Life Stories of Friends and Enemies*. Laurel-Leaf, 1996.

Bohrer, Melissa Lukeman. *Glory, Passion, and Principle: The Story of Eight Remarkable Women at the Core of the American Revolution*. Atria Books, 2003.

Bolden, Tonya, ed. *33 Things Every Girl Should Know about Women's History: From Suffragettes to Skirt Lengths to the E.R.A.* Crown, 2002.

Bolt, Robert. *A Man for All Seasons: A Play in Two Acts*. Vintage Books, 1960.

Bradbury, Ray. *Fahrenheit 451*. Del Ray, 1953.

Bradley, James, with Ron Powers, adapted by Michael French. *Flags of Our Fathers: Heroes of Iwo Jima*. Delacorte, 2001.

Bradley, Kimberly Brubaker. *For Freedom: The Story of a French Spy*. Delacorte, 2003.

Brenaman, Miriam. *Evvy's Civil War*. Speak, 2002.

Breslin, Theresa. *Remembrance*. Delacorte, 2002.

Bridgers, Sue Ellen. *All We Know of Heaven*. Banks Channel Books, 1996.

_____. *Permanent Connections*. Banks Channel Books, 1987.

Bridgman, Roger. *1000 Inventions and Discoveries*. DK, 2002.

Bronte, Charlotte. *Jane Eyre*. 1847.

Brooks, Bruce. *Midnight Hour Encores*. HarperTrophy, 1986.

_____. *The Moves Make the Man*. HarperTrophy, 1984.

_____. *What Hearts*. HarperTrophy, 1992.

_____. *Vanishing*. HarperTempest, 1999.

Brooks, Kevin. *Kissing the Rain*. Push, 2004.

_____. *Lucas*. Chicken House, 2003.

Brooks, Martha. *True Confessions of a Heartless Girl*. Farrar, Straus & Giroux, 2003.

Bruchac, Joseph. *Code Talker: A Novel about the Navajo Marines of World War Two*. Dial, 2005.

_____. *Sacajawea: The Story of Bird Woman and the Lewis and Clark Expedition*. Scholastic Signature, 2000.

Brugman, Alyssa. *Finding Grace*. Delacorte, 2004.

_____. *Walking Naked*. Delacorte, 2004.

Buckley, Gail. *American Patriots: The Story of Blacks in the Military from the Revolution to Desert Storm.* Crown, 2003.

Bunting, Eve. *The Wall.* Clarion, 1990.

Burg, David F. *The Great Depression: An Eyewitness History.* Facts on File, 1996.

Buss, Fran Leeper. *Journey of the Sparrows.* Puffin, 1991.

Butcher, Kristin. *Zee's Way.* Orca Soundings, 2004.

Cadnum, Michael. *The Book of the Lion.* Puffin, 2000.

_____. *In a Dark Wood.* Puffin, 1998.

Cameron, Sara. *Out of War: True Stories from the Front Lines of the Children's Movement for Peace in Colombia.* United Nations Publications, 2001.

Camus, Albert. *The Stranger.* Vintage Books, 1946.

Capek, Michael. *Murals: Cave, Cathedral, to Street.* Lerner Publishing Group, 1996.

Carbone, Elisa. *Stealing Freedom.* Dell Yearling, 1998.

Card, Orson Scott. *Ender's Game.* Starscape, 1985.

Carlsson, Janne. *Camel Bells.* Groundwood, 2004.

Cart, Michael, ed. *Love and Sex: Ten Stories of Truth.* Simon Pulse, 2001.

Carter, Alden R. *Bull Catcher.* Scholastic, 1997.

_____. *Up Country.* Puffin, 1989.

Carter-Scott, Chérie. *If High School Is a Game, Here's How to Break the Rules: A Cutting Edge Guide to Becoming Yourself.* Delacorte, 2001.

Carvell, Marlene. *Who Will Tell My Brother?* Hyperion, 2002.

Cary, Lorene. *Black Ice.* Vintage, 1992.

Chambers, Aidan. *Postcards from No Man's Land.* Dutton, 2002.

Chbosky, Stephen. *The Perks of Being a Wallflower.* MTV Books, 1999.

Cheaney, J. B. *The Playmaker.* Yearling, 2000.

Chen, Da. *China's Son: Growing Up in the Cultural Revolution.* Delacorte, 2001.

Cheng, Andrea. *Marika.* Front Street, 2002.

Cheripko, Jan. *Imitate the Tiger.* Boyds Mills Press, 1996.

_____. *Rat.* Boyds Mills Press, 2002.

Chotjewitz, David. *Daniel Half Human and the Good Nazi.* Trans. Doris Orgel. Atheneum, 2004.

Chute, Nevil. *On the Beach.* Ballantine, 1957.

Clinton, Catherine. *The Black Soldier: 1492 to the Present.* Houghton Mifflin, 2000.

Cochran, Thomas. *Roughnecks.* Harcourt, 1997.

Coerr, Eleanor. *Sadako and the Thousand Paper Cranes.* Puffin, 1977.

Cohn, Marthe. *Behind Enemy Lines: The True Story of a French Jewish Spy in Nazi Germany.* Harmony Books, 2002.

Cole, Brock. *Celine.* Sunburst, 1989.

_____. *The Facts Speak for Themselves.* Puffin, 1997.

Collier, James Lincoln, and Christopher Collier. *My Brother Sam Is Dead.* Scholastic, 1974.

Collins, Pat Lowery. *Just Imagine.* Houghton Mifflin, 2001.

Colman, Penny. *Girls: A History of Growing Up Female in America.* Scholastic, 2003.

_____. *Where the Action Was: Women War Correspondents in World War II.* Crown, 2002.

Coman, Carolyn. *Many Stones.* Speak, 2000.

Cooley, Beth. *Ostrich Eye.* Delacorte, 2004.

Cooney, Caroline B. *Driver's Ed.* Laurel-Leaf, 1994.

_____. *Goddess of Yesterday.* Laurel-Leaf, 2002.

_____. *Operation Homefront.* Laurel-Leaf, 1992.

_____. *The Terrorist.* Scholastic, 1997.

Cooper, Michael L. *Dust to Eat: Drought and Depression in the 1930s.* Clarion, 2004.

_____. *Fighting for Honor: Japanese Americans and World War II.* Clarion, 2001.

_____. *Remembering Manzanar: Life in a Japanese Relocation Camp.* Clarion, 2002.

Cooper, Susan. *King of Shadows.* Aladdin, 1999.

Cormier, Robert. *The Chocolate War.* Knopf, 1974.

_____. *Frenchtown Summer.* Laurel-Leaf, 1999.

_____. *Heroes: A Novel.* Laurel-Leaf, 1998.

_____. *I Am the Cheese.* Laurel-Leaf, 1977.

_____. *The Rag and Bone Shop.* Laurel-Leaf, 2001.

_____. *Tenderness.* Laurel-Leaf, 1997.

_____. *Tunes for Bears to Dance To.* Laurel-Leaf, 1992.

_____. *We All Fall Down.* Laurel-Leaf, 1991.

Corrigan, Eireann. *You Remind Me of You: A Poetry Memoir.* Scholastic Push, 2002.

Couper, Heather, and Nigel Henbest. *Black Holes.* DK, 1996.

Cox, Clinton. *Come All You Brave Soldiers: Blacks in the Revolutionary War.* Scholastic, 1999.

Crane, Stephen. *The Red Badge of Courage.* 1895.

Creech, Sharon. *Heartbeat.* HarperCollins, 2004.

_____. *Walk Two Moons.* HarperTrophy, 1994.

Crew, Linda. *Children of the River.* Laurel-Leaf, 1998.

Crist-Evans, Craig. *Amaryllis.* Candlewick, 2003.

Crowe, Chris. *Getting Away with Murder: The True Story of the Emmett Till Case.* Phyllis Fogelman Books, 2003.

_____. *Mississippi Trial, 1955.* Speak, 2002.

Crutcher, Chris. *Athletic Shorts: Six Short Stories.* HarperTempest, 1991.

_____. *Chinese Handcuffs.* Laurel-Leaf, 1989.

_____. *The Crazy Horse Electric Game.* Laurel-Leaf, 1987.

_____. *Ironman.* Laurel-Leaf, 1995.

_____. *Running Loose.* HarperTempest, 1983.

_____. *Staying Fat for Sarah Byrnes.* HarperCollins, 1993.

_____. *Stotan!* HarperTempest, 1986.

_____. *Whale Talk.* Laurel-Leaf, 2001.

Cummings, Priscilla. *Saving Grace.* Dutton, 2003.

Curtis, Christopher Paul. *Bucking the Sarge.* Wendy Lamb Books, 2004.

_____. *Bud, Not Buddy.* Dell Yearling, 1999.

_____. *The Watsons Go to Birmingham—1963.* Bantam, 1995.

Cushman, Karen. *The Ballad of Lucy Whipple.* HarperTrophy, 1996.

_____. *Catherine, Called Birdy.* HarperTrophy, 1995.

_____. *The Midwife's Apprentice.* HarperTrophy, 1995.

Daly, Maureen. *Seventeenth Summer.* Archway, 1943.

Danticat, Edwidge. *Behind the Mountains*. Scholastic, 2002.

_____. *The Farming of Bones: A Novel*. Penguin, 1998.

Dash, Joan. *The Longitude Prize*. Farrar, Straus & Giroux, 2000.

_____. *The World at Her Fingertips: The Story of Helen Keller*. Scholastic, 2001.

De Camillo, Kate. *A Tale of Despereaux*. Candlewick, 2003.

DeFelice, Cynthia. *Nowhere to Call Home*. HarperCollins, 1999.

Delaney, Mark. *Pepperland*. Peachtree, 2004.

Del Calzo, Nick, and Peter Collier. *Medal of Honor: Portraits of Valor beyond the Call of Duty*. Artisan, 2003.

Denenberg, Barry. *All Shook Up: The Life and Death of Elvis Presley*. Scholastic, 2001.

_____. *The Journal of Ben Uchida: Citizen 13559, Mirror Lake Internment Camp, California, 1942*. Scholastic, 1999.

_____. *The Journal of William Thomas Emerson: A Revolutionary War Patriot, Boston, Massachusetts, 1774*. Scholastic, 1998.

_____. *Shadow Life: A Portrait of Anne Frank and Her Family*. Scholastic, 2005.

_____. *Voices from Vietnam*. Scholastic, 1994.

Desetta, Al, and Sybil Wolin, eds. *The Struggle to Be Strong: True Stories by Teens about Overcoming Tough Times*. Free Spirit Press, 2000.

Dessen, Sarah. *Dreamland*. Speak, 2000.

_____. *Someone Like You*. Speak, 1998.

_____. *This Lullaby*. Speak, 2002.

Deuker, Carl. *Heart of a Champion*. HarperTrophy, 1993.

_____. *High Heat*. Houghton Mifflin, 2003.

_____. *Night Hoops*. HarperTrophy, 2000.

_____. *Painting the Black*. HarperTrophy, 1997.

Dickens, Charles. *Great Expectations*. 1860–61.

_____. *A Tale of Two Cities*. 1959.

Dickinson, Peter. *Eva*. Laurel-Leaf, 1988.

Donnelly, Jennifer. *A Northern Light*. Harcourt, 2003.

Dorros, Arthur. *Under the Sun*. Abrams, 2004.

Douglas, John. *The Great Depression*. Chelsea House, 1996.

Draper, Sharon M. *Romiette and Julio*. Simon Pulse, 1999.

_____. *Tears of a Tiger*. Simon Pulse, 1994.

Drill, Esther, Heather McDonald, and Rebecca Odes. *The Looks Book: A Whole New Approach to Beauty, Body Image, and Style*. Penguin, 2002.

Drucker, Malka. *Jacob's Rescue: A Holocaust Story*. Dell Yearling, 1993.

Duncan, Lois. *Killing Mr. Griffin*. Laurel-Leaf, 1978.

DuPrau, Jeanne. *The City of Ember*. Random House, 2003.

_____. *The People of Sparks*. Random House, 2004.

Durbin, William. *The Journal of C.J. Jackson, A Dust Bowl Migrant, Oklahoma to California, 1935*. Scholastic, 2002.

Durrett, Deanne. *Unsung Heroes of World War II: The Story of the Navajo Code Talkers*. Facts on File, 1998.

Easton, Kelly. *Life History of a Star*. Simon Pulse, 2001.

_____. *Walking on Air*. McElderberry Books, 2004.

Edelman, Bernard, ed. *Dear America: Letters Home from Vietnam*. W. W. Norton, 1989.

Eliot, George. *Silas Marner.* 1861.

Elliott, L. M. *Under a War-Torn Sky.* Hyperion, 2001.

Ellison, Ralph. *The Invisible Man.* Vintage Books, 1947.

Enzensberger, Hans Magnus. *The Number Devil: A Mathematical Adventure.* Henry Holt, 1998.

Esckilsen, Erik E. *Offsides.* Houghton Mifflin, 2004.

Farmer, Nancy. *A Girl Named Disaster.* Puffin, 1996.

_____. *The House of the Scorpion.* Atheneum, 2002.

Farrell, Jaqueline. *The Great Depression.* Lucent Books, 1996.

Farrell, Jeanette. *Invisible Allies: Microbes That Shape Our Lives.* Farrar, Straus & Giroux, 2005.

Farrell, Mame. *And Sometimes Why.* Farrar, Straus & Giroux, 2001.

Fernley, Fran. *I Wrote on All Four Walls: Teens Speak Out on Violence.* Annic Press, 2004.

Ferris, Jean. *Bad.* Sunburst, 1998.

_____. *Eight Seconds.* Puffin, 2000.

_____. *Of Sound Mind.* Farrar, Straus & Giroux, 2001.

Fiedler, Lisa. *Dating Hamlet: Ophelia's Story.* Henry Holt, 2002.

Filipovic, Zlata. *Zlata's Diary: A Child's Life in Sarajevo.* Penguin, 1994.

Fitzgerald, F. Scott. *The Great Gatsby.* Scribner's, 1925.

Flake, Sharon G. *Who Am I without Him? Short Stories about Girls and the Boys in Their Lives.* Hyperion, 2004.

Fleischman, Paul. *Bull Run.* HarperTrophy, 1993.

_____. *Mind's Eye.* Laurel-Leaf, 1999.

_____. *Saturnalia.* HarperTrophy, 1990.

_____. *Whirligig.* Laurel-Leaf, 1998.

Fleming, Candace. *Ben Franklin's Almanac: Being a True Account of the Good Gentleman's Life.* Atheneum, 2003.

Flinn, Alex. *Breaking Point.* HarperTempest, 2002.

_____. *Breathing Underwater.* HarperTempest, 2001.

_____. *Nothing to Lose.* HarperCollins, 2004.

Fogelin, Adrian. *The Big Nothing.* Peachtree, 2004.

Foote, Shelby. *Shiloh.* Vintage, 1985.

Forbes, Esther. *Johnny Tremain.* Dell Yearling, 1943.

Fougard, Athol. *"Master Harold"...and the Boys.* Viking Press, 1982.

Fox, Paula. *The Eagle Kite.* Laurel-Leaf, 1995.

_____. *Monkey Island.* Dell Yearling, 1991.

_____. *The Slave Dancer.* Laurel-Leaf, 1973.

Fradin, Denis Brindell. *My Family Shall Be Free! The Life of Peter Still.* HarperCollins, 2001.

Fradin, Denis Brindell, and Judith Bloom Fradin. *Fight On! Mary Church Terrell's Battle for Integration.* Clarion, 2003.

Frank, Anne. *Anne Frank: The Diary of a Young Girl.* Prentice Hall (K–12), 1947.

Frank, E. R. *America.* Atheneum, 2002.

_____. *Friction.* Simon Pulse, 2003.

Frank, Hillary. *Better than Running at Night.* Houghton Mifflin, 2002.

Frank, Lucy. *I Am an Artichoke.* Laurel-Leaf, 1995.

Franzen, Jonathan. *The Corrections.* St. Martins Press, 2001.

Freedman, Russell. *In Defense of Liberty: The Story of America's Bill of Rights.* Holiday House, 2003.

_____. *The Life and Death of Crazy Horse.* Scholastic, 1996.

Fremon, David K. *The Great Depression in American History.* Enslow, 1997.

_____. *Japanese-American Internment in American History.* Enslow, 1996.

Freymann-Wehr, Garret. *My Heartbeat.* Speak, 2002.

Fritz, April Young. *Praying at the Sweetwater Motel.* Hyperion, 2003.

Gaines, Ernest J. *The Autobiography of Miss Jane Pitman.* Bantam, 1971.

_____. *A Lesson before Dying.* Vintage Books, 1977.

Gallo, Donald R., ed. *Destination Unexpected.* Candlewick, 2003.

_____, ed. *First Crossing: Stories about Teen Immigrants.* Candlewick, 2004.

_____, ed. *No Easy Answers: Short Stories about Teenagers Making Tough Choices.* Laurel-Leaf, 1997.

_____, ed. *On the Fringe.* Speak, 2001.

_____, ed. *Ultimate Sports: Short Stories by Outstanding Writers for Young Adults.* Laurel-Leaf, 1995.

Gantos, Jack. *Hole in My Life.* Farrar, Straus & Giroux, 2002.

_____. *Joey Pigza Loses Control.* HarperTrophy, 2000.

_____. *Joey Pigza Swallowed the Key.* HarperTrophy, 1998.

Garden, Nancy. *Dove and Sword: A Novel of Joan of Arc.* Point Signature, 1995.

_____. *The Year They Burned the Books.* Farrar, Straus & Giroux, 1999.

Gardner, John. *Grendel.* Vintage Books, 1971.

Garner, Eleanor Ramrath. *Eleanor's Story: An American Girl in Hitler's Germany.* Peachtree, 1999.

Gavin, Jamila. *Coram Boy.* Farrar, Straus & Giroux, 2001.

Geras, Adele. *Troy.* Harcourt, 2001.

Gibbons, Kaye. *Ellen Foster.* Vintage, 1988.

Giblin, James Cross. *The Life and Death of Adolf Hitler.* Clarion, 2002.

_____. *When Plague Strikes: The Black Death, Smallpox, AIDS.* HarperTrophy, 1995.

Gies, Miep, with Alison Leslie Gold. *Anne Frank Remembered.* Simon & Schuster, 1988.

Giles, Gail. *Playing in Traffic.* Roaring Brook, 2004.

_____. *Shattering Glass.* Simon Pulse, 2002.

Glenn, Mel. *Jump Ball: A Basketball Season in Poems.* Dutton, 1997.

_____. *Split Image: A Story in Poems.* HarperTempest, 2000.

_____. *Who Killed Mr. Chippendale?* Puffin, 1996.

Going, K. L. *Fat Kid Rules the World.* Speak, 2003.

Gold, Alison Leslie. *A Special Fate: Chiune Sugihara: Hero of the Holocaust.* Scholastic, 2000.

Golding, William. *Lord of the Flies.* Perigee, 1954.

Goldman, Peter, and Tony Fuller. *Charlie Company: What Vietnam Did to Us.* Quill, 1983.

Goobie, Beth. *Flux.* Orca, 2004.

_____. *The Lottery.* Orca, 2002.

Goodall, Jane. *The Chimpanzees I Love: Saving Their World and Ours.* Scholastic, 2001.

Granfield, Linda. *I Remember Korea: Veterans Tell Their Stories of the Korean War, 1950–53.* Clarion, 2004.

Grant, R. G. *The Great Depression*. Barrons Educational Series, 2003.

Greenberg, Jan. *Heart to Heart: New Poems Inspired by Twentieth-Century Art*. Harry N. Abrams, 2001.

_____. *Romare Bearden: Collage of Memories*. Harry N. Abrams, 2003.

Greenberg, Jan, and Sandra Jordan. *Andy Warhol: Prince of Pop*. Delacorte, 2004.

_____. *Chuck Close: Up Close*. DK, 1998.

_____. *Frank O. Gehry: Outside In*. DK, 2000.

_____. *Runaway Girl: The Artist Louise Bourgeois*. Harry N. Abrams, 2003.

_____. *Vincent Van Gogh: Portrait of an Artist*. Dell Yearling, 2001.

Greenberg, Joanne. *I Never Promised You a Rose Garden*. New American Library, 1964.

Greenberg, Martin, and Larry Segriff, eds. *Future Wars*. DAW, 2003.

Greene, Bette. *The Drowning of Stephan Jones*. Laurel-Leaf, 1991.

Greenfeld, Howard. *After the Holocaust*. Greenwillow, 2001.

Gregory, Kristiana. *Across the Wide and Lonesome Prairie: The Oregon Trail Diary of Hattie Campbell, 1847*. Scholastic, 1997.

_____. *The Winter of the Red Snow: The Revolutionary War Diary of Abigail Jane Stewart, Valley Forge, Pennsylvania, 1777*. Scholastic, 1996.

Grimes, Nikki. *Bronx Masquerade*. Penguin Putnam, 2002.

Guest, Judith. *Ordinary People*. Penguin, 1976.

Gutsche, Henry. *Hitler's Willing Warrior*. Royal Fireworks Press, 2003.

Haddix, Margaret Peterson. *Don't You Dare Read This, Mrs. Dunphrey*. Simon Pulse, 1996.

_____. *Just Ella*. Aladdin Library, 1999.

_____. *Takeoffs and Landings*. Aladdin, 2001.

Hahn, Mary Downing. *Hear the Wind Blow*. Clarion, 2003.

_____. *Promises to the Dead*. HarperTrophy, 2000.

Hale, Marian. *The Truth about Sparrows*. Henry Holt, 2004.

Hall, Eleanor J. *The Lewis and Clark Expedition*. Lucent Books, 1995.

Halliday, John. *Shooting Monarchs*. Margaret K. McElderberry Books, 2003.

Halvorson, Marilyn. *Bull Rider*. Orca Soundings, 2003.

Hamilton, Virginia. *Anthony Burns: The Defeat and Triumph of a Fugitive Slave*. Laurel-Leaf, 1988.

_____. *Many Thousand Gone: African Americans from Slavery to Freedom*. Knopf, 2003.

Hanauer, Cathi. *My Sister's Bones*. Delta, 1996.

Hansberry, Lorraine. *A Raisin in the Sun*. Vintage, 1959.

Hansen, Joyce. *Which Way Freedom?* HarperTrophy, 1986.

Hardman, Ric Lynden. *Sunshine Rider: The First Vegetarian Western*. Laurel-Leaf, 1998.

Harlow, Joan Hiatt. *Shadows on the Sea*. Aladdin, 2003.

Harrar, George. *Not as Crazy as I Seem*. Houghton Mifflin, 2003.

Hartinger, Brent. *Geography Club*. HarperTempest, 2003.

_____. *The Last Chance Texaco*. HarperTempest, 2004.

Haruf, Kent. *Plainsong*. Vintage Books, 1999.

Haseley, Dennis. *The Amazing Thinking Machine*. Dial, 2002.

Haskins, James. *One Love, One Heart: A History of Reggae*. Jump at the Sun, 2002.

_____. *One Nation under a Groove: Rap Music and Its Roots*. Jump at the Sun, 2000.

Hautman, Pete. *Sweetblood*. Simon Pulse, 2003.

Hawk, Tony, with Sean Mortimer. *Tony Hawk: Professional Skateboarder*. Harper-Collins, 2002.

Hawthorne, Nathaniel. *The Scarlet Letter*. 1850.

Head, Ann. *Mr and Mrs Bo Jo Jones*. Signet, 1967.

Heller, Joseph. *Catch-22*. Simon & Schuster, 1961.

Hemingway, Ernest. *A Farewell to Arms*. Scribner's, 1929.

_____. *For Whom the Bell Tolls*. Scribner's, 1940.

_____. *The Old Man and the Sea*. Scribner's, 1952.

Henderson, Aileen Kilgore. *Hard Times for Jake Smith*. Milkweed Editions, 2004.

Henson, Heather. *Making the Run*. HarperTempest, 2002.

Hentoff, Nat. *The Day They Came to Arrest the Book*. Laurel-Leaf, 1982.

_____. *Jazz Country*. HarperCollins, 1965.

Hersey, John. *Hiroshima*. Vintage Books, 1946.

Hesse, Karen. *Aleutian Sparrow*. Aladdin, 2003.

_____. *The Cats in Krasinski Square*. Scholastic, 2004.

_____. *Letters from Rifka*. Hyperion, 1992.

_____. *A Light in the Storm: The Civil War Diary of Amelia Martin, Fenwick Island, Delaware, 1861*. Scholastic, 1999.

_____. *Out of the Dust*. Scholastic, 1997.

_____. *Phoenix Rising*. Puffin, 1994.

_____. *Stowaway*. Aladdin, 2000.

_____. *Witness*. Scholastic, 2001.

Hesser, Terry Spencer. *Kissing Doorknobs*. Laurel-Leaf, 1998.

Hiaasen, Carl. *Hoot*. Knopf, 2002.

Hillerman, Tony, with photographs by Frank Kessler. *Kilroy Was There*. Kent State University Press, 2004.

Hines, Sue. *Out of the Shadows*. HarperTempest, 2000.

Hinton, S. E. *The Outsiders*. Puffin, 1967.

Hite, Sid. *The Journal of Rufus Rowe: The Battle of Fredericksburg, Bowling Green, Virginia, 1862*. Scholastic, 2003.

Hobbs, Valerie. *Letting Go of Bobby James, or How I Found My Self of Steam*. Frances Foster Books, 2004.

_____. *Sonny's War*. Farrar, Straus & Giroux, 2002.

Hobbs, Will. *Beardance*. Aladdin, 1993.

_____. *Bearstone*. Aladdin, 1989.

_____. *Downriver*. Laurel-Leaf, 1991.

_____. *Down the Yukon*. HarperTrophy, 2001.

_____. *Far North*. Avon Camelot, 1997.

_____. *Jackie's Wild Seattle*. HarperTrophy, 2003.

_____. *Jason's Gold*. HarperTrophy, 1999.

_____. *Leaving Protection*. HarperCollins, 2004.

_____. *The Maze*. HarperTrophy, 1998.

_____. *River Thunder*. Laurel-Leaf, 1997.

_____. *Wild Man Island*. HarperTrophy, 2002.

Holm, Anne. *I Am David*. Harcourt, 2004.

Holt, Kimberly Willis. *My Louisiana Sky*. Dell Yearling, 1998.

_____. *When Zachary Beaver Came to Town*. Yearling, 1999.

Homer. *The Odyssey*.

Homes, A. M. *Jack*. Vintage, 1989.

Hoose, Phillip. *The Race to Save the Lord God Bird*. Farrar, Straus & Giroux, 2004.

Horvath, Polly. *The Canning Season*. Farrar, Straus & Giroux, 2003.

Hosseini, Khaled. *The Kite Runner*. Riverhead Books, 2003.

Houston, Jeanne Wakatsuki, and James D. Houston. *Farewell to Manzanar: A True Story of Japanese American Experience during and after the World War II Internment*. Laurel-Leaf, 1973.

Howe, James. *The Misfits*. Aladdin, 2001.

Howe, Peter. *Shooting Under Fire: The World of the War Photographer*. Artisan, 2002.

Hrdlitschka, Shelley. *Kat's Fall*. Orca, 2004.

_____. *Dancing Naked*. Orca, 2002.

Hudson, Jan. *Sweetgrass*. Putnam, 1989.

Huff, G. Daniel. *For Love or Honor*. Self-published, 2001.

Hughes, Dean. *Soldier Boys*. Simon Pulse, 2001.

Hughes, Pat. *Guerrilla Season*. Farrar, Straus & Giroux, 2003.

Hunt, Irene. *No Promises in the Wind*. Berkley Publishing Group, 1970.

Hurston, Zora Neale. *Their Eyes Were Watching God*. Perennial Press, 1937.

Huxley, Aldous. *Brave New World*. Perennial, 1932.

Ingold, Jeanette. *The Big Burn*. Harcourt, 2002.

_____. *Mountain Solo*. Harcourt, 2003.

_____. *Pictures, 1918*. Puffin, 1998.

_____. *The Window*. Harcourt, 1996.

Innocenti, Robert. *Rose Blanche*. Creative Editions/Harcourt Brace, 1985.

Isaacs, Anne. *Torn Thread*. Scholastic, 2000.

Janeczko, Paul B., with illustrations by Jenna LaReau. *Top Secret: A Handbook of Codes, Ciphers, and Secret Writing*. Candlewick, 2004.

Janke, Katelan. *Survival in the Storm: The Dust Bowl Diary of Grace Edwards, Dalhart, Texas, 1935*. Scholastic, 2002.

Jenkins, A. M. *Damage*. HarperTempest, 2001.

Jensen, Kathryn. *Pocket Change*. Scholastic, 1989.

Jiang, Ji-Li. *Red Scarf Girl: A Memoir of the Cultural Revolution*. HarperTrophy, 1997.

Johnson, Angela. *The First Part Last*. Simon Pulse, 2003.

_____. *Toning the Sweep*. Scholastic, 1993.

Johnson, Charles. *Soulcatcher: And Other Stories*. Harvest Books, 2001.

Johnson, Kathleen Jeffrie. *The Parallel Universe of Liars*. Laurel-Leaf, 2002.

_____. *Target*. Roaring Brook, 2003.

Johnson, Spencer. *Who Moved My Cheese? for Teens: An A-Mazing Way to Change and Win!* Putnam, 2002.

Johnston, Tim. *Never So Green*. Farrar, Straus & Giroux, 2002.

Johnston, Tony. *The Harmonica*. Charlesbridge, 2004.

Jones, Patrick. *Things Change*. Walker Books, 2004.

Keizer, Garret. *God of Beer*. HarperTempest, 2002.

Kelley, William Melvin. *A Different Drummer*. Anchor, 1962.

Kerr, M. E. *Deliver Us from Evie*. HarperTrophy, 1994.

_____. *Gentlehands.* Bantam, 1978.

_____. *Linger.* HarperTrophy, 1993.

_____. *Slap Your Sides.* HarperTrophy, 2001.

Kerrod, Robin. *The Way Science Works.* DK, 2002.

Kesey, Ken. *One Flew over the Cuckoo's Nest.* New American Library, 1962.

King, Casey, and Linda Barrett Osborne. *Oh, Freedom! Kids Talk About the Civil Rights Movement with the People Who Made It Happen.* Knopf, 1997.

Kingsolver, Barbara. *The Poisonwood Bible.* HarperTorch, 1998.

Klass, David. *California Blue.* Scholastic, 1994.

_____. *Danger Zone.* Scholastic, 1996.

_____. *Home of the Braves.* Farrar, Straus & Giroux, 2002.

_____. *Wrestling with Honor.* Scholastic, 1989.

_____. *You Don't Know Me.* HarperTempest, 2001.

Klause, Annette Curtis. *The Silver Kiss.* Laurel-Leaf, 1990.

Klein, Gerda Weissmann. *All but My Life: A Memoir.* Hill and Wang, 1995.

Koertge, Ron. *The Brimstone Journals.* Candlewick, 2001.

_____. *Margaux with an X.* Candlewick, 2004.

_____. *Shakespeare Bats Cleanup.* Candlewick, 2003.

_____. *Stoner & Spaz.* Candlewick, 2002.

Koja, Kathe. *The Blue Mirror.* Frances Foster/Farrar, Straus & Giroux, 2004.

_____. *Talk.* Farrar, Straus & Giroux, 2005.

Koller, Jackie French. *Nothing to Fear.* Gulliver Books, 1993.

Konigsburg, E.L. *Silent to the Bone.* Aladdin, 2000.

Korman, Gordon. *Jake, Reinvented.* Hyperion, 2003.

_____. *Son of the Mob.* Hyperion, 2002.

Kositsky, Lynne. *The Thought of High Windows.* Kids Can Press, 2004.

Krisher, Trudy. *Spite Fences.* Laurel-Leaf, 1994.

Kuhn, Betsy. *Angels of Mercy: The Army Nurses of World War II.* Atheneum, 1999.

Kurtz, Jane. *The Storyteller's Beads.* Gulliver Books, 1998.

Kushner, Tony, and Maurice Sendak. *Brundibar.* Michael diCapua Books, 2003.

Kyi, Tanya. *Truth.* Orca Soundings, 2003.

Laird, Christa. *But Can the Phoenix Sing?* HarperTrophy, 1995.

Lasky, Kathryn. *Beyond the Burning Time.* Scholastic Point, 1994.

_____. *Beyond the Divide.* Simon Pulse, 1983.

_____. *Christmas After All: The Great Depression Diary of Minnie Swift—Indianapolis, Indiana, 1932.* Scholastic, 2001.

_____. *Elizabeth I: Red Rose of the House of Tudor, England, 1544.* Scholastic, 1999.

_____. *The Journal of Augustus Pelletier: The Lewis and Clark Expedition, 1804.* Scholastic, 2000.

_____. *A Journey to the New World: The Diary of Remember Patience Whipple, Mayflower, 1620.* Scholastic, 1996.

_____. *Mary, Queen of Scots: Queen without a Country, France, 1553.* Scholastic, 2002.

_____. *Memoirs of a Bookbat.* Harcourt, 1994.

_____. *True North: A Novel of the Underground Railroad.* Scholastic, 1996.

Lauber, Patricia. *Hurricanes: Earth's Mightiest Storms.* Scholastic, 1996.

Lavender, William. *Just Jane: A Daughter of England Caught in the Struggle of the American Revolution.* Gulliver Books, 2002.

Lawrence, Iain. *B for Buster*. Delacorte, 2004.

_____. *The Buccaneers*. Dell Yearling, 2001.

_____. *Lord of the Nutcracker Men*. Laurel-Leaf, 2001.

_____. *The Wreckers*. Dell Yearling, 1998.

Lawrence, Jerome, and Robert E. Lee. *Inherit the Wind*. Bantam, 1955.

Lawton, Clive A. *Auschwitz: The Story of a Nazi Death Camp*. Candlewick, 2002.

_____. *Hiroshima: The Story of the First Atom Bomb*. Candlewick, 2004.

Lazan, Marion Blumenthal, and Lila Perl. *Four Perfect Pebbles: A Holocaust Story*. HarperTrophy, 1996.

Leapman, Michael. *Witnesses to War: Eight True-Life Stories of Nazi Persecution*. Puffin, 1998.

Lee, Harper. *To Kill a Mockingbird*. Little, Brown, 1960.

Lee, Marie G. *Finding My Voice*. HarperTrophy, 1992.

_____. *Necessary Roughness*. HarperTrophy, 1996.

Lester, Julius. *Othello: A Novel*. Scholastic, 1995.

_____. *To Be a Slave*. Puffin, 1968.

_____. *When Dad Killed Mom*. Harcourt, 2001.

Levenkron, Steven. *The Best Little Girl in the World*. Warner Books, 1978.

Levine, Ellen. *Darkness over Denmark: The Danish Resistance and the Rescue of the Jews*. Holiday House, 2000.

_____. *Freedom's Children: Young Civil Rights Activists Tell Their Own Stories*. Puffin, 1993.

_____. *The Journal of Jedediah Barstow: An Emigrant on the Oregon Trail, 1848*. Scholastic, 2002.

Levine, Gail Carson. *Dave at Night*. HarperTrophy, 1999.

_____. *The Two Princesses of Bamarre*. HarperTrophy, 2001.

Levithan, David. *Boy Meets Boy*. Knopf, 2003.

_____. *The Realm of Possibility*. Knopf, 2004.

Levitin, Sonia. *Room in the Heart*. Puffin, 2003.

Lindquist, Susan Hart. *Summer Soldiers*. Dell Yearling, 1999.

Lipsyte, Robert. *The Brave*. HarperTrophy, 1991.

_____. *The Chemo Kid*. HarperTrophy, 1992.

_____. *The Chief*. HarperTrophy, 1993.

_____. *The Contender*. HarperTrophy, 1967.

_____. *Warrior Angel*. HarperTrophy, 2003.

Lobel, Anita. *No Pretty Pictures: A Child of War*. HarperTrophy, 1998.

_____. *Potatoes, Potatoes*. Greenwillow, 2004.

London, Jack. *The Call of the Wild*. Prentice Hall, 1903.

Lowry, Lois. *Gathering Blue*. Laurel-Leaf, 2000.

_____. *The Giver*. Laurel-Leaf, 1993.

_____. *Messenger*. Houghton Mifflin, 2004.

_____. *Number the Stars*. Laurel-Leaf, 1989.

Lubar, David. *Hidden Talents*. Tor, 1999.

Lunn, Janet. *The Hollow Tree*. Perfection Learning, 1999.

Lupica, Mike. *Travel Team*. Philomel, 2004.

Lynch, Chris. *Freewill*. HarperTempest, 2001.

_____. *Gold Dust*. HarperTrophy, 2000.

_____. *Iceman*. HarperTrophy, 1994.

_____. *Shadow Boxer.* HarperTrophy, 1993.

_____. *Slot Machine.* HarperTrophy, 1995.

Mack, Tracy. *Birdland.* Scholastic, 2003.

_____. *Drawing Lessons.* Scholastic Signature, 2000.

Mackler, Carolyn. *The Earth, My Butt, and Other Big Round Things.* Candlewick, 2003.

_____. *Vegan Virgin Valentine.* Candlewick, 2004.

Macy, Sue, ed. *Girls Got Game: Sports Stories and Poems.* Henry Holt, 2001.

Maestro, Betsy. *The Story of Clocks and Calendars: Marking a Millennium.* HarperTrophy, 1999.

Mah, Adeline Yen. *Chinese Cinderella: The True Story of an Unwanted Daughter.* Laurel-Leaf, 1999.

Mahy, Margaret. *Memory.* Laurel-Leaf, 1987.

Malmgren, Dallin. *The Ninth Issue.* Laurel-Leaf, 1989.

Marsden, John. *So Much to Tell You.* Fawcett, 1989.

_____. *Tomorrow: When the War Began.* Laurel-Leaf, 1993.

Marsh, Carole. *Unidentified Flying Objects and Extra Terrestrial Life.* 21st Century Books, 1997.

Marshall, Kathryn. *In the Combat Zone: An Oral History of American Women in Vietnam: 1966–1975.* Little, Brown, 1987.

Martin, Ann M. *A Corner of the Universe.* Scholastic, 2002.

Masoff, Joy. *Colonial Times: 1600–1700.* Scholastic, 2000.

Mason, Bobbie Ann. *In Country.* Perennial Press, 1986.

Masters, Edgar Lee. *Spoon River Anthology.* Touchstone, 1915.

Mastoon, Adam. *The Shared Heart: Portraits and Stories Celebrating Lesbian, Gay, and Bisexual Young People.* HarperTempest, 1997.

Matas, Carol. *After the War.* Simon Pulse, 1996.

_____. *Daniel's Story.* Scholastic, 1993.

_____. *In My Enemy's House.* Simon Pulse, 1999.

_____. *The War Within: A Novel of the Civil War.* Aladdin, 2001.

Matthews, Andrew. *The Flip Side.* Laurel-Leaf, 2003.

Mazer, Harry. *A Boy at War: A Novel of Pearl Harbor.* Aladdin, 2001.

_____. *A Boy No More.* Simon & Schuster, 2004.

_____. *The Last Mission.* Laurel-Leaf, 1979.

_____. *The Wild Kid.* Aladdin, 1998.

Mazer, Norma Fox. *Good Night, Maman.* HarperCollins, 1999.

_____. *Out of Control.* Avon Flare, 1993.

_____. *When She Was Good.* Scholastic, 1997.

Mazer, Norma Fox, and Harry Mazer. *Bright Days, Stupid Nights.* Laurel-Leaf, 1992.

McCloud, Bill. *What Should We Tell Our Children about Vietnam?* University of Oklahoma Press, 1989.

McCormick, Patricia. *Cut.* Push/Scholastic, 2000.

McDonald, Joyce. *Devil on My Heels.* Delacorte, 2004.

_____. *Swallowing Stones.* Laurel-Leaf, 1997.

McElvaine, Robert S. *The Great Depression: America, 1929–1941.* Times Books, 1993.

McEwan, Ian. *Atonement: A Novel.* Anchor Books, 2002.

McGill, Alice. *Miles' Song*. Scholastic, 2000.

McKissack, Fredrick, Jr. *Black Hoops: The History of African Americans in Basketball*. Scholastic, 1999.

McKissack, Patricia C. *A Picture of Freedom: The Diary of Clotee, a Slave Girl, Belmont Plantation, Virginia, 1859*. Scholastic, 1997.

McKissack, Patricia C., and Fredrick L. McKissack. *Sojourner Truth: Ain't I a Woman?* Scholastic, 1992.

McKissack, Patricia C., and Fredrick McKissack Jr. *Black Diamond: The Story of the Negro Baseball Leagues*. Polaris, 1994.

McKissack, Patricia C., and Arlene Zarembka. *To Establish Justice: Citizenship and the Constitution*. Knopf, 2004.

McLaren, Clemence. *Waiting for Odysseus*. Simon Pulse, 2000.

McMullan, Margaret. *How I Found the Strong*. Houghton Mifflin, 2004.

McNamee, Graham. *Acceleration*. Wendy Lamb Books, 2003.

McPherson, James M. *Fields of Fury: The American Civil War*. Atheneum, 2002.

McWhorter, Diane. *A Dream of Freedom: The Civil Rights Movement from 1954 to 1968*. Scholastic, 2004.

Mead, Alice. *Girl of Kosovo*. Dell Yearling, 2001.

Meltzer, Milton. *Ain't Gonna Study War No More: The Story of America's Peace Seekers*. Landmark Books, 1985.

_____. *Driven from the Land: The Story of the Dust Bowl*. Benchmark Books, 2000.

_____. *Never to Forget: The Jews of the Holocaust*. HarperCollins, 1976.

_____. *Rescue: The Story of How Gentiles Saved Jews in the Holocaust*. HarperCollins, 1988.

Meyer, Carolyn. *Beware, Princess Elizabeth*. Gulliver Books, 2001.

_____. *Doomed Queen Ann*. Gulliver Books, 2002.

_____. *Mary, Bloody Mary*. Gulliver Books, 1999.

_____. *Patience, Princess Catherine*. Gulliver Books, 2004.

_____. *White Lilacs*. Gulliver Books, 1993.

Meyer, Louis A. *Bloody Jack: Being an Account of the Curious Adventures of Mary "Jacky" Faber, Ship's Boy*. Harcourt, 2002.

Mikaelsen, Ben. *Petey*. Hyperion, 1998.

_____. *Red Midnight*. RAYO, 2002.

_____. *Touching Spirit Bear*. HarperTrophy, 2001.

_____. *Tree Girl*. HarperCollins, 2004.

Miklowitz, Gloria D. *The Enemy Has a Face*. Eerdmans, 2003.

_____. *Masada: The Last Fortress*. Eerdmans, 1998.

Miller, Arthur. *The Crucible*. Penguin, 1982.

_____. *Death of a Salesman*. Penguin, 1949.

Miller, Mary Beth. *Aimee*. Speak, 2002.

Minchin, Adele. *The Beat Goes On*. Simon & Schuster, 2004.

Moore, Peter. *Blind Sighted*. Speak, 2002.

Morgenstern, Julie, and Jessi Morgenstern-Colon. *Organizing from the Inside Out for Teenagers: The Foolproof System for Organizing Your Room, Your Time, and Your Life*. Owl Books, 2002.

Moriarty, Jaclyn. *The Year of Secret Assignments*. Scholastic, 2004.

Morpurgo, Michael. *Private Peaceful*. Scholastic, 2004.

Morrison, Toni. *Beloved*. Plume, 1998.

_____. *The Bluest Eye.* Penguin, 1969.

Moses, Sheila P. *I, Dred Scott: A Fictional Slave Narrative Based on the Life and Legal Precedent of Dred Scott.* Margaret K. McElderberry Books, 2005.

Moskin, Marietta D. *I Am Rosemarie.* Replica Books, 1972.

Mosley, Walter. *47.* Little, Brown, 2005.

Moss, Marissa. *Hannah's Journal: The Story of an Immigrant Girl.* Silver Whistle Books, 2000.

_____. *Rachel's Journal: The Story of a Pioneer Girl.* Sagebrush, 1998.

Muhlberger, Richard. *What Makes a Degas a Degas?* Viking, 1993.

_____. *What Makes a Monet a Monet?* Viking, 1993.

_____. *What Makes a Rembrandt a Rembrandt?* Viking, 1993.

_____. *What Makes a Van Gogh a Van Gogh?* Viking, 1993.

Mulvey, Deb. *We Had Everything but Money.* Crescent Books, 1992.

Murphy, Jim. *An American Plague: The True and Terrifying Story of the Yellow Fever Epidemic of 1793.* Clarion, 2003.

_____. *The Journal of James Edmond Pease: A Civil War Union Soldier, Virginia, 1863.* Scholastic, 1998.

_____. *The Long Road to Gettysburg.* Clarion, 1992.

_____. *West to a Land of Plenty: The Diary of Teresa Angelino Viscardi, New York to Idaho Territory, 1883.* Scholastic, 1992.

_____. *A Young Patriot: The American Revolution as Experienced by One Boy.* Houghton Mifflin, 1996.

Murphy, Virginia Reed, with letters by James Reed, ed. Karen Zeinert. *Across the Plains in the Donner Party.* Ye Galleon Press, 1996.

Murray, Jaye. *Bottled Up.* Puffin, 2003.

Myers, Walter Dean. *Amistad: A Long Road to Freedom.* Puffin, 1998.

_____. *Antarctica: Journeys to the South Pole.* Scholastic, 2004.

_____. *Fallen Angels.* Scholastic, 1988.

_____. *The Glory Field.* Scholastic, 1994.

_____. *The Greatest: Muhammad Ali.* Scholastic Signature, 2001.

_____. *The Journal of Biddy Owens: The Negro Leagues—Birmingham, Alabama, 1948.* Scholastic, 2001.

_____. *The Journal of Scott Pendleton Collins, A World War II Soldier, Normandy, France, 1944.* Scholastic, 1999.

_____. *Monster.* HarperCollins, 1999.

_____. *Patrol: An American Soldier in Vietnam.* HarperCollins, 2002.

_____. *Shooter.* Amistad, 2004.

_____. *Slam!* Point Signature, 1996.

_____. *Somewhere in the Darkness.* Apple, 1992.

Myracle, Lauren. *Kissing Kate.* Puffin, 2003.

Na, An. *A Step from Heaven.* Speak, 2001.

Naidoo, Beverly. *No Turning Back: A Novel of South Africa.* HarperTrophy, 1997.

_____. *The Other Side of Truth.* HarperTrophy, 2001.

Napoli, Donna Jo. *Daughter of Venice.* Laurel-Leaf, 2002.

_____. *Stones in Water.* Puffin, 1997.

Neimark, Anne E. *The Life of Woody Guthrie: There Ain't Nobody That Can Sing Like Me.* Atheneum, 2002.

Nelson, Marilyn. *Carver: A Life in Poems.* Front Street, 2001.

Nelson, Peter. *Left for Dead: A Young Man's Search for Justice for the USS Indianapolis*. Delacorte, 2002.

Nir, Yehuda. *The Lost Childhood: A World War II Memoir*. Scholastic, 2002.

Nishi, Dennis. *Life during the Great Depression*. Lucent Books, 1998.

Nix, Garth. *Shade's Children*. Eos, 1997.

Nolan, Han. *Born Blue*. Harcourt, 2001.

_____. *If I Should Die before I Wake*. Harcourt, 1994.

Normandin, Christine, ed. *Spirit of the Cedar People: More Stories and Paintings of Chief Lelooska*. Diane Publishing, 1998.

Nye, Naomi Shihab. *Habibi*. Aladdin, 1997.

Oates, Joyce Carol. *Big Mouth and Ugly Girl*. HarperTempest, 2002.

_____. *Freaky Green Eyes*. HarperTempest, 2003.

O'Brien, Robert C. *Z for Zachariah*. Simon Pulse, 1975.

O'Brien, Tim. *The Things They Carried*. Broadway Books, 1981.

Oneal, Zibby. *In Summer Light*. Starfire, 1985.

O'Neill, Eugene. *Ah, Wilderness!* Samuel French, 1939.

_____. *Mourning Becomes Electra*. In *Three Plays: Desire Under the Elms / Strange Interlude / Mourning Becomes Electra*. Vintage Books, 1931.

Opdyke, Irene Gut, with Jennifer Armstrong. *In My Hands: Memories of a Holocaust Rescuer*. Anchor, 1999.

Orgel, Doris. *The Devil in Vienna*. Dial, 1978.

Orlev, Uri. *The Island on Bird Street*. Houghton Mifflin, 1984.

_____. *The Man from the Other Side*. Puffin, 1991.

_____. *Run, Boy, Run*. Trans. Hillel Halkin. Houghton Mifflin, 2003.

Orr, Wendy. *Peeling the Onion*. Laurel-Leaf, 1997.

Orwell, George. *1984*. Signet, 1949.

Osa, Nancy. *Cuba Fifteen*. Delacorte, 2003.

Osborne, Mary Pope. *Favorite Medieval Tales*. Hyperion, 1998.

_____. *My Secret War: The World War II Diary of Madeline Beck, Long Island, New York, 1941*. Scholastic, 2000.

Palmer, Laura. *Shrapnel in the Heart: Letters and Remembrances from the Vietnam Veterans Memorial*. Vintage, 1987.

Park, Linda Sue. *A Single Shard*. Dell Yearling, 2001.

_____. *When My Name Was Keoko*. Dell Yearling, 2002.

Parker, Margaret Hundley. *KISS Guide to Fitness*. DK, 2002.

Parks, Rosa, with Jim Haskins. *Rosa Parks: My Story*. Puffin, 1992.

Partridge, Elizabeth. *Restless Spirit: The Life and Work of Dorothea Lange*. Puffin, 1998.

_____. *This Land Was Made for You and Me: The Life and Songs of Woody Guthrie*. Viking, 2002.

Patent, Dorothy Hinshaw. *Biodiversity*. Clarion, 1996.

Paterson, Katherine. *Jip: His Story*. Puffin, 1997.

_____. *Lyddie*. Puffin, 1991.

_____. *Park's Quest*. Puffin, 1988.

_____. *Parzival: The Quest of the Grail Knight*. Puffin, 1998.

Paulsen, Gary. *The Beet Fields: Memories of a Sixteenth Summer*. Laurel-Leaf, 2000.

_____. *Caught by the Sea: My Life on Boats*. Laurel-Leaf, 2001.

_____. *The Crossing*. Laurel-Leaf, 1987.

_____. *The Island.* Laurel-Leaf, 1988.

_____. *The Monument.* Dell Yearling, 1991.

_____. *Mr. Tucket.* Dell Yearling, 1968.

_____. *Nightjohn.* Laurel-Leaf, 1993.

_____. *Puppies, Dogs, and Blue Northers.* Dell Yearling, 1996.

_____. *Sarny: A Life Remembered.* Laurel-Leaf, 1997.

_____. *Soldier's Heart: Being the Story of the Enlistment and Due Service of the Boy Charley Goddard in the First Minnesota Volunteers.* Laurel-Leaf, 1998.

_____. *Voyage of the Frog.* BantamDoubledayDell, 1989.

_____. *Winterdance: The Fine Madness of Running the Iditarod.* Harvest, 1994.

_____. *Woodsong.* Aladdin, 1990.

Pearsall, Shelley. *Trouble Don't Last.* Knopf, 2002.

Pearson, Mary E. *Scribbler of Dreams.* Harcourt, 2001.

Peck, Richard. *The Last Safe Place on Earth.* Laurel-Leaf, 1995.

_____. *A Long Way from Chicago.* Puffin, 1998.

_____. *Remembering the Good Times.* Laurel-Leaf, 1985.

_____. *The River between Us.* Puffin, 2003.

_____. *Unfinished Portrait of Jessica.* Laurel-Leaf, 1991.

_____. *A Year Down Yonder.* Puffin, 2000.

Peck, Robert Newton. *A Part of the Sky.* Random House, 1994.

Pederson, Stephanie. *KISS Guide to Beauty.* Penguin, 2001.

Perez, Marlene. *Unexpected Development.* Roaring Brook, 2004.

Peters, Julie Ann. *Luna.* Little, Brown, 2004.

Philbrick, Nathaniel. *Revenge of the Whale: The True Story of the Whaleship* Essex. Puffin, 2002.

Philbrick, Rodman. *Freak the Mighty.* Blue Sky Press, 1993.

_____. *The Journal of Douglas Allen Deeds: The Donner Party Expedition, 1846.* Scholastic, 2001.

_____. *The Last Book in the Universe.* Blue Sky Press, 2000.

_____. *Max the Mighty.* Point Signature, 1998.

_____. *The Young Man and the Sea.* Blue Sky Press, 2004.

Philip, Neil, ed., with illustrations by Michael McCurdy. *War and the Pity of War.* Houghton Mifflin, 1998.

Pierce, Meredith Ann. *Treasure at the Heart of the Tanglewood.* Firebird, 2001.

Platt, Richard. *Eureka! Great Inventions and How They Happened.* Kingfisher, 2003.

Plum-Ucci, Carol. *The Body of Christopher Creed.* Harcourt, 2000.

_____. *The She.* Harcourt, 2003.

_____. *What Happened to Lani Garver.* Harcourt, 2002.

Porter, Tracey. *Treasures in the Dust.* HarperTrophy, 1997.

Potok, Chaim. *The Chosen.* Fawcett, 1967.

Powell, Randy. *Run if You Dare.* Farrar, Straus & Giroux, 2001.

_____. *Three Clams and an Oyster.* Farrar, Straus & Giroux, 2002.

_____. *Tribute to Another Dead Rock Star.* Sunburst, 1999.

Pressler, Mirjam. *Anne Frank: A Hidden Life.* Puffin, 2000.

_____. *Malka.* Speak, 2001.

_____. *Shylock's Daughter.* Dial, 2001.

Prose, Francine. *After.* HarperCollins, 2003.

Pullman, Phillip. *Ruby in the Smoke*. Laurel-Leaf, 1985.

_____. *Shadow in the North*. Random House, 1988.

_____. *Tiger in the Well*. Random House, 1991.

Randle, Kristin D. *Breaking Rank*. HarperTempest, 1999.

Rapp, Adam. *33 Snowfish*. Candlewick, 2003.

Ratcliffe, Jane. *The Free Fall*. Henry Holt, 2001.

Reeder, Carolyn. *Before the Creeks Ran Red*. HarperCollins, 2003.

Rees, Celia. *Pirates!* Bloomsbury, 2003.

Rees, Douglas. *Lightning Time*. Puffin, 1997.

Reeve, Philip. *Mortal Engines*. HarperCollins/Eos, 2003.

Reit, Seymour. *Behind Rebel Lines: The Incredible Story of Emma Edmonds, Civil War Spy*. Gulliver Books, 1988.

Remarque, Erich Maria. *All Quiet on the Western Front*. 1929.

Renault, Mary. *The King Must Die*. Vintage Books, 1958.

Rinaldi, Ann. *An Acquaintance with Darkness*. Gulliver Books, 1997.

_____. *Amelia's War*. Scholastic, 1999.

_____. *A Break with Charity: A Story about the Salem Witch Trials*. Gulliver Books, 1992.

_____. *Girl in Blue*. Scholastic, 2001.

_____. *Hang a Thousand Trees with Ribbons: The Story of Phillis Wheatley*. Gulliver Books, 1996.

_____. *In My Father's House*. Scholastic Point, 1992.

_____. *The Journal of Jasper Jonathan Pierce: A Pilgrim Boy, Plymouth, 1620*. Scholastic, 2001.

_____. *Keep Smiling Through*. Gulliver Books, 1996.

_____. *The Last Silk Dress*. Laurel-Leaf, 1988.

_____. *Numbering All the Bones*. Jump at the Sun/Hyperion, 2002.

_____. *A Stitch in Time: A Quilt Trilogy*. Scholastic Point, 1994.

_____. *Wolf by the Ears*. Scholastic Point, 1991.

Ripslinger, Jon. *How I Fell in Love and Learned to Shoot Free Throws*. Roaring Brook, 2003.

Ritter, John H. *Choosing Up Sides*. Putnam, 1998.

_____. *Over the Wall*. Puffin, 2000.

Ritter, Lawrence S. *The Story of Baseball*. 3rd rev. and expanded ed. HarperTrophy, 1983.

Roach, Mary. *Stiff: The Curious Lives of Human Cadavers*. W. W. Norton, 2003.

Robinet, Harriette Gillem. *Walking to the Bus-Rider Blues*. Aladdin, 2000.

Rochman, Hazel, and Darlene Z. McCampbell, eds. *Bearing Witness: Stories of the Holocaust*. Orchard, 1995.

_____, eds. *Leaving Home: Stories*. HarperCollins, 1997.

Rogasky, Barbara. *Smoke and Ashes: The Story of the Holocaust*. Holiday House, 1988.

Rosoff, Meg. *How I Live Now*. Wendy Lamb Books, 2004.

Ross, Ramon Royal. *Harper & Moon*. Camelot, 1995.

Rostand, Edmond. *Cyrano de Bergerac*. 1897.

Rostkowski, Margaret I. *After the Dancing Days*. HarperTrophy, 1986.

Rubin, Susan Goldman. *Art against the Odds: From Slave Quilts to Prison Paintings*. Crown, 2004.

Russo, Marisabina. *Always Remember Me: How One Family Survived World War II.* Atheneum, 2005.

Russo, Richard. *Empire Falls.* Vintage Books, 2001.

Ryan, Pam Muñoz. *Esperanza Rising.* Scholastic, 2000.

Ryan, Sara. *Empress of the World.* Penguin, 2001.

Rylant, Cynthia. *A Blue-Eyed Daisy.* Aladdin, 2000.

_____. *I Had Seen Castles.* Harcourt, 1993.

Sacher, Louis. *Holes.* Dell Yearling, 1998.

Salinger, J. D. *The Catcher in the Rye.* Little, Brown, 1951.

Salisbury, Graham. *Eyes of the Emperor.* Wendy Lamb Books, 2005.

_____. *Lord of the Deep.* Laurel-Leaf, 2001.

_____. *Under the Blood-Red Sun.* Dell Yearling, 1994.

Sanchez, Alex. *Rainbow Boys.* Simon Pulse, 2001.

_____. *Rainbow High.* Simon Pulse, 2003.

_____. *So Hard to Say.* Simon & Schuster, 2004.

Santiago, Esmeralda. *When I Was Puerto Rican.* Vintage Books, 1993.

Sappéy, Maureen Stack. *Letters from Vinnie.* Front Street, 1999.

Saramago, Jose. *Blindness.* Harvest Books, 1998.

Schmidt, Gary D. *Anson's Way.* Puffin, 1999.

Scieszka, Jon, and Lane Smith. *Math Curse.* Viking, 1995.

_____. *Science Verse.* Viking, 2004.

_____. *Seen Art?* Viking, 2005.

Sebold, Alice. *The Lovely Bones.* Back Bay Books, 2002.

Sender, Ruth Minsky. *The Cage.* Aladdin, 1986.

Severance, John. *Braving the Fire.* Clarion, 2002.

Shakespeare, William. *Hamlet.*

_____. *Julius Caesar.*

_____. *King Lear.*

_____. *The Merchant of Venice.*

_____. *A Midsummer Night's Dream.*

_____. *Othello.*

_____. *Romeo and Juliet.*

Shange, Ntozake. *Betsey Brown.* Picador USA, 1985.

Shepard, Jim. *Project X.* Knopf, 2004.

Sherlock, Patti. *Letters from Wolfie.* Viking, 2004.

Sherrow, Victoria. *Encyclopedia of Youth and War: Young People as Participants and Victims.* Oryx, 2000.

Siegel, Aranka. *Upon the Head of a Goat: A Childhood in Hungary, 1939–1944.* Sunburst, 1981.

Siegelson, Kim L. *Trembling Earth.* Philomel, 2004.

Simmons, Michael. *Pool Boy.* Roaring Brook, 2003.

Simon, Seymour. *The Universe.* HarperTrophy, 1998.

Singer, Marilyn, ed. *Face Relations: 11 Stories about Seeing beyond Color.* Simon & Schuster, 2004.

Singh, Simon. *The Code Book: How to Make It, Break It, Hack It, Crack It.* Delacorte, 2002.

Sis, Peter. *The Tree of Life: A Book Depicting the Life of Charles Darwin, Naturalist, Geologist and Thinker.* Farrar, Straus & Giroux, 2003.

Slade, Arthur G. *Dust*. Wendy Lamb Books, 2003.

Sleator, William. *Others See Us*. Puffin, 1997.

Slepian, Jan. *The Alfred Summer*. Puffin, 1980.

Smiley, Jane. *A Thousand Acres*. Ivy Books, 1991.

Smith, Sherri L. *Lucy the Giant*. Laurel-Leaf, 2002.

Sones, Sonya. *Stop Pretending: What Happened When My Big Sister Went Crazy*. HarperTempest, 1999.

Sophocles. *Antigone*.

_____. *Oedipus Rex*.

Soto, Gary. *Jesse*. Scholastic, 1994.

Spiegelman, Art. *Maus: A Survivor's Tale*. Random House, 1986.

_____. *Maus II*. Pantheon, 1993.

Spinelli, Jerry. *Milkweed*. Knopf, 2003.

_____. *Night of the Whale*. Laurel-Leaf, 1985.

_____. *Stargirl*. Knopf, 2000.

_____. *Wringer*. HarperTrophy, 1997.

Spooner, Michael. *Daniel's Walk*. Henry Holt, 2001.

Stamaty, Mark Alan. *Alia's Mission: Saving the Books of Iraq*. Knopf, 2004.

Stanley, Diane. *Michelangelo*. HarperTrophy, 2000.

Stanley, Jerry. *I Am an American: A True Story of Japanese Internment*. Crown, 1994.

Staples, Suzanne Fisher. *Shabanu: Daughter of the Wind*. Laurel-Leaf, 1989.

Steger, Will, and Jon Bowermaster. *Over the Top of the World: Explorer Will Steger's Trek across the Arctic*. Scholastic, 1997.

Steinbeck, John. *The Grapes of Wrath: John Steinbeck Centennial Edition (1902–2002)*. Penguin, 1939.

_____. *Of Mice and Men*. Penguin, 1937.

_____. *The Pearl*. Penguin, 1948.

Stevenson, Robert Louis. *Treasure Island*. 1883.

Stevermer, Caroline. *River Rats*. Magic Carpet Books, 1992.

Stewart, Ross. *Causes and Consequences of the Great Depression*. Raintree/Steck-Vaughn, 1998.

Strasser, Todd. *Can't Get There from Here*. Simon & Schuster, 2004.

_____. *Give a Boy a Gun*. Simon Pulse, 2000.

_____. *The Wave*. Laurel-Leaf, 1981.

Sweeney, Joyce. *Players*. Winslow Press, 2000.

_____. *Waiting for June*. Marshall Cavendish, 2003.

Talbert, Marc. *The Purple Heart*. HarperCollins, 1992.

Tamar, Erika. *The Midnight Train Home*. Knopf, 2000.

_____. *The Things I Did Last Summer*. Harcourt, 1994.

Tan, Amy. *The Joy Luck Club*. Prentice Hall, 1989.

Tang, Greg. *Math Appeal: Mind-Stretching Math Riddles*. Scholastic, 2003.

Tashjian, Janet. *Fault Line*. Henry Holt, 2003.

_____. *The Gospel According to Larry*. Laurel-Leaf, 2001.

_____. *Multiple Choice*. Apple Signature, 1999.

_____. *Vote for Larry*. Henry Holt, 2004.

Taylor, Kim. *Cissy Funk*. HarperCollins, 2001.

Taylor, Mildred D. *The Land*. Speak, 2001.

_____. *Roll of Thunder, Hear My Cry.* Puffin, 1976.

Taylor, Theodore. *Air Raid—Pearl Harbor! The Story of December 7, 1941.* Gulliver Books, 1971.

_____. *The Bomb.* HarperTrophy, 1995.

Taylor, William. *Jerome.* Alyson, 1999.

Tekavec, Valerie. *Teenage Refugees from Bosnia-Herzegovina Speak Out.* Globe Fearon, 1995.

Terkel, Studs. *Hard Times: An Oral History of the Great Depression.* New Press, 1986.

Terry, Wallace, ed. *Bloods: An Oral History of the Vietnam War by Black Veterans.* Ballantine, 1992.

Testa, Maria. *Almost Forever.* Candlewick, 2003.

Thimmesh, Catherine, with illustrations by Melissa Sweet. *The Sky's the Limit: Stories of Discovery by Women and Girls.* Houghton Mifflin, 2002.

Thomas, Rob. *Rats Saw God.* Simon Pulse, 1996.

Thoreau, Henry David. *Walden.* 1854.

Trembath, Don. *The Popsicle Journal.* Orca, 2001.

Trueman, Terry. *Cruise Control.* HarperTempest, 2004.

_____. *Inside Out.* HarperTempest, 2003.

_____. *Stuck in Neutral.* HarperTempest, 2000.

Tryszynska-Frederick, Luba, and Michelle Roehm. *Luba: The Angel of Bergen-Belsen.* Tricycle Press, 2003.

Tunnell, Michael O., and George W. Chilcoat. *The Children of Topaz: The Story of a Japanese-American Internment Camp Based on a Classroom Diary.* Holiday House, 1996.

Turner, Ann. *Learning to Swim: A Memoir.* Scholastic, 2000.

Twain, Mark. *The Adventures of Huckleberry Finn.* 1884.

Uchida, Yoshiko. *The Invisible Thread: An Autobiography.* HarperTrophy, 1991.

Uys, Errol Lincoln. *Riding the Rails: Teenagers on the Move during the Great Depression.* Routledge, 1999.

Veciana-Suarez, Ana. *Flight to Freedom.* Scholastic, 2002.

Voigt, Cynthia. *Izzy, Willy-Nilly.* Simon Pulse, 1986.

_____. *When She Hollers.* Scholastic, 1994.

Volavkova, Hana, ed. *I Never Saw Another Butterfly: Children's Drawings and Poems from Terezan Concentration Camp, 1942–1944.* Schoken Books, 1971.

Vonnegut, Kurt, Jr. *Slaughterhouse-Five.* Dell, 1968.

Vreeland, Susan. *Girl in Hyacinth Blue.* Penguin, 1999.

Walker, Alice. *The Color Purple.* Pocket Books, 1982.

Walker, Paul Robert. *Hoop Dreams.* Turner Publishing, 1995.

Walker, Richard. *Encyclopedia of the Human Body.* DK, 2002.

Wallace, Ian. *The Man Who Walked the Earth.* Groundwood, 2003.

Wallace, Rich. *Losing Is Not an Option.* Knopf, 2003.

_____. *Playing without the Ball: A Novel in Four Quarters.* Laurel-Leaf, 2000.

_____. *Restless: A Ghost's Story.* Speak, 2003.

_____. *Shots on Goal.* Knopf, 1998.

_____. *Wrestling Sturbridge.* Laurel-Leaf, 1996.

Walter, Mildred Pitts. *The Girl on the Outside.* Scholastic Point, 1982.

Warren, Andrea. *Escape from Saigon: How a Vietnam War Orphan Became an American Boy.* Farrar, Straus & Giroux, 2004.

_____. *Surviving Hitler: A Boy in the Nazi Death Camps*. HarperCollins, 2001.

Wassiljewa, Tatjana. *Hostage to War: A True Story*. Polaris, 1997.

Watkins, T.H. *The Hungry Years: A Narrative History of the Great Depression in America*. Owl Books, 1999.

Watkins, Yoko Kawashima. *So Far from the Bamboo Grove*. Harper Tempest, 1986.

Weaver, Beth Nixon. *Rooster*. Winslow Press, 2001.

Weaver, Will. *Claws*. HarperCollins, 2003.

_____. *Farm Team*. HarperTrophy, 1995.

_____. *Hard Ball*. HarperTrophy, 1998.

_____. *Memory Boy*. HarperTrophy, 2001.

_____. *Striking Out*. HarperTrophy, 1993.

Weeks, Sarah. *So B. It*. HarperCollins, 2004.

Werlin, Nancy. *Double Helix*. Sleuth/Puffin, 2004.

Westall, Robert. *Blitzcat*. Scholastic, 1989.

_____. *Gulf*. Egmont Children's Books, 1995.

_____. *The Machine-Gunners*. Ace, 1975.

Wharton, Edith. *Ethan Frome*. 1911.

Whelan, Gloria. *Burying the Sun*. HarperCollins, 2004.

_____. *Homeless Bird*. HarperTrophy, 2000.

White, Ellen Emerson. *The Journal of Patrick Seamus Flaherty, United States Marine Corps, Khe Sanh, Vietnam, 1968*. Scholastic, 2002.

_____. *The Road Home*. Point Signature, 1995.

_____. *Where Have All the Flowers Gone? The Diary of Molly MacKenzie Flaherty, Boston, Massachusetts, 1968*. Scholastic, 2002.

White, Ruth. *Memories of Summer*. Laurel-Leaf, 2000.

Whitmore, Arvella. *The Bread Winner*. Sandpiper/Houghton Mifflin, 1990.

Wiesel, Elie. *Night*. Bantam, 1960.

Wilder, Thornton. *Our Town*. Perennial Press, 1938.

Wilhelm, Doug. *Raising the Shades*. Farrar, Straus & Giroux, 2001.

Williams, Laura E. *Behind the Bedroom Wall*. Milkweed Editions, 1996.

Williams, Tennessee. *The Glass Menagerie*. Penguin, 1945.

Williams-Garcia, Rita. *Every Time a Rainbow Dies*. HarperTempest, 2001.

_____. *Like Sisters on the Homefront*. Puffin, 1995.

Wilson, August. *The Piano Lesson*. Plume, 1990.

Wilson, John. *And in the Morning*. Kids Can Press, 2003.

Winick, Judd. *Pedro and Me: Friendship, Loss, and What I Learned*. Henry Holt, 2000.

Wisler, G. Clifton. *When Johnny Went Marching Home: Young Americans Fight the Civil War*. HarperCollins, 2001.

Wittlinger, Ellen. *Gracie's Girl*. Aladdin, 2000.

_____. *Hard Love*. Simon Pulse, 1999.

_____. *Heart on My Sleeve*. Simon Pulse, 2004.

_____. *Razzle*. Simon Pulse, 2001.

_____. *Zigzag*. Simon & Schuster, 2003.

Wolf, Allan. *New Found Land: Lewis and Clark's Voyage of Discovery*. Candlewick, 2004.

Wolff, Virginia Euwer. *Bat 6*. Scholastic, 1998.

_____. *Make Lemonade.* Scholastic, 1993.

_____. *The Mozart Season.* Scholastic, 1991.

_____. *Probably Still Nick Swansen.* Simon Pulse, 1988.

_____. *True Believer.* Simon Pulse, 2001.

Woodson, Jacqueline. *Hush.* Speak, 2002.

_____. *If You Come Softly.* Puffin, 1998.

_____. *Locomotion.* Putnam, 2003.

_____. *Miracle's Boys.* Puffin, 2000.

Wright, Richard. *Black Boy.* Perennial Press, 1945.

Wulffsen, Don. *Soldier X.* Speak, 2001.

Yancey, Diane. *Life during the Dust Bowl.* Lucent, 2004.

Yep, Laurence. *Dragon's Gate.* HarperTrophy, 1993.

Yolen, Jane. *Briar Rose.* Tor, 1992.

_____. *The Devil's Arithmetic.* Puffin, 1988.

Young, Cathy, ed. *One Hot Second: Stories about Desire.* Laurel-Leaf, 2002.

Zindel, Paul. *The Gadget.* Laurel-Leaf, 2001.

Zusak, Marcus. *Fighting Ruben Wolfe.* Scholastic, 2000.

REFERENCE BOOKS AND MONOGRAPHS

Applebee, Arthur N. *A Study of Book-Length Works Taught in High School English Courses.* Albany: State University of New York, 1989.

Aronson, Marc. *Exploding the Myths: The Truth about Teenagers and Reading.* Lanham, MD: Scarecrow Press, 2001.

Authors and Artists for Young Adults. Farmington Hills, MI: Thompson Gale, 2001.

Barnhouse, Rebecca. *Recasting the Past: The Middle Ages in Young Adult Literature.* Portsmouth, NH: Boynton/Cook-Heinemann, 2000.

Beers, Kylene. *When Kids Can't Read—What Teachers Can Do: A Guide for Teachers, 6–12.* Portsmouth, NH: Heinemann, 2002.

Beers, Kylene, and Teri S. Lesesne, eds. *Books for You: An Annotated Booklist for Senior High.* 14th ed. Urbana, IL: National Council of Teachers of English, 2001.

Beers, Kylene, and Barbara G. Samuels, eds. *Into Focus: Understanding and Creating Middle School Readers.* Norwood, MA: Christopher-Gordon Publishers, 1998.

Bishop, Rudine Sims. *Presenting Walter Dean Myers.* Boston: Twayne, 1991.

Bodart, Joni Richards. *Booktalk!* 5 vols. New York: Wilson, 1980–93.

_____. *Booktalking the Award Winners.* 4 vols. New York: Wilson, 1994–98.

_____. *Radical Reads: 101 YA Novels on the Edge.* Lanham, MD: Scarecrow Press, 2002.

Booth, David. *Even Hockey Players Read: Boys, Literacy, and Learning.* York, ME: Stenhouse, 2002.

Bott, C. J. *The Bully in the Book and in the Classroom.* Lanham, MD: Scarecrow Press, 2004.

Bouricius, Ann. *The Romance Readers' Advisory: The Librarian's Guide to Love in the Stacks.* Chicago: American Library Association, 2000.

Bowman, Cynthia Ann, ed. *Using Literature to Help Troubled Teenagers Cope with Health Issues.* Westport, CT: Greenwood, 2000.

Brouse, Ann, ed. *Talk It Up! Book Discussion Programs for Young People.* Albany: New York Library Association, 1999.

Brown, Jean E., and Elaine C. Stephens, eds. *United in Diversity: Using Multicultural Young Adult Literature in the Classroom.* Urbana, IL: National Council of Teachers of English, 1998.

_____. *Your Reading: An Annotated Booklist for Middle School and Junior High.* 11th ed. Urbana, IL: National Council of Teachers of English, 2003.

Brown, Joanne, and Nancy St. Clair. *Declarations of Independence: Empowered Girls in Young Adult Literature, 1990–2001.* Lanham, MD: Scarecrow Press, 2002.

Buker, Derek M. *The Science Fiction and Fantasy Readers' Advisory: The Librarian's Guide to Cyborgs, Aliens, and Sorcerers.* Chicago: American Library Association, 2002.

Bushman, John H., and Kay Parks Bushman. *Using Young Adult Literature in the English Classroom.* 2nd ed. Englewood Cliffs, NJ: Prentice Hall, 1997.

Carlsen, G. Robert. *Books and the Teenage Reader.* 2nd rev. ed. New York: Bantam, 1980.

Carlsen, G. Robert, and Anne Sherrill. *Voices of Readers: How We Come to Love Books.* Urbana, IL: National Council of Teachers of English, 1988.

Carroll, Pamela S., ed. *Using Literature to Help Troubled Teenagers Cope with Societal Issues.* Westport, CT: Greenwood, 1999.

Carter, Betty B., with Sally Estes and Linda Waddle, eds. *Best Books for Young Adults.* 2nd ed. Chicago: American Library Association, 2000.

Charles, John, Joanna Morrison, and Candace Clark. *The Mystery Readers' Advisory: The Librarian's Clues to Murder and Mayhem.* Chicago: American Library Association, 2002.

Clyde, Laurel, and Marjorie Lobban, eds. *Out of the Closet and into the Classroom: Homosexuality in Books for Young People.* 2nd ed. Melbourne, Australia: Thorpe, 1996.

Crowe, Chris. *More than a Game: Sports Literature for Young Adults.* Lanham, MD: Scarecrow Press, 2004.

Darby, Mary Ann, and Miki Pryne. *Hearing All the Voices: Multicultural Books for Adolescents.* Lanham, MD: Scarecrow Press, 2002.

Day, Frances Ann. *Lesbian and Gay Voices: An Annotated Bibliography and Guide to Literature for Children and Young Adults.* Westport, CT: Greenwood Press, 2000.

Dickerson, Constance B. *Teen Book Discussion Groups @ the Library.* New York: Neal-Schuman Publishers, 2004.

Donelson, Kenneth L., and Alleen Pace Nilsen. *Literature for Today's Young Adults.* 7th ed. Boston: Allyn and Bacon, 2004.

Dresang, Eliza T. *Radical Change: Books for Youth in a Digital Age.* New York: Wilson, 1999.

Elliott, Joan B., and Mary M. Dupuis, eds. *Young Adult Literature in the Classroom: Reading It, Teaching It, Loving It.* Newark, DE: International Reading Association, 2002.

Ericson, Bonnie O., ed. *Teaching Reading in High School English Classes.* Urbana, IL: National Council of Teachers of English, 2001.

Estes, Sally, ed. *Growing Up Is Hard to Do.* Chicago: American Library Association, 1994.

Gallo, Donald R., ed. *Authors' Insights: Turning Teenagers into Readers and Writers.* Portsmouth, NH: Heinemann, 1992.

Gill, David Macinnis. *Graham Salisbury: Island Boy.* Lanham, MD: Scarecrow Press, 2005.

Glasgow, Jacqueline N. *Using Young Adult Literature: Thematic Activities Based on Gardner's Multiple Intelligences.* Norwood, MA: Christopher-Gordon, 2002.

Gregg, Gail P., and Pamela S. Carroll, eds. *Books and Beyond: Thematic Approaches to Teaching Literature in High School.* Norwood, MA: Christopher-Gordon, 1998.

Hall, Susan. *Using Picture Books to Teach Literary Devices: Recommended Books for Children and Young Adults.* Vol. 3. Phoenix: Oryx Press, 2001.

Herald, Diana Tixier. *Genreflecting: A Guide to Reading Interests in Genre Fiction.* Westport, CT: Libraries Unlimited, 1995.

Hipple, Ted, ed. *Writers for Young Adults.* 3 vols. New York: Scribner's, 1997.

_____, ed. *Writers for Young Adults, Supplement I.* New York: Scribner's, 2000.

Isaac, Megan Lynn. *Heirs to Shakespeare: Reinventing the Bard in Young Adult Literature.* Portsmouth, NH: Heinemann, 2000.

Jones, Patrick, Michele Gorman, and Tricia Suellentrop. *Connecting Young Adults and Libraries: A How-To-Do-It Manual.* 3rd ed. New York: Neal-Schuman, 1998.

Jones, Patrick, Patricia Taylor, and Kirsten Edwards. *A Core Collection for Young Adults.* New York: Neal-Schuman Publishers, 2003.

Jung, C. G. *The Archetypes and the Collective Unconscious.* Princeton, NJ: Princeton University Press, 1969.

Kaplan, Jeffrey S., ed. *Using Literature to Help Troubled Teenagers Cope with Identity Issues.* Westport, CT: Greenwood, 1999.

Kaywell, Joan F., ed. *Adolescent Literature as a Complement to the Classics.* 4 vols. Norwood, MA: Christopher-Gordon Publishers, 1993–2000.

_____, ed. *Using Literature to Help Troubled Teenagers Cope with Family Issues.* Westport, CT: Greenwood, 1999.

Kravitz, Nancy. *Censorship and the School Library Media Center.* Westport, CT: Libraries Unlimited, 2002.

Lesesne, Teri S. *Making the Match: The Right Book for the Right Reader at the Right Time, Grades 4–12.* York, ME: Stenhouse, 2003.

Lesesne, Teri S., and Rosemary Chance. *Hit List for Young Adults 2: Frequently Challenged Books.* Chicago: American Library Association, 2002.

Makowski, Silk. *Serious about Series: Evaluations and Annotations of Teen Fiction in Paperback Series.* Lanham, MD: Scarecrow, 1998.

Marcus, Leonard S., ed. *Author Talk.* New York: Simon and Schuster, 2000.

McCaffery, Laura Hibbets. *Building an ESL Collection for Young Adults: A Bibliography of Recommended Fiction and Nonfiction for Schools and Public Libraries.* Westport, CT: Greenwood, 1998.

Monseau, Virginia R., and Gary M. Salvner, eds. *Reading Their World: The Young Adult Novel in the Classroom.* 2nd ed. Portsmouth, NH: Heinemann, 2000.

Pennac, Daniel. *Better than Life.* York, ME: Stenhouse/Pembroke, 1999.

Pipkin, Gloria, and Releah Lent. *At the Schoolhouse Gate: Lessons in Intellectual Freedom.* Portsmouth, NH: Heinemann, 2002.

Probst, Robert E. *Response and Analysis: Teaching Literature in Secondary School.* 2nd ed. Portsmouth, NH: Heinemann, 2004.

Reeves, Anne R. *Adolescents Talk about Reading: Exploring Resistance to and Engagement with Text.* Newark, DE: International Reading Association, 2004.

Reichman, Henry. *Censorship and Selection: Issues and Answers for Schools.* 3rd ed. Chicago: American Library Association, 2001.

Reid, Louann, with Jamie Hayes Neufeld, eds. *Rationales for Teaching Young Adult Literature.* Portland, ME: Calendar Islands, 1999.

Reid, Suzanne. *Book Bridges for ESL Students: Using Young Adult and Children's Literature to Teach ESL Students.* Lanham, MD: Scarecrow Press, 2002.

Reynolds, Marilyn. *I Won't Read and You Can't Make Me: Reaching Reluctant Teen Readers.* Portsmouth, NH: Heinemann, 2004.

Rochman, Hazel. *Against Borders: Promoting Books for a Multicultural World.* Chicago: American Library Association, 1993.

Rosenblatt, Louise M. *Literature as Exploration.* 4th ed. New York: Modern Language Association, 1983.

_____. *The Reader, the Text, the Poem.* Carbondale, IL: Southern Illinois University Press, 1978.

Saricks, Joyce G. *Readers' Advisory Guide to Genre Fiction.* Chicago: American Library Association, 2001.

Schall, Lucy. *Booktalks and More: Motivating Teens to Read.* Westport, CT: Libraries Unlimited, 2003.

Schon, Elizabeth. *The Best of the Latino Heritage: A Guide to the Best Juvenile Books about Latino People and Cultures.* Lanham, MD: Scarecrow Press, 1996.

Something about the Author (SATA) series. Farmington Hills, MI: Gale Research Company, various years.

St. James Guide to Young Adult Writers. Detroit: St. James Press, 1999.

Stover, Lois T. *Young Adult Literature: The Heart of the Middle School Curriculum.* Portsmouth, NH: Heinemann, 1996.

Stover, Lois Thomas. *Jacqueline Woodson: The Real Thing.* Lanham, MD: Scarecrow Press, 2004.

Stringer, Sharon A. *Conflict and Connection: The Psychology of Young Adult Literature.* Portsmouth, NH: Heinemann, 1997.

Sullivan, Edward T. *The Holocaust in Literature for Youth.* Lanham, MD: Scarecrow Press, 1999.

_____. *Reaching Reluctant Young Adult Readers: A Handbook for Librarians and Teachers.* Lanham, MD: Scarecrow Press, 2002.

Tuccillo, Diane. *Library Teen Advisory Groups: A VOYA Guide.* Lanham, MD: Scarecrow Press, 2004.

Willis, Arlette Ingram, ed. *Teaching Multicultural Literature in Grades 9–12: Moving beyond the Canon.* Norwood, MA: Christopher-Gordon, 1998.

Young Adult Library Services Association (YALSA) and Patrick Jones. *New Directions for Library Service to Young Adults.* Chicago: American Library Association, 2002.

Zvirin, Stephanie, ed. *The Best Years of Their Lives: A Resource Guide for Teenagers in Crisis.* 2nd ed. Chicago: American Library Association, 1996.

ARTICLES, POEMS, SHORT STORIES, AND CHAPTERS FROM BOOKS

Carlsen, G. Robert. "Literature Is." *English Journal* 63 (February 1974): 23–27.

Davis, Terry. "In the Valley of Elephants." In *On the Edge: Stories at the Brink,* ed. Lois Duncan (New York: Simon Pulse, 2000), 196–209.

Gallo, Donald R. "Listening to Readers: Attitudes toward the Young Adult Novel." In *Reading Their World,* ed. Virginia R. Monseau and Gary M. Salvner (Portsmouth, NH: Boynton/Cook, 1992), 17–27.

George, Phil. "Battle Won Is Lost." In *Zero Makes Me Hungry,* ed. Edward Lueders and Primus St. John (Glenview, IL: Scott, Foresman and Co., 1976), 106.

Jarrell, Randall. "The Death of the Ball Turret Gunner." In *The Complete Poems,* by Randall Jarrell (New York: Farrar, Straus & Giroux, 1969), 144.

Mazer, Harry. "Furlough 1944." In *Sixteen: Short Stories by Outstanding Writers for Young Adults,* ed. Donald R. Gallo (New York: Laurel-Leaf, 1984), 83–91.

Owen, Wilfred. "Dulce et Decorum Est." Various texts, 1920.

Salisbury, Graham. "Waiting for the War." In *Time Capsule: Short Stories about Teenagers throughout the Twentieth Century,* ed. Donald R. Gallo (New York: Laurel-Leaf, 1999), 88–107.

Sandburg, Carl. "Grass." In *Harvest Poems: 1910–1960,* by Carl Sandburg (San Diego: Harcourt Brace, 1960), 51–52.

Sullivan, Anne McCrary. "The Natural Reading Life: A High School Anomaly." *English Journal* 80 (October 1991): 40–46.

Vogel, Mark, and Don Zancanella. "The Story World of Adolescents in *and* out of the Classroom." *English Journal* 80 (October 1991): 54–60.

WEB SITES

The American Experience: Surviving the Dust Bowl. http://www.pbs.org/wgbh/amex/dustbowl/.

A Depression Art Gallery. http://www.english.uiuc.edu/maps/depression.art-gallery.htm.

The Depression in the United States—An Overview. http://www.english.uiuc.edu/maps/depression/overview.htm.

Photographs of the Great Depression. http://history1900s.about.com/library/photos/blyindexdepression.htm.

In Praise of Shantytowns by Jeb Blount. http://www.nextcity.com/main/town/2shanty.htm.

Voices from the Dust Bowl: The Charles L. Todd and Robert Sonkin Migrant Worker Collection. http://memory.loc.gov/ammem/afctshtml/tshome.html.

VIDEOS AND DVDS

Riding the Rails by Michael Uys and Lexy Lovell. Videocassette (1997) and DVD (2003). Produced by Out of the Blue Productions, distributed by WGBH.

INDEX

About the Authors

SARAH K. HERZ taught English in the Westport, Connecticut, school system for 24 years. She frequently conducts workshops at English and library conferences and staff development meetings. An article reviewer for *English Journal* and the *ALAN Review*, Herz has served on the Board of Directors of the Connecticut Council of Teachers of English and the Assembly on Literature for Adolescents of NCTE (ALAN). She was a recipient of fellowships from the National Endowment for the Humanities and the Connecticut Humanities Council.

DONALD R. GALLO is a former junior high school English teacher, reading specialist, and university professor who has become the country's foremost anthologist of short stories for young adults. His most recent anthologies are *Destination Unexpected, First Crossing: Stories about Teen Immigrants,* and *What Are You Afraid Of?* He is the recipient of the ALAN Award for Outstanding Contributions to Young Adult Literature as well as the Ted Hipple Service Award for exemplary service and dedication to ALAN. Along with his writing, Gallo also interviews notable authors for Authors4Teens.com.